Camp

Woss L.

Gold

River

Muchalat L.

Conuma River

Upana L.

Heber R.

Head B

Hisnit

Tlupana In.

GOLD
RIVER

Bligh I.

Gore I

Muchalat Inlet

Matchlee Bay

Jacklah R.

quot

Escalante Pt.

Hesquiat
Peninsula

NOOTKA SOUND EXPLORED

A Westcoast History

Laurie Jones

published by

Ptarmigan Press
Campbell River, British Columbia, Canada

Canadian Cataloguing in Publication Data

Jones, Laurie, 1953–
  Nootka Sound Explored

  Includes bibliographical references and index.
  ISBN 0-919537-24-3

  1. Nootka Sound Region (B.C.)—History.
2. Kyuquot Sound Region (B.C.)—History.
I. Title.
FC3845.N65J65   1991   971.1'2   C91-091275-0
F1089.N8J65   1991

Copyright © 1991 Laurie Jones and the Regional District of Comox-Strathcona.

First Edition published August 1991.

Designed and produced by Kask Graphics Ltd., Campbell River, British Columbia, Canada.
Printed in Hong Kong.

Contents

CHAPTER 1   INTRODUCTION

There are many stories to be written about the west coast of Vancouver Island, British Columbia. This book is only one of those stories. It attempts to present, for the first time, a cohesive form for understanding the historical development of the Nootka Sound and Kyuquot Sound region. It is not, however, a definitive history of the west coast. There is no such thing. There are as many histories of a place as there are people who have lived there and continue to live there. Each story presents a slightly different perspective, provides a slightly different meaning to events.

This book does not fully address all of the perspectives found on the west coast: women's stories, the Native story, the rich and complex mix of other cultures. These can only be touched on. Each requires its own book, and, in the best of all possible worlds, a book is required on each. This history should be considered as a beginning, with other stories by other people to follow.

Similarly, there is no such thing as "finishing" the story of Nootka Sound; there is only a decision to stop writing. The history continues, and there will always be something more to write about, some new story to tell. In writing this manuscript, the purpose has been to document and record the historical development of the region, from the time of contact to the present. It is not intended to be a specific and local history of day-to-day occurrences. Each community deserves to have its own unique story told. Those are different kinds of projects, however, and are best undertaken by local residents who have a deep and intimate knowledge of the more contemporary developments of their towns.

Geography

The Nootka and Kyuquot Sound region encompasses some 71,000 hectares (175,440 acres) of land from the western boundary of Strathcona Park to the Pacific Ocean. It extends from Muchalat Inlet and Escalante Point in the south, to Brooks Peninsula in the north. Backed by the steep slopes of the Vancouver Island Range, and facing the open Pacific, it's an area characterized by a rugged terrain with long deep inlets penetrating inland, protected from the fierce winter storms which pound the rocky shores and beaches of the outer coast.

Of its total land mass, less than 6 per cent, or 10,000 acres, is estimated to be suitable for human habitation and development.[1] Most of the developable land is located on river estuaries, the deltas at the heads of inlets, and in the tiny bays and coves along the inside waterways. Over the years, it is here that Native villages, fish plants, logging camps, and mill towns have been established. Today, the main settlements in the region are at Tahsis, Zeballos, Gold River, and Kyuquot.

The geography of the Nootka and Kyuquot Sound area has figured largely in isolating the region from the rest of the world, and reinforcing a regional perspective. Dependent on a resource-based economy, and restricted by the rugged terrain, communities have in common similar economic and geographic concerns, and a shared history. Nonetheless, the development of Nootka Sound has been largely

Nootka Sound, 1988. Aerial view looking north up Tahsis Inlet.　　　　　Laurie Jones photo.

influenced by external factors and decisions. World market conditions, government policies, and international politics have played key roles in affecting events and activities within the region.

A Resource-Based Economy

The controlling force behind the region's development has been a resource-based economy. In the 18th century, Nootka Sound was the hub of a thriving maritime fur trade. British and American traders were getting top dollar in Asian markets for west coast sea otter pelts. Later, fishing, logging, prospecting, and mining became the focus for small-scale industry. Canneries, floatcamps, and mining operations flourished, and tiny settlements soon grew up around them.

Historically, be it logging, fishing, or fur trading, the success or failure of the dominant industry has determined the extent to which the region's communities have thrived. Today, the close relationship between resource-base and community is more apparent than ever. A single resource - forestry - and a single company dominate the economy. Canadian Pacific Forest Products Ltd., a major international forest company, is the largest single employer in the region. It controls Tree Farm License #19 and, through its logging, sawmill, and pulp mill operations, provides employment to the majority of residents in Tahsis, Zeballos, and Gold River. Modernization of the sawmill in Tahsis and expansion of the pulp mill in Gold River indicate the company's economic commitment to the region.

The reliance on forestry is changing, albeit slowly. Exploration drilling shows promise for re-opening the gold mines in Zeballos. And in the region generally, the potential for aquaculture and tourism is being considered for development. All suggest that a more diverse future may be on the horizon.

Transportation

Accessibility and transportation are two of the primary factors affecting the region's development. In particular, the maritime link has played an instrumental role in shaping the settlement of the sound. Long before Europeans claimed these shores as their own, the Indians were travelling up and down the coast in sturdy canoes - trading with their neighbors to the north and south, harvesting seafood, and navigating expertly between the shoals and reefs of the the open Pacific, and the protected fjords. First approaches by the Spanish and the British were by sea, not by the mountainous overland route travelled by explorers to settle the interior valleys and river mouths of the province's mainland. Later, fish processing plants and logging operations relied on the water to move goods to market and to connect them socially to the wider world "outside." Today, the waterways continue to be a major link to international export markets for lumber and pulp, the region's economic mainstays.

For many years, the small remote settlements along the west coast of Vancouver Island depended solely on the CPR steamship *S.S. Princess Maquinna* for freight and transportation.[2] Built in Esquimalt and launched in 1913, the *Maquinna* plied the waters of the west coast until 1952. She made the run from Victoria to Port Alice every ten days, carrying supplies, mail, and passengers.

For people living in the logging camps, canneries, and small communities along her route, the *Maquinna* was a lifeline. Food was ordered from Woodward's department store and delivered by ship. Mail arrived every ten days. And it was the *Maquinna* that brought hundreds of miners and loggers and sawmill workers out to work on the west coast.

In 1952, the reliable but aging steamship made its last regular run. She was converted into an ore carrier, renamed the *Taku*, and served her final years carrying ore from Alaska to Tacoma.

The *S.S. Princess Norah*, a sister ship, relieved the *Maquinna* during her annual overhaul, and, for two summers, served as an additional ship on the run. The *Norah* was later put into service on CPR's Alaskan route.

S.S. Princess Maquinna *calling in at a coastal fish camp. Photograph by John Perry.*   Royal B.C. Museum, Ethnology Division.

When the *Maquinna* was retired from service, Northland Navigation took over the original CPR run. Based in Port Alberni, the *Northland Prince* operated for a few years, mainly as a freight service, before eventually being discontinued in the early 1960s.

The *Uchuck III*, based in Gold River and owned by Nootka Sound Marine Services, now provides the only regularly scheduled freight and passenger service between Gold River, Tahsis, Kyuquot, and Friendly Cove. Like her predecessors, she too services the logging camps and Indian villages along the coast. Originally based in Port Alberni, Nootka Sound Marine commenced service March 18, 1960, with the *Uchuck II*, an old West Vancouver ferry built in 1925. It made weekly trips into the area, delivering freight, groceries, and visitors, then returned to Port Alberni. In 1962, the boat's owners, Esson Young and George McCandless, purchased a former U.S. Navy minesweeper, renamed it the *Uchuck III*, and added it to the run.

The dependency on marine transportation has lessened considerably since the construction of roads in the 1970s. At the same time, however, the withdrawal of steamship service contributed to the changing settlement patterns. With the consolidation of industry, people abandoned the small coastal settlements in favor of more centralized communities. Flying, a much faster alternative to boat travel, became more affordable and offered competition to the steamship lines. In the 1960s, airlines offered daily direct flights between the Nootka

Playing shuffleboard aboard the S.S. Princess Maquinna, *circa 1936.*
Laura Anderson photo.

Sound region and Vancouver. The demand for coastal shipping dwindled until finally, it was cancelled altogether. Deprived of regular boat service, the remaining outposts closed down.

Today, a network of gravel logging roads and paved secondary highways connect the communities of Tahsis, Gold River, and Zeballos to Highway 19 - the primary transportation route on the more populated east coast of Vancouver Island. The major centers of Vancouver and Victoria - once a four-day trip by steamship - are now a day's drive away. And Campbell River, the major service center for the North Island, can be reached in less than three hours from any of the three main communities.

Many smaller settlements, however, remain inaccessible by land. People living along the outer coast, in logging camps, and in the tiny communities of Esperanza, Queen's Cove, and Kyuquot, must still rely on floatplanes or boats - services which are often disrupted by stormy weather and high seas. The *Uchuck III*, which continues to serve these communities, has also capitalized on a growing interest in sightseeing and coastal cruising. Many of the *Uchuck's* passengers are tourists, eager to take in the spectacular scenery and wildlife of the west coast.

The Project

Nootka Sound Explored is part of a larger project which was commissioned, in 1987, by the West Coast Committee of the Regional District of Comox-Strathcona, a group representing the communities of Gold River, Tahsis, and Zeballos, and the outlying unincorporated areas of Esperanza, Nuchatlitz, and Kyuquot.[3] They felt that their history, the story of who they are and how they developed, was important, and worth preserving. They undertook not only to record that history, but to make it available to the public in the form of a 90-minute video, "Nootka Sound Explored," completed in May, 1988, a short, introductory guide to the history of the region, and this book.

The fieldwork and research took place over a period of two years, from May, 1987 to July, 1989. I also spent two summers in Tahsis in 1985 and 1986. During that time, I lived and worked in the region for the period May to August, 1985 and again in 1986, and from June, 1987, until April, 1988. I made my home in Tahsis and regularly visited the other communities in the region where I stayed at the homes of the mayors and their families. Upon moving out of the region in 1988, I returned frequently to attend community events, conduct interviews, make public presentations, and collect further information.

Gravel road from Gold River to Tahsis. Conuma Peak in the distance, 1988.   Laurie Jones photo.

Although I was first hired by the Regional District in 1987, it was not my first association with the region. I had worked for the village of Tahsis in the summers of 1985 and 1986 to establish a community archives and to research the local history of the town. The Tahsis project required organizing written and photographic material donated to the village by Canadian International Paper Company Ltd. (now Canadian Pacific Forest Products Ltd.), and interviewing early residents.

During those two summers, I lived in Tahsis, a community of about 1,000 people. Both summers were spent in vacant teacherages on School Hill, so named because it was once the site of the town's elementary school. When a new elementary-secondary school was built in 1970, the old school was demolished and the site was used for teacherages: five mobile homes and a modular triplex owned by the school district to provide subsidized housing to teachers and their families.

The community leaders who spearheaded the regional project were keenly interested in documenting the history of the region because they saw it as a means of reinforcing a collective identity. Initially, they wanted to capitalize on the region's role in European history as the place where Captain Cook landed, thereby establishing the first contact between Europe and western Canada, and as the place where Spain and Britain argued over territorial rights to the Pacific.

The history of the three communities is inextricably intertwined. The pulp and paper mill at Gold River, for example, is dependent, to some degree, on woodfibre supplied by the loggers and sawmill workers living and working in Tahsis and Zeballos. And the contemporary history of the area can only be understood by going back to the development of logging, and to the establishment of Tahsis.

The industrial development of Tahsis begins with the construction of a sawmill at the head of Tahsis Inlet in 1945. The mill was the foundation of what, through a process of corporate takeovers and mergers, has led to the economic domination of the region by Canadian Pacific Forest Products, Ltd. Stages in the town's development are marked by the move from a company-owned town to incorporated municipality, and by the opening of a road connecting Tahsis to Gold River and the east coast of the island.

Zeballos has two histories. Today, the community is a logging camp and log sort for CPFP, and a base for renewed gold mining activities in the area. But the history the town prefers to present to the public is the history of Zeballos as a gold rush town. By-laws require that all commercial and public buildings have house fronts in the style of the gold mining era of 1930-1938. During the period of my research, the mayor and council were debating how best to construct sidewalks for their tiny community which would be in keeping with its earlier era. Yet, Zeballos today and Zeballos yesterday are two separate realities. Only one person in the town remains from the heady days of the gold rush. The majority of the townspeople are loggers and fishermen and exploration miners.

Gold River, an "instant town," was planned and built around a pulp mill in 1965. It also has two separate and distinct histories. One is the history of the Beach Camp, a logging camp on the site of what is now the pulp mill. Former Beach Camp residents recall a sense of community and history not shared by the town's present residents. The other history, the most recent one, has to do with the opening of the pulp mill in 1967 when an influx of pulp mill workers and their families swelled the population of the former logging camp.

Gold River is the youngest of the three communities. Although human occupancy in the immediate area can be traced back several thousands of years before European contact, the "remembered" history of the non-Native population only goes back to 1953, and the recorded history of the town itself begins in 1965. This relative newness made it difficult at first for local residents to understand what relevance the project had to their lives. They firmly believed that their town had no history; "history" seemed to mean being able to trace a continual line of settlement back for generations, to their great-grandfathers' or great-great-grandfathers' time.

A fourth history is the history of the Native people in the region. In Nootka Sound there are a number of Native communities whose way of life has been drastically altered as a result of European contact and settlement. Theirs is a contemporary history of disenfranchisement, racism, poverty, and the struggle to reclaim their cultural traditions.

Research - Documentary

In the course of the research, many trips were made to the Provincial Archives in Victoria, and to the libraries and special collections at the University of B.C. and Simon Fraser University. The most well-documented period in any consistent and analytical form is the period of initial European contact and the maritime fur trade between the Natives and the Spanish, British, and American ships that stopped in at Nootka Sound during the late 18th Century. Journals and diaries kept by ships' captains, officers, botanists, and priests - all well-educated and trained in their profession - have been preserved. Most are readily available to the public through reprints and transcripts in the Provincial Archives and university libraries. Many have been published in book form. These are all first-person accounts and as such, often reveal more about the writer's culture and background, his interpretation of events, than about the meaning of the events themselves. This is particularly true of the accounts of northwest coast Native culture which, when first encountered by strangers from another culture, is nearly incomprehensible. Many secondary sources have also been written about the early contact period, providing analyses and a synthesis of the period.

The Provincial Archives of B.C. in Victoria was consulted for both its written as well as its visual records. At the University of B.C., the Special Collections division has some good primary material on the fishing industry in the area. Libraries at UBC and Simon Fraser University were used to consult primary and secondary works.

The chapter on the area's original inhabitants is drawn largely from Philip Drucker's study, *The Northern and Central Nootkan Tribes* (1951), as well as from the works of Gilbert Malcolm Sproat, Susan Kenyon, A. Y. Arima, John Mills, Michael Folan, Richard Inglis, and James C. Haggarty. Due to changes in the form for spelling Native words, readers may notice different versions of words referring to places, rivers and culture groups. For consistency, I have chosen to use the spelling which is most preferred by the Native people themselves.

As for the period of contact, in order to capture the flavor of those early years, I have used direct quotes from explorers' journals. These quotes may seem awkward and difficult to read at first, as they are written in the language and style of the period. But I feel it is well worth the effort, as they provide a first-hand account of the region, told in the words of the people who were there at the time.

Friendly Cove lighthouse. The lighthouse was built in 1911 and is one of the few remaining manned light stations on B.C.'s coast.
Vancouver Sun photo.   Tahsis Archives.

Newspaper articles and local newspapers, including those published by the communities themselves as well as the company newspaper, were also reviewed, particularly for the local perspective on events and issues in their communities. The community newspapers were a tremendous source of information. Until recently, each community had its own local newspaper. Today, the *Gold River Record*, published every two weeks, is the main newspaper for the region.

Several popular histories have been written over the past 30 years: George Nicholson's *Vancouver Island's West Coast*; Margaret Sharcott's *A Place of Many Winds*; Bethine Flynn, *The Flying Flynns* and *Flynn's Cove*; *Splendour from the Sea*, by Phillip Keller, and *Bull of the Woods*, by Gordon Gibson, founder of Tahsis Company. Company reports and records, government reports, statistics, and so on, rounded out the documentary research.

Personal photographs have been used with the kind permission of their owners: Laura Anderson, Bruce Davies, Kathleen Davies, John Perry, Elvera Ericson, and Bud and Alice Young. Other photographs come from the Provincial Archives of British Columbia, the Ethnology Division of the Royal British Columbia Museum, the Campbell River Museum and Archives, the Village of Gold River, and the Village of Tahsis Archives.

Research - Oral Accounts

What truly makes the history come alive are the people who shared their experiences with me. Many people were interviewed in the course of this project, and their contributions have provided an important perspective on the region's development. The Nootka Sound story could not have been told without their participation. They gave generously and warmly of their time, their hospitality, and their memories. There are too many to list here (see Appendix A at back of book), but I am indebted to each and every person who consented to share their stories with me, no matter how long or short those stories may have been.

I don't think they ever thought of themselves as "storytellers." What they gave me was their own, personal account of their experiences. In the telling, and retelling, they have truly become storytellers. Through their life stories, anecdotes, and personal observations, the intimate details of life on the coast emerged. First person accounts added meaning to the otherwise dry and formal accounts of the written record.

Sense of Community

In the process of "doing" the research—talking to people, asking questions, participating in community life—residents began to develop an interest in their own history, leading to the initiation of various local history projects throughout the region. The three communities on the west coast of Vancouver Island have since undertaken another joint project, this time to organize a 1992 celebration as part of the bicentennial of Captain George Vancouver's circumnavigation of Vancouver Island. In addition, each community has gone on to develop individual community projects.

In Tahsis, a local citizens' group formed to preserve and renovate an old bunkhouse building for use as a local museum, tourist information centre, and campus for North Island College. The Tahsis Historical and Archives Society raised close to $3,000 in local funds and was formally placed in charge of the operation of the local museum.

In Gold River, cases were designed and a permanent exhibit of artifacts was set up in the village hall. The nearly defunct Nootka Sound Historical Society, which had been maintained in name only, was revived. One of the buildings from the original logging camp was moved from its site at the logging division to a new site at the entrance to town where it was turned into an information booth featuring exhibits and photographs of the community.

Zeballos' historical society raised local funds to purchase and restore a building used as a hospital and doctor's clinic during the first years of the mining boom. The building will be used as a small museum and as the base for the historical society.

All three historical groups have been assisted, supported, and encouraged by their village councils. Through financial help, official representation on the boards, and through administrative support, local history has been given a position of prominence and importance in the region.

Acknowledgements

Many people contributed, in one way or another, to the writing of this book. To all of them, I give my thanks and appreciation, with a special thanks to Jim Fiddick, Maxine McCrae, Gerry Hill, Laura Fenton, Diane Crowhurst, Pat and Adolf Eichmeyer, Canadian Pacific Forest Products Ltd., and its predecessor, Canadian International Paper Ltd., and McAdam Resources Ltd.

Background research and the preparation of material was made possible, in part, through the financial assistance of the Ministry of Municipal Affairs, Recreation and Culture through the British Columbia Heritage Trust and B.C. Lotteries. Many thanks to J. Pauline Rafferty and Susan Irvine, who introduced me to Tahsis, and to Cliff Hewitt and Neil Wilton for their continuing support.

I would also like to thank the members of the West Coast Committee, past and present, who invited me into their communities: Anne Fiddick, mayor of Gold River and chairman of the committee; Tom McCrae, former mayor of Tahsis; Mary Gedlaman, former Tahsis councillor and now mayor of Tahsis; John Crowhurst, former mayor of Zeballos; and Brian Witt, representative of the outlying areas. Their initiative made this project possible.

I am also grateful to Dr. Richard Inglis, head of ethnology at the Royal B.C. Museum, for his reading of the manuscript and his discussion of the Native history. His comments were thought-provoking and provided me with another perspective on the impact of European culture on Native culture.

Finally, a special thanks to Ron Trepanier for his partnership and support in the course of this work. He was constant companion, colleague, video producer, and proof-reader, and provided an invaluable critique of the manuscript through its various stages.

Notes

[1] Regional District of Comox-Strathcona, *A Report on Land Use and Resources Within the Region* (Courtenay: 1975), p. 56.

[2] For further reading on the steamship service to the west coast of Vancouver Island, see Norman R. Hacking and W. Kaye Lamb, *The Princess Story: A Century and a Half of West Coast Shipping* (Vancouver: 1974). See also Ruth Greene, *Personality Ships of British Columbia* (West Vancouver: 1969).

[3] Regional districts are a level of the provincial government which represent the unincorporated areas in a particular region. On August 19, 1965, the Regional District of Comox-Strathcona became the first regional district to be incorporated in B.C. It includes two mid-sized urban centers on the east coast of Vancouver Island, Campbell River and Courtenay, as well as several smaller communities, including Tahsis, Gold River, and Zeballos on the west coast.

CHAPTER 2   THE FIRST INHABITANTS

Friendly Cove and Nootka Sound are often called the "Birthplace of B. C.," a title which refers to the region's role in European history. The written history credits Spanish explorers and British navigator Captain James Cook with "discovering" the west coast. But, what was a discovery for them was old and familiar territory to the original inhabitants of the region: the Native people. As Nick Howard, a young Mowachaht who grew up in Friendly Cove and Gold River, puts it:

"Our understanding is that Captain Cook came in a weird boat, in a weird design - y'know, it held so many people - and he was the one lost. We were there all the time. We weren't lost. We were on our land."[1]

Most of our recorded knowledge of British Columbia's Indian people has been documented from the perspective of non-Indians. It begins with the arrival of the European explorers and fur traders: the one was searching for new lands to claim, the other was looking for resources to exploit. They had the means to record their observations in writing, observations which have come to shape our interpretation of the past, and, more importantly, shape our understanding of the Native way of life.

These accounts, for all their scientific data and information, tell only part of the story. Recently, there's been a strong and growing popular interest in learning the other part. Anthropologists - whose role has traditionally been to study and document other cultures - are now finding new audiences for their work. Historians, with their generally conservative approach to history as told by the dominant world view, are also considering other perspectives. Working-class histories, women's stories, first person oral accounts, and community histories are increasingly finding their way into schools and bookstores across the country. And Native people themselves want to know more about their past as told from their own point of view: the "white man's" stories rarely do justice to the richness and depth of Native culture.

"I've read these books and a lot of times I get that feeling, you know: what's my history on my right side, according to my elders, what they've told me. And I've read the other side of the culture, history from the white man. Different altogether," says Sam Johnson. "They wrote the history on one side, what they saw of my Native people, Indian people. But the history lies here hidden."[2]

Sam Johnson is a Mowachaht elder now living at the A'haminaquus reserve near Gold River. He was born on January 27, 1916, in his parents' house at Friendly Cove. His mother was a Mowachaht from Marvinas Bay; his father was from the Hesquiat tribe. Sam says that, before the white man came, things were different for his people:

"Because they had everything out here. They didn't depend on a general store or Super Valu. The food was right out here... They chewed on roots in order to stay healthy. They chewed on herbs, plants, medicine. They lived a good life. But, this generation, we are far - what you might call, our canoe is tipping over. We're drifting away from our culture, drifting away from our language, our tradition, our laws of our society, ancient society. It's disappearing."[3]

Political and Territorial Divisions

People have been living on the west coast of Vancouver Island for thousands of years. Archaeological records of the main village of Yuquot at Friendly Cove show that the site is at least 4,200 years old, and researchers suggest that it is one of the earliest and longest continuously inhabited sites on the outer coast.[4] More recent archaeological surveys by the Royal British Columbia Museum have identified hundreds of other village sites, fishing stations, and burial grounds between Estevan Point and Brooks Peninsula.[5] According to Dr. Richard Inglis, head of ethnology at the RBCM, this latest information indicates that the Yuquot site is not as unique as was originally thought. It is probably, in fact, only one of many ancient sites along the coast that have a record of long and continuous human occupancy.[6]

Historically, the first inhabitants of Nootka Sound have been referred to as the Nootka, a name given them by Captain James Cook when his expedition first arrived at Yuquot, in 1778. The British, however, didn't know the Native language and the locals didn't know English. The two groups communicated by gestures and by simple drawings scratched in the earth. This resulted, naturally enough, in misunderstandings about what kind of information was being asked and what the answers were. One theory, put forward by Gilbert Malcolm Sproat, government agent and businessman on the west coast of Vancouver Island from 1860-1865, is that the name 'nootka' came from the word 'noochee' (nutci), meaning mountain.[7] Father Augustin Joseph Brabant, resident priest at Hesquiat from 1874-1900, whose territory included Friendly Cove, suggests that Nootka is derived from 'nootk-sitl' meaning to go around or make a circuit, and was used either to indicate that Yuquot was situated on an island, or as a way of telling the European sailors to circle around into the shelter of the cove.[8] Sam Johnson says the name has another meaning, one which comes from the Native word for the C-shaped bay at Friendly Cove, meaning "circle bay."[9]

Regardless of the origin of the word 'nootka,' it was not an indigenous name for the area, nor was it the name used by the local inhabitants to refer to themselves. The term Nootka Indian, or Nootkan, came from the colloquial name of the sound, which was also variously named King George's Sound by Captain Cook, and San Lorenzo de Nuca by the Spanish. The widespread use of 'Nootka' as the name of the people continued until late into the present century when it was changed to West Coast and, finally, Nuu-chah-nulth. As well, quite early on in the fur trading period, the Native people themselves began to refer to themselves as Nootkans.[10] Later, the designation was applied to the language and culture

Titled "At Nootka," American photographer Edward S. Curtis took this photo of two Mowachaht men in 1914. Provincial Archives of B.C.

group of all tribes living along the west coast of Vancouver Island from Bamfield in Clayoquot Sound, to Brooks Peninsula at the northern edge of Kyuquot Sound.

Within the Nootka culture group, a significant linguistic and cultural division occurred at Estevan Point on the tip of Hesquiat Peninsula. Jutting out into the ocean, the peninsula forms the southern entrance to Nootka Sound and is a natural geographical barrier separating groups living along the northern coast from those in the south. Tribes north of Estevan spoke what Phillip Drucker identified as a northern dialect of the Nootka language, while their neighbors to the south, in Clayoquot and Barkley Sounds, spoke a central dialect.[11] Included in the northern grouping are the present-day Mowachaht, Muchalat, Ehattesaht-Queen's Cove, Nuchatlaht, Checleset, and Kyuquot.

Tribes in the north had frequent contact with their Kwa-kwa-la speaking neighbors in Quatsino Sound and Nimpkish Lake. Overland trails from Tahsis to Woss Lake, and from Muchalat Lake up the Nimpkish River, linked the Mowachaht and Muchalat people with the Kwakwa'kawak[w] on the north end of the island.[12] Another trail at Tahsish in Kyuquot Sound provided the Kyuquot and Checleset tribes a similar link with the Nimpkish. Over the years, through trade and intermarriage, west coast families acquired various cultural traditions from the Kwakwa'kawak[w], such as dances, songs, and property rights, just as the Kwakwa'kawak[w] picked up traditions belonging to the people living in Nootka and Kyuquot Sounds. Well-known amongst the Kwakwa'kawak[w] today is the Friendship Dance, a dance which was given to them by the westcoast people and is often performed at modern potlatches and feasts.

Today, the northern tribes belong to the Nuu-chah-nulth Tribal Council, a political and administrative organization based in Port Alberni. The Tribal Council was established in the early 1960s, to represent all fourteen bands on the west coast of Vancouver Island, including Ahousaht, Ditidaht, Ehattesaht, Hesquiat, Kyuquot,

Two Mowachaht women wearing full cedar bark outfits and carrying food-gathering baskets. Originally titled "On the Shores of Nootka," this photo was taken by Edward S. Curtis in 1914.

Provincial Archives of B.C.

Mowachaht, Nuchatlaht, Ohiaht, Opetchesaht, Sheshaht, Tla-o-qui-aht, Toquaht, Uchucklesaht, and Ucluelet. As a co-ordinating body, the council administers federal government programs and represents Native people on issues which concern them.

The name "Nuu-chah-nulth" was chosen to replace "West Coast people," a term used for a short period of time in the 1970s and then discarded. The Tribal Council - and people - wanted a traditional name, one which would more aptly represent their Native identity. Nuu-chah-nulth, meaning "people living all along the mountains," comes from the word 'nutci' and refers to the Vancouver Island Range, a chain of rugged mountains which runs down the center of the island and forms the eastern boundary of the coastal territories. That narrow strip of land, bounded on one side by the open Pacific and on the other by the steep, densely-forested mountains, is home to the Nuu-chah-nulth people.

Social Organization

Prior to European contact, and as with most northwest coast culture groups, the original inhabitants did not refer to themselves by one all-encompassing group name. Rather, they identified themselves as separate and independent local groups. Fiercely territorial, their strongest ties were with land, family, and their immediate environment. Their concept of collective membership was fairly loose, extending only so far as a general reference to "people who we can understand."[13]

The local group was the basic unit of social organization. These were small, family-related groups which owned specific salmon fishing sites at rivers along the shores of the inlets. Each group was named for the place it came from, attaching the suffix "ath" (modern usage "aht") to mean "people of" or "belonging to" a particular place. Thus, the Mowachaht took their name from the local group site "mowatca," meaning "place where the deer come." Strong ties to the land were strengthened by kinship ties. Certain territorial rights and privileges, such as the right to take fish from a particular salmon stream, and the right to hunt whales and other sea mammals, were passed on through marriage and inheritance.

"The importance of our land was, before your people came, we lived our land," says Sam Johnson, "Like, animals: we didn't have to kill any species. We were lectured, through the old people, to never kill a young one because they're going to produce. They used to tell us that. 'Just weed out the old ones; take it home.'

"Mind you, a long time ago, they used to talk to that animal. 'I want your meat.' Talking to his spirit. 'You're going to be

Maquinna, a high ranking chief of the Mowachaht, grew to be a powerful leader during the European fur trade period. Original drawing by Spanish priest Tomas de Suria, 1791.

Provincial Archives of B.C.

useful to my family. You're going to provide for my family. And I'm thanking god that you are given to me as sacrifice.' That was the song, from our teachings. Everything you do, everything's got spirit. Like, when you're going to fall a cedar, you talk to that cedar. You're going to travel - 'I'm going to make a canoe out of you. You're going to be useful, you're not going to die.' That was the word, talking to that tree."[14]

Conventional knowledge suggests that the west coast people were migratory and followed a seasonal round of food-gathering. During winter, several local groups or "families" would come together at a common winter tribal village where each group had their own house site. In the spring, they broke up into individual groups to fish and gather food along the inlets, converging in one main village during the summer to form a confederacy.

Discussions with Dr. Inglis, however, suggest that the traditional patterns may have been very different. Much of our understanding comes from documents written during the initial period of contact, he says. An article written by Inglis and James Haggarty in 1985 suggests that, by assuming that these early descriptions reflect traditional cultural patterns, we have failed to recognize the magnitude and intensity of cultural change in Nootka Sound.[15]

The authors go on to say that the seasonal round of activities occurred as a direct result of the European presence.[16] According to archaelogical evidence, prior to the arrival of the trading ships, there were numerous relatively small, independent groups living in year-round villages and making full use of the resources within their territorial range.[17] The seasonal round began shortly after initial contact with the Europeans as a strategy for dealing with the new economic resource. Traditional subsistence activities gave way to the more immediate need to supply the trading vessels with fresh fish, meat, berries, and vegetables. Sea mammal hunters paid less attention to catching whales and sea lions, concentrating instead on honing their skills to hunt sea otters.

The people of Yuquot, led by Maquinna, a high-ranking chief of the Mowachaht, were the first to fully exploit this new resource, growing to become a powerful - and prosperous - force on the coast. Maquinna had the advantage of owning the rights to the Friendly Cove area, and thus could control access to the lucrative trade. Political, social, and economic changes during the relatively short period of the fur trade irrevocably altered the traditional patterns of the culture.

The Mowachaht

The Mowachaht, one of the most powerful confederacies on the coast, consisted of the Tlupana Arm group, led by Tlupana-nutl, said to be second to Maquinna, and the Tahsis-Nootka Sound group, led by Maquinna. The winter tribal village of the Tlupana Arm group was located at the mouth of Hoiss Creek (o'wis), with local group sites and fishing stations at Hisnit Inlet (hisnit), Head Bay at the mouth of the Sucwoa River (tsaxho) and Canton Creek (ta'atis), the Conuma River at Moutcha Bay (mowatca), and the Tlupana River at Nesook (nisaq).

Local group sites of the Nootka Sound-Tahsis Inlet branch were located at Tahsis (tacis), Blowhole Bay (hatoq), Lloyd Creek (amitsa), Tsowwin River (tsawun), Kendrick Creek (luis), and Marvinas Bay (mawun). Their tribal winter village was originally at Coopte on the northeast entrance to Tahsis Inlet. Shortly before the Europeans arrived, they began wintering at the head of Tahsis Inlet (tacis) near the mouth of the Leiner River, an extremely rich salmon fishing stream.

Originally, the Tlupana Arm group did not have a summer village site on the outer coast. During the European period, however, they were given house sites at

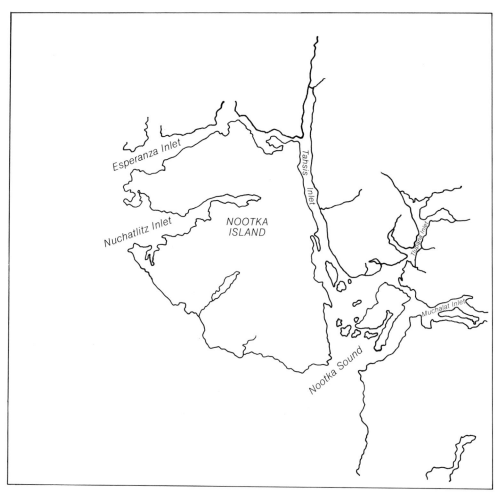

Mowachaht territory

Yuquot by Maquinna. The confederacy then took the name Mowachaht from the Tlupana Arm group *mowatca* meaning "place where the deer come to drink."

During the initial period of contact with the Europeans, Maquinna continued to use the outside village sites at Bajo Point (e'as) and either Beano or Callicum Creek. These two villages on the outside of Nootka Island were most likely the original outside village sites of an ancient group of people who lived on the outer coast year round. These outer coast people eventually joined groups which had inside properties, moving to the more protected inlets during the winter.

In the 1890s, the Muchalaht moved down to join the Mowachaht at Friendly Cove, and in 1935, the Mowachaht and Muchalaht tribes formally amalgamated. Their name was officially changed to the Mowachaht Band in the 1950s. To this day, the Muchalaht, who were given house sites at Yuquot, have retained their separate potlatch seats and traditions.

Friendly Cove

In 1789, the Spanish arrived to build a garrison at Friendly Cove. Shortly after, Maquinna moved his people to the other side of the island to what was likely an ancient fishing site. The move may have been partly in reaction to the murder of Callicum, a high-ranking Mowachaht, by a Spanish crew member, and partly due to the takeover of Yuquot. According to Esteban José Martínez, commandant at the fort, the Spanish were given the land at Yuquot by Maquinna.[18] There is some

Village at Yuquot (Friendly Cove) showing traditional house frames along the embankment. Photo by Richard Maynard, HMS Boxer *expedition,1874.*   Royal B.C. Museum, Ethnology Division.

indication, however, that Maquinna and his people had very little choice in the matter. When Martínez arrived at Nootka in May, 1789, he immediately set his men to the task of clearing the land and erecting buildings for the fort. His diary makes no mention of Maquinna or any other Indian granting the land to the Spanish. Nor does Martínez mention asking permission to build: he just does it. The reference to Maquinna "giving" the land to Martínez comes on August 25, 1789, nearly four months after Martínez' arrival.

Archibald Menzies, a British botanist with Captain George Vancouver's expedition to the west coast, visited Maquinna's new home on the outside coast in 1792. Setting out on foot the morning of May 21st, 1792, Menzies soon arrived at what he calls the Village of Caaglee which was:

"about three Miles from the Cove where Maquinna & his Tribe generally reside during the summer months for the conveniency of fishing in the Bay, ever since they were deprivd of the place which the Spaniards at present occupy, They had removd thither from their winter quarters situated in the back parts of the Sound a few days before our arrival with all their effects which were now arrangd & the Village reestablished."[19]

"The shore here is facd with high picked rocks irregularly piled over one another & the inland Country seems to be a continuation of the same rugged bottom coverd over with a thin layer of black vegetable mould which affords nourishment to a stinted forest of pinery, whose scrubby appearance evidently indicates both the poverty of the Soil & the violence of the Southern gales to which they are very much exposed. The interstices between the Trees was so filled up with underwood & Moss that it often conceald from our view the lurking dangers to which we were every moment exposd in tumbling over precipices or into Cavities & holes amongst rugged Rocks in this pathless forest...In the whole of our journey beyond the Village of Caaglee I saw not a spot of ground that even the most laborious industry could render Arable."[20]

When the Spanish finally departed in 1795, Maquinna returned to Yuquot, quickly distributing what remained of the fort among his tribe. Over the years, Friendly Cove has continued to be the main village site for the Mowachaht, although seasonal employment and food harvesting have taken people away from time to time. In 1917, Nootka Packing Company built a cannery and later, a reduction plant around the corner at Boca del Infierno Bay. Many of the Friendly Cove people were hired on at the cannery, living at the fish plant during the fishing season and returning to Friendly Cove in the winter. The fish processing plant and steamship stop became known as Nootka. While there, the Native workers lived in what was called the "Indian camp," a section of the cannery which consisted of a few communal family houses and several small, two- and three-room cabins. The buildings were plain and simple. Made from rough lumber, there was no indoor plumbing, and electricity was reserved for the managers and store-keeper: workers living in the Indian community and in the bunkhouses for Japanese and Chinese workers, had oil or gas lamps for light and wood-burning stoves for heat and cooking.[21]

When the cannery closed down in the 1950s, the Mowachahts returned to Friendly Cove where they had always kept their homes, and where they had returned each year during the off-seasons. Life resumed. Commercial and food fishing continued to play a major role in the economy of the small community. Regular transportation and freight services were provided by the *Uchuck*. The Catholic

View of Yuquot, 1874. HMS Boxer *at anchor in the bay.*

Yuquot, 1896. Photo by Edgar Fleming, Laing expedition. Note the change to the more modern house styles with vertical siding and sloped roofs.   Provincial Archives of B.C.

Yuquot, circa 1928. Roman Catholic Church and rectory are seen at the far right corner of the cove. Large house with three-cornered roof belonged to Captain Jack, a high ranking chief of the Mowachaht.   Provincial Archives of B.C.

Church operated well into the 1960s, moving its day school from Nootka Cannery to Yuquot. Most older children, however, were forced to leave their homes to attend residential schools near Tofino, returning to Friendly Cove only in the summers and during Christmas vacations. The loss of the children took an emotional toll on the community, as did the geographical isolation from the centers of economic activity. The Department of Indian Affairs began to pressure them to move out of Friendly Cove and closer to a larger community, one with more services and greater opportunity for employment.

During this same period, the federal government and the Mowachaht Band negotiated to lease several acres of land at the mouth of the Gold River to the East Asiatic Company for construction of the Gold River pulp mill. The land is part of the A'haminaquus reserve and is traditional Muchalaht territory. Opened in 1967, the mill is now owned by Canadian Pacific Forest Products Ltd., a multi-national corporation which controls the cutting rights to most of the timber in the Nootka and Kyuquot Sound area.

The Department of Indian Affairs succeeded in convincing the Mowachaht Band to relocate. In 1968, the Band voted in favour of moving to A'haminaquus, an old Muchalaht village site at the mouth of the Gold River and across the highway from the new pulp mill. The following year, the federal government completed construction on seven houses in the "instant village" at the mouth of the Gold River. By then, the Catholic Church at Friendly Cove had closed down, and with it, the day school which had been operating sporadically during the 1960s.

Friendly Cove is currently the year-round home of Ray Williams and his family. They are self-appointed caretakers of their tribe's ancestral land. As anyone will tell you, Friendly Cove or, rather, Yuquot, is not abandoned, despite its lack of population. It remains, and will continue to remain, the traditional home of the Mowachaht, no matter how far afield current generations may roam to seek employment or adventure. The ties to the land are strong. Today, Friendly Cove is used for Band retreats, annual summer Youth Camps, and food gathering. At the time of this writing, an archaeological dig has attracted much local attention and interest, and the Band plans, one day, to build a museum and cultural centre on the site of the Mowachahts' traditional village.

The Muchalaht

The Muchalaht groups lived along Muchalat Arm and inland, up the Gold River Valley. Some of their tribal winter sites have been identified as being located at the mouth of Mooyah River (mo'ya), Silverado

Muchalat Arm (A'haminaquus). Woman and baby. Photo by Edgar Fleming, Laing expedition, 1896. Newcombe Collection.

Royal B.C. Museum, Ethnology Division.

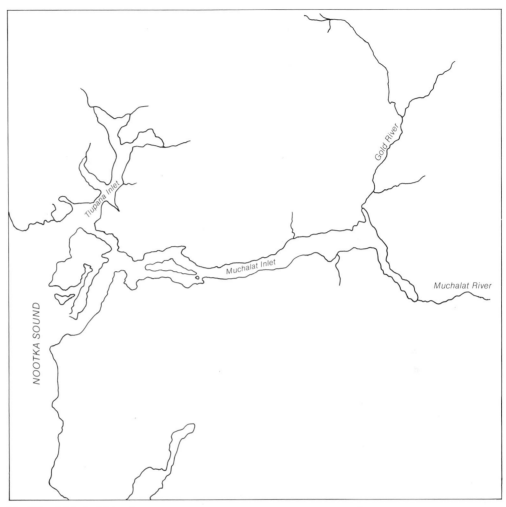

Traditional Muchalat territory.

River on Kings Passage (a'os), Hanna Creek (tcecis), Kleeptee River (clipti), the mouth of Burman River at the head of Matchlee Bay (matcli), A'haminaquus at Gold River, and tsaxana at the juncture of the Gold and Heber Rivers, near the site of the modern town of Gold River. They also had several camp sites at McCurdy Creek (moktas), Jacklah River (tcexla), and hiluwe'ta, located inland on the Gold River.

At one time, the Muchalaht group consisted of several small, independent local groups affiliated through marriage and kinship. Shortly after European contact, however, they joined together for mutual defense against outside attacks. Other, more powerful, tribes coveted their rich salmon fishing streams and periodically attacked the Muchalaht in hopes of taking over their territory. The Gold River was a particularly abundant salmon stream, and hence an extremely desirable site.

The strict dependency and reliance on marine resources of most coastal groups did not extend to the Muchalaht. Located some distance away from the outer coast, they didn't have direct access to resources on the outer coast, such as whales and other sea mammals. What they got was through trade or family connections. By the late 1800s and early 1900s, the Muchalaht didn't have any sites on the outer coast and it is not known if they ever did. They seemed to have made more use of land game than did the coastal tribes, hunting grouse in the fall, and elk and deer in the winter to supplement their diet of fish, seaweed, shellfish, and berries.

At one time, the Muchalahts' fiercest enemies were the Mowachaht, the Nimpkish, and the Hopatcisaht. The Gold River was one of the few sockeye spawning streams in the region, and was coveted by several groups, including the Mowachaht to the west, at the entrance to the sound, the Nimpkish to the northeast, and the Hopatcisaht at Sproat Lake to the south. During the first half of the 19th century, devastating attacks by their enemies reduced the Muchalaht people from over 400 to less than a hundred. The remainder joined together for mutual protection, taking their name from the local group at Matchlee Bay. They temporarily vacated their villages at the lower end of Muchalat Arm and moved deep up the inlet for safety.

Over the years, as peace was restored, they gradually regained confidence and moved back down the inlet to their old village sites. Eventually, through a series of inter-marriages, an alliance was formed between the Muchalaht and the Mowachaht. Good relations were finally established in the latter part of the 1890s when a Mowachaht chief died, leaving no immediate heir. The next in line was a Muchalaht man who moved from the head of Muchalat Inlet to Friendly Cove, bringing most of the Muchalaht with him.[22]

Several families, however, remained at the A'haminaquus site. Sam Johnson says a few of the elders had houses there, and it continued to be used during the fishing season as a major fishing camp. A photograph from the 1930s shows a fishing weir in place on the river just up from the canyon. Another photograph shows houses along the river delta.

Today's descendants of the Muchalaht tribe live with the descendants of the original Mowachaht tribe. For administrative purposes, and according to federal legislation, they are members of the Mowachaht Indian Band. Culturally and socially, however, they retain their allegiances to Muchalaht bloodlines, stories, and traditions. When they moved to Friendly Cove, they were not given potlatch seats or ranked housing. They have their own seats, and their own ties to the land.

A'haminaquus at the mouth of the Gold River, 1930.   Campbell River and District Museum and Archives.

Spearing salmon on the Gold River near the Muchalat Village site of A'haminaquus. Photo by Gordon Smith. Campbell River and District Museum and Archives.

Recently, the Muchalaht-Mowachaht returned to a political system of hereditary chiefs and an appointed council.

Today, the Muchalaht-Mowachaht alliance is looking toward the future and the role events in the past have played in crucial developments affecting their tribes. Several Band administrations have expressed concern over the way in which their land was leased to the East Asiatic Company to build a pulp mill, saying that their people weren't properly consulted in the negotiations. There has also been concern expressed over some of the the terms of the contract, including the issue of Native employment opportunities at the mill. At the same time, many of the villagers don't like their proximity to a pulp mill which has been charged with violating anti-pollution laws.

A'haminaquus is the ancestral home of the Muchalaht. Friendly Cove, or Yuquot, belongs to the Mowachaht. One day, say the Mowachaht, we will go home. Today, say the Muchalaht, we are home.

The Nuchatlaht

Several different groups inhabited the Esperanza Inlet area at the northern end of Nootka Island. They are now organized into two tribes, the Nuchatlaht, and the Ehattesaht. The Nuchatlaht territory included local group sites in Nuchatlitz Inlet at the entrance to Port Langford (lupatcsis), the head of Inner Basin (co'oma), and the head of Mary Basin (yutckhtok); the head of Espinosa Arm (olaktci); the east side of Catala Island (tcisyo'qwis); and along the south shore of Esperanza Inlet at Saltery Bay (aqi), Owossitsa Creek (o'astea) and Brodick Creek (tca'la). Their tribal winter villages were at Port Langford (apaqtu), Chum Creek (tcatcatcinik) in Espinosa Arm, and the head of Port Eliza (dhkac). In the summer, the confederacy moved to Nutcal at the entrance to Nuchatlitz Inlet, a rocky promontory off the northwest tip of Nootka Island.

Until very recently, the Nuchatlaht made their permanent home at Nutcal. At one time, it was a tiny but thriving community. There was even a weekly movie night, says Walter Michael Jr. who grew up in Nutcal. Everyone attended, from the elders

Village of Nuchatlitz, circa 1910.   Royal B.C. Museum, Ethnology Division.

Village of Nuchatlitz at entrance to Esperanza Inlet, circa 1988.   Don Dwulit photo.

right down to the toddlers and nursing babes in arms. In the 1800s, sealing schooners stopped in regularly to take on men and canoes for the Bering Sea. Steamships made regular deliveries of supplies and mail. A trading post and store bought furs and supplied the village with goods such as rice, flour, canned milk, and other household items. For many years, resident priests ran a Catholic mission church and day school at Nutcal which became a base for serving the Nuchatlaht and Ehattesaht tribes. Later, the canneries and reduction plants along Esperanza Inlet, Espinosa Arm, and Port Eliza provided opportunities for employment and socializing.

That all began to change in the 1940s and 50s. The reduction plants began to close and the steamship service was discontinued, depriving the small, remote villages along the coast of a vital transportation and communication link. The church and school closed down, and children were forced to leave their homes for much of the year to attend school in the town of Campbell River where they were boarded out. After much debate, the Band decided to relocate the village. According to some of the elders, the decision was based primarily on the desire to have their children with them, and the need to be closer to health care and other services. In 1987, they vacated their ancestral village and moved to Oclucje, a former winter home at the head of Espinosa Arm. There, connected by logging road to Zeballos and Highway 19, the main highway on Vancouver Island, they are closer to schools, stores, and services.

Many of the homes at Oclucje are brand new, built especially for the move. Others were floated up from their original sites at Nutcal and put on new foundations. The community is built on a gentle slope above the bay, facing south. Each house commands a breathtaking view down the inlet and across to distant mountains and islands. On the other side of the inlet, a few yards down from the village, is Chum Creek, another former winter site, and an ideal fishing stream. Since the relocation, says Walter Michael Jr., more and more of their people want to move back from the cities and towns on the east coast of the island. At the time I visited Oclucje, in the summer of 1988, two new houses were under construction, and the Band was on the waiting list for additional housing. They had a waiting list themselves, for people anxious to return home to their families and fellow tribe members.

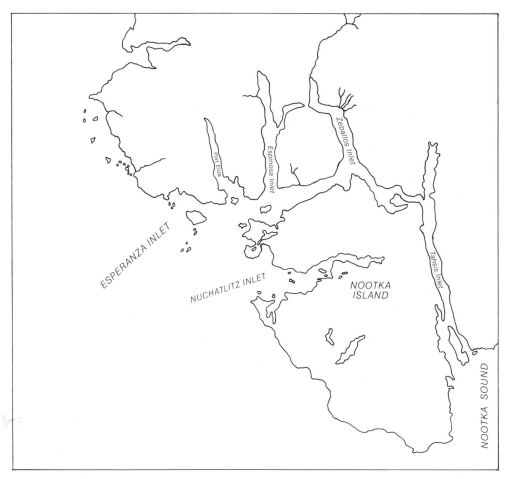

Ehattesaht and Nuchatlaht territory.

Queen's Cove

History suggests that at some point before European contact, a small tribe had two village sites at Chenakent, popularly known as Queen's Cove (tcinexnit), and maxteas, both located at the mouth of Port Eliza. The Queen's Cove group was apparently an independent tribe which maintained friendly relations with both the Ehattesaht and Nuchatlaht groups. In the mid-1880's, the Queen's Cove groups amalgamated with the Ehattesaht. Decimated by disease and war, they joined the larger group for protection and support. They did not receive any potlatch seats from the Ehattesaht, and retained their own bloodline. The Ehattesaht-Queen's Cove group resides primarily at Queen's Cove, bound together by marriage and family ties, and by a shared political and administrative structure.

The Ehattesaht

According to Drucker, the Ehattesaht was a confederacy of nine local groups which wintered at Hohk near the mouth of Ehattesaht Creek and spent the summers at Tatchu Point (tatcu). Local group sites were at Graveyard Bay (huphol), Mamat Creek at Little Espinosa (litcya), Ceepeecee (haqumts), Barr Creek (atcin), Little Zeballos River (icsa), the west side of Catala Island (woxne'a), and the head of Zeballos Arm (ehetis). Their name is derived from ehetis, the local group site at Zeballos. They also had a camp site at o'pnit near the entrance to Esperanza Inlet and in the middle of Nuchatlaht territory.

Queen Mary totem pole, 1962.

Photos courtesy of Shelagh Graham.

Hohk is best known to area residents for the totem pole which stood watch over the inlet for many years. The pole was raised at the beginning of this century by a high-ranking Ehattesaht woman married to Old Captain Jack. She was popularly known by her English name, Queen Mary. According to Moses Smith, an Ehattesaht elder living at Queen's Cove, Queen Mary had the pole carved in her honor because she had no offspring and she wanted to leave something behind to commemorate her bloodline.

"After that totem pole was carved," Moses said, "Then she gave the potlatch and raised the totem pole. That potlatch and the raising of that totem pole was strictly, absolutely, in her own honor. No body else's."[23]

Several carvers worked on the original pole, including Old David John from Ehattesaht who carved the Sun design, Victor Jim (Mituunii), also from Ehattesaht, Kakawin Chiiltt, Kakawin, and Tommy McLean who was originally from Ehattesaht but later transferred into the Friendly Cove Band.[24]

The pole was removed in 1985 after Moses raised concern over its deteriorating condition. "I began to worry about that totem pole," he said, "All at once it began to deteriorate very, very fast. So I made an approach to the leaders of the Ehattesaht people that we should save the totem pole."[25]

Eventually, arrangements were made to have the pole taken down and placed in the Provincial Museum in Victoria for safekeeping, despite a strong feeling among some elders that it would be taboo to remove the pole from its original site. In September 1985, the pole was carefully removed, a delicate undertaking that involved a team from the provincial museum, local logging contractor Ed Rowsell, the *Uchuck III*, and several local residents. Many people in the area recall the poignant sight of the *Uchuck* sailing down the passage with its fragile cargo strapped to the deck. When the boat docked at Gold River, the pole was lifted onto a flatbed truck and securely fastened. The remainder of the trip to Victoria was made by road.

The Provincial Museum had a replica carved by Nuu-chah-nulth carvers Art Thompson and Tim Paul. After much debate and consultation among elders and band members, it was decided that the new pole be erected at Ehetis at the head of Zeballos Inlet, rather than at its original site at Hohk. The decision may have had to do, in part, with the tribe's plans to relocate to Ehetis, a traditional winter village site. On September 30, 1988, the new pole returned to Esperanza Inlet where it was raised in the traditional fashion. Tragically, a few weeks after the ceremony, the pole was blown down in a windstorm and destroyed.

Relationship to the Environment

There existed a powerful unity between the people of the coast, the land and sea, and the spiritual realm. There was a strong maritime bond: they depended on the sea for food, travelled by water, and made their homes at the water's edge. They were mainly hunters of sea mammals -

Raising of the new pole at Ehetis near Zeballos, September 30, 1988.

Laurie Jones photos.

Ehattesaht village at Hokh. Photo from Gus Cox, Indian Agent.   Royal B.C. Museum, Ethnology Division.

whales, hair seals, sea lions, porpoises - and were particularly known for their whaling skills. Salmon, herring, kelp, shellfish, and mollusks, were other main sources of food, supplemented by berries and roots. They knew their world intimately. Their knowledge of the sea was unsurpassed. Every reef, every current, every beach and cliff along the outside coast was known. Every river, stream, inlet, cove, and bay was familiar. Everything had a name, and everything was owned.

On the west coast, the world was categorized as "outside" (kla'a) and "inside" (hilstis): outer coast and inner coast. Activities were organized around food resources. Winters were spent gathered in several main tribal villages located deep in the inside coast, protected from the fierce winter storms which blew in from the open seas. In March, the tribes broke up into several smaller family units and moved down the inlets to their fishing stations. Late spring and early summer were spent gathering food: they hunted sea mammals, fished, and collected mollusks and kelp.

The thick undergrowth of the rainforest made the interior lands almost impenetrable. Steep mountains and snow-covered peaks rising up from the shores of the inlets made access almost impossible. There were only a few overland trails, connecting the people on the west coast of the island with their neighbors to the east: Tahsish Arm to Nimpkish, Tahsis River to Woss Lake, Gold River to Sproat Lake, and Muchalat Lake to Nimpkish Lake.

The forests were utilized, however, for a very important resource: the cedar tree. Called the "tree of life," the red cedar provided the coastal people with bark for clothing, withes and roots for baskets, and wood for shelters and canoes. The yellow cedar too was used, and was especially good for carving. As Hilary Stewart notes in her book, *Cedar: Tree of Life to the Northwest Coast Indians,* every part of the cedar tree was used, including the outer and inner bark, the wood, the branches and withes, and the roots. Taking only what they needed, they left the tree standing, returning to the water's edge to work on their products.

The Indians held a great respect for everything living, firmly believing in their own "oneness" with the world. Land, sea, sky, mountains, rivers, plants, and animals:

all were related, and all were to be honored and revered. They believed in a world beneath the sea which was inhabited by the Salmon People, Herring People, and Whale People. When in their undersea homes, these supernatural beings looked and behaved exactly like humans, shedding their animal forms upon their return from the human world.

In the time before the influence of Christianity was felt, the coastal peoples believed that the spirits of these supernatural beings needed to be honored and appeased in order to ensure future abundance of food and to gain their cooperation in fishing and food-gathering. Two such important rituals were the First Salmon ceremony to honor the first salmon run up the rivers, and the purification rites practiced by sea mammal hunters in preparation for a successful hunt.

Whaler's Washing Shrine near Yuquot (Friendly Cove). Photo by George Hunt, circa 1903.

American Museum of Natural History.

Catholic Church and Rectory built by Father Brabant at Friendly Cove.

Royal B.C. Museum, Ethnology Division.

Whaler's Shrine

Shrines were another important aspect of Nootkan religious life and, according to Drucker, were made and used to "bring" a variety of important foods. For example, a shrine near A'haminaquus was used in a ritual to bring sockeye salmon up Muchalat Inlet to the mouth of the Gold River.[27]

A similar shrine, used by whalers, was located on a small island in Jewitt Lake at Friendly Cove. The first European to see and describe the shrine was de Roquefeuil, a French navigator and scientist who saw the shrine in 1817:

"The Indians call by the name of tche-ha the shed which serves as the burying place of the great chiefs of Nootka only. At the entrance of the shed there are five rows of wooden statues, rudely carved, extending to the other extremity, where there is a kind of cabinet decorated with human skulls. Several of these statues wear the distinctive features of a man, and even have natural hair. A gallery of human bones marks the limits of the shed. Opposite the entrance there are eight large whales made of wood, placed in a line, on the back of each, skulls are symmetrically arranged..."[28]

The Whaler's Shrine at Jewitt Lake is said to be the most significant monument of any kind from the west coast of North America. At one time, some anthropologists and historians believed that the presence of shrines in the Nootka Sound area linked the Mowachaht to the whaling cults of the Bering Sea. The shrine was removed in 1904 by George Hunt, assistant to Franz Boas, renowned ethnographer who at the time was studying the Kwakwa'kwak^w on the north eastern end of Vancouver Island. Hunt purchased the shrine and shipped it back east to the American Museum of Natural History in New York.

The questions surrounding the shrine's removal, however, have never been fully dealt with. Who sold it? Did they have the authority to sell it? Why was it removed in the first place? Over the years, there has been a growing concern by both Native and non-Native about the loss of northwest coast culture and the ethics of collecting. In 1984, the historical significance of the Whaler's Shrine was officially recognized by the Historic Sites and Monuments Board of Canada, and by the provincial Ministry of the Environment. In 1989, the Mowachaht entered into a working relationship with the American Museum of Natural History to discuss the future of the shrine, including the possibility of carving a replica to return to Friendly Cove. The American Museum in New York, along with representatives from the Royal B.C. Museum in Victoria, are actively engaged in the process to repatriate, in some form, part of the culture that was taken away.

Cultural Change

The coming of the European way of life significantly changed and eventually destroyed the integrity of the northwest coast Native culture. Warfare, and diseases such as smallpox, diphtheria, tuberculosis, and venereal diseases decimated the population and weakened important social structures, including the potlatch system. Traditional hunter-gatherer patterns, irrevocably altered by the economic boon of the maritime fur trade, were further eroded by industrialization. Finally, through the implementation of government colonization plans and the Indian land reserve system, Native use of the land was restricted.

In the late 1800s, Bishop Seghers and Father Augustin Joseph Brabant, became the first missionaries to visit the west coast since the Spanish left Friendly Cove in 1795. They arrived in 1874, travelling up the west coast of the island aboard a trading ship operated by Captain William Spring. On that first trip to the northern coast, they visited Friendly Cove, Esperanza Inlet, and Kyuquot Sound. Later that year Father Brabant founded the Roman Catholic mission at Hesquiat, where he was based for the next 15 years. His mission included the territory covered by Nootka and Kyuquot Sounds.

During his time on the coast, Father Brabant kept a diary, filled with somewhat sporadic entries, and containing references and observations on his work among the Nootka and Kyuquot people. A few years after establishing the Mission at Hesquiat,

Catholic Church at Friendly Cove, 1968. Photo by John Smyly.   Royal B.C. Museum, Ethnology Division.

Brabant built a small chapel and rectory house at Friendly Cove. In 1880, a Mission and Indian school was built at Kyuquot Sound. The resident priest was Father Nicolaye, followed by Father Lemmens, both of whom also maintained diaries while stationed in Kyuquot.

Christie Residential School

One of the most brutal attacks on the Native culture was the implementation of the Indian residential school system, widely promoted throughout the province by all religious denominations. Among the first schools on Vancouver Island was the Christie Indian Residential School, built in 1890. Located on Meares Island in Clayoquot Sound, the school was intended to indoctrinate Indian children into the white man's culture by instilling Christian principles and behavior. Native children from Friendly Cove, Esperanza Inlet, and Kyuquot Sound, were removed from their families and sent to live at the residential school, where they were forbidden to speak their own language.

The Christie Residential School operated until 1974 when it was finally closed down. The main school building burned to the ground in 1976. It's legacy remains, however, burned indelibly into the memories of the children who attended the school and who can no longer speak their language.

"I got spanked for speaking Indian, in my language," said Sam Johnson, "First day I was there. That's how strict it was. Father Charles - he spoke Indian after that! My cousin down-island, he started laughing. 'He's talking Indian,' he said. Father Charles, he spoke our language."[29]

Sam was seven years old when he was sent to the residential school. Many Indian children were taken away when they were four or five years old. Ben Jack, hereditary chief of the Mowachaht Band, says the residential school system and the loss of the language destroyed their culture.

"A lot of our people, because of our parents going to residential schools, they were really frowned on talking our own language," he said, "So they were forced to speak English. And when my brothers and them went to a residential school, they came home and tried to speak our language. They lost the dialect, and the parents usually laughed at them because they weren't speaking it right any more, they weren't pronouncing words right. That whole residential school system hurt us."[30]

Christie Residential School, circa 1894.   Royal B.C. Museum, Ethnology Division.

Modern Times

In 1871, the colonies of Vancouver Island and the mainland joined together as one province and entered confederation with Canada. Colonization plans were stepped up, as was pressure on the government to reach an agreement over the issue of Indian land. In 1872, Dr. I.W. Powell was appointed B.C.'s Commissioner of Indian Affairs responsible for Vancouver Island and the Northwest Coast. In 1874, he made a trip to Nootka and Kyuquot Sounds aboard the *H.M.S. Boxer*, taking with him photographer Richard Maynard. Many of our earliest photographic records of the area were made at this time.

Shortly after the establishment of the West Coast Agency of Indian Affairs, in 1881, the process of laying out the bulk of the land reserves in the Nootka and Kyuquot Sounds was undertaken. Unlike Native groups in other parts of the country, coastal Indians were not "driven from their home territories and placed on reservations."[31] In laying out the reserves, the government made an attempt to recognize the existing land use patterns of the aboriginal population. The Mowachaht, Muchalaht, Nuchatlaht, Ehattesaht, Checleset and Kyuquot people were allocated land in places that had been identified as their traditional village sites, hunting grounds,and fishing areas, a plan which resulted in the creation of several small reserves scattered over the region. What the government did not settle at the time was the question of Indian rights to the land, a question which today continues to plague Native and non-Native relations.

In the region today, Native people live in settlements that are separate from white communities, yet too small to be self-sufficient. The Mowachaht live nine miles away from the modern white community of Gold River, and across the road from a multi-million dollar pulp mill. Their reserve land is at the mouth of the Gold River, the traditional Muchalaht village site of A'haminaquus. The community consists of some twenty or so houses, a community hall, the band administration office, and two double-wide trailers used by visiting federal and provincial government workers from public health, social services, and Indian Affairs.

The tiny community of about 140 people doesn't have its own school, a store, or other amenities such as hotel, post office, cafe, etc.. Children attend school in Gold River and their parents do their shopping at the town's stores or drive into

A'haminaquus village, Gold River, 1988.   Laurie Jones photo.

Campbell River, 60 miles away. Some families live in the town of Gold River, but, as in many small towns in B.C., there continues to be difficulty in the integration of Native and non-Native communities.

Responding to changing economic conditions, the Nuchatlaht recently moved to Oclucje at the head of Espinosa Inlet. The logging community of Zeballos, where their children attend school, is a 20-minute drive away by gravel logging road.

The village of Nutcal at Nuchatlitz is no longer inhabited year-round. Nor, with the exception of the Ray Williams family, is Friendly Cove. The Ehattesaht Band Council's office is located in Campbell River where the majority of their band members live. At the time of this writing, they are in the process of moving back to their ancestral home at Ehetis at the head of Zeballos Inlet. It's only a matter of time before the people of Queen's Cove, the last remaining village in Nootka Sound, will also choose to live closer to the schools, stores and services provided by the larger centers.

Along with centralization into single villages, the changing economic, political, and social patterns created changes in Native society. Wage labor replaced food gathering, and people began taking jobs in the resource-based industries which dominated the economy of the west coast: seal hunting, commercial fishing, canning and fish processing, and picking fruit and hops.

Seal hunting was one of the first such industries to use Indian labor from the west coast of Vancouver Island. Trading schooners heading to the hair seal grounds in the Bering Sea stopped in at villages in Nootka Sound, Esperanza Inlet, and Kyuquot Sound to take on Native men as hunters. They were required to pay their own room and board, and supply their own canoes and hunting gear. In return, they were paid for each seal pelt they brought in. They were out for several months at a time, returning to their villages with several hundred dollars in cash earnings. Similarly, fruit and hop pickers moved to the Fraser Valley and the Puget Sound area for several months of the year, returning home to the Nootka Sound when the fruit season was over.

Today, Native people in Nootka Sound are struggling to revive their lost heritage and culture. Through language programs and Native studies curriculum in the schools, the popular interest in Native art and design, and through the practice of the modern potlatch, they are able to pass on to their children the stories and traditions of their ancestors. They too, like the rest of us, are concerned with the fundamental issues of modern industrial life: employment, the environment, and the quality of life:

"It'd be pretty hard for us to go back to history and say we want to be downright Mowachaht and go back exactly the way we were," said Nick Howard. "Who's going to walk around half-naked in cedar bark outfits, you know. Or who's going to ride around in a canoe from Friendly Cove to the Bering Sea again. That's never going to happen. Today, we're going to have to go back to admitting who we are today. We're a brand of Mowachaht people. We are Mowachaht. But we're a new brand that's adapted to a society that's given to us."[32]

Writing, or rather, attempting to write the Native story is a difficult task. It is not my intent here to "tell the Native story," just as I will never be able to completely tell the story of Tahsis or Zeballos or Gold River. What I hope to have done is raise an awareness of some of the social and economic forces which have shaped the Native community and have brought Native and non-Natives to where we are today. To understand the Native story, and to appreciate each other's place in that story, we must begin to break down the barriers between the two separate and distinct histories.

Notes

[1] Interview, Nick Howard (Gold River: April 28, 1988).

[2] Interview, Sam Johnson (Gold River: April 11, 1988).

[3] Interview, Sam Johnson (Friendly Cove: April 22, 1988).

[4] Barbara Efrat and William Langlois, *nut-ka: The History and Survival of Noot-kan Culture* (Victoria: 1978), p. 1.

[5] Conversation, James C. Haggerty, Head of the Archaeology Division, Royal B.C. Museum (Victoria: January 26, 1989).

[6] Conversation, Richard Inglis, Head of the Ethnology Division, Royal B.C. Museum (Victoria: August 1990).

[7] G.M. Sproat, *The Nootka: Scenes and Studies of Savage Life*, ed. Charles Lillard (Victoria: 1987), p. 10.

[8] A. J. Brabant in Captain John T. Walbran, *British Columbia Coast Names* (Vancouver: 1971), p. 359.

[9] Johnson interview, April 11, 1988.

[10] William J. Folan, *The Community, Settlement and Subsistence Patterns of the Nootka Sound Area* (University of Southern Illinois: 1972), p. 36.

[11] Philip Drucker, *The Northern and Central Nootkan Tribes* (Washington D.C.: 1951), pp. 3-4.

[12] Formerly Kwakiutl and Kwakwelth, the Kwakwa'kwak^w, meaning "Kwa-kwa-la speaking people," inhabit the northeast coast of Vancouver Island and the adjacent area of mainland British Columbia. At the turn of the century, German anthropologist Franz Boas gave to the group as a whole the name "Kwakiutl" after one of the small tribes on the northern tip of Vancouver Island. The term Kwakwa'kwak^w is generally preferred by anthropologists and the people themselves.

[13] Drucker, p. 3.

[14] Johnson interview, April 11, 1988.

[15] Richard I. Inglis and James C. Haggarty, *Cook to Jewitt: Three Decades of Change in Nootka Sound, Selected Papers of the Fifth North American Fur Trade Conference* (Montreal: 1985), p. 194.

[16] Ibid., p. 195.

[17] Ibid., p. 221.

[18] Esteban José Martínez, *Diary of the Voyage of Don Esteban José Martínez...in 1789* (Provincial Archives of British Columbia, Victoria), p. 172.

[19] Archibald Menzies, *Menzies Journal of Vancouver's Voyage: 1790-1792* (PABC, Victoria), p. 580.

[20] Ibid., p. 581.

[21] Fire insurance plans, Special Collections, University of B.C. Main Library (Vancouver).

[22] Drucker, p. 231.

23 Interview, Moses Smith (Royal B.C. Museum, Victoria: September, 1985).

24 Royal B.C. Museum, Anthropological Collections Section, Victoria, B.C. Information from the backs of photographs. Information provided by Mr. and Mrs. Joseph Smith, Queen's Cove, August 1976.

25 Interview, RBCM, 1985.

26 Hilary Stewart, *Cedar: Tree of Life to the Northwest Coast Indians* (Vancouver: 1984).

27 Drucker, p. 172.

28 de Roquefeuil, *A Voyage to the Northwest Coast of America in 1823*, p. 102.

29 Johnson interview, April 22, 1988.

30 Interview, Ben Jack (A'haminaquus: April 11, 1988).

31 Wilson Duff, *The Indian History of British Columbia, Volume 1: The Impact of the White Man* (Victoria: 1977), p. 50.

32 Howard interview, April 28, 1988.

Nootka Sound is best known for the key role it played in world affairs during the period 1774 to 1795. During that time, it was the center of a thriving fur trade and became the focal point of a bitter struggle between Spain and Britain over control of the Pacific northwest. Britain eventually won that struggle, and western Canada's future as a British colony was sealed: the entire west coast lands, from the Columbia River to Alaska - were granted to the British Empire.

The dispute, now known as the Nootka Controversy, went on for several years and was finally settled in the European courts, far from the site of contention. Then, as now, the development of the area was tied to external factors: the development of Vancouver Island and British Columbia; international markets; and political decisions made by foreign governments who had an economic stake in the north Pacific coast.

People have been living on the outer coast of Vancouver Island for thousands of years. Long before the first European sailing ship anchored off Friendly Cove on Nootka Sound, the ancestors of today's Nuu-chah-nulth people were hunting sea mammals along the outer coast, fishing for salmon at the mouths of rivers, and cutting cedar trees to construct their marvelous whaling canoes. Until the latter part of the 18th century, they were unaware of European nation states, Asian markets, and political struggles over lucrative trade routes. Their primary contact was with neighboring tribes to the south and north along the coast who had a similar lifestyle and shared a common interest in the sea.

That all changed with the arrival of Spanish and British sailing ships. The European presence signaled the beginning of a new phase in the development of the region. Nootka Sound - remote, isolated, self-contained - was quickly drawn into the realm of the "known" world and swept up in events outside its geographical boundaries and beyond its control.

The Perez Expedition

The first recorded arrival was a Spanish expedition to the north Pacific coast under the command of Juan José Perez Hernandez. He anchored his vessel, the *Santiago,* just outside the entrance to Nootka Sound on the afternoon of August 8th, 1774. Two Roman Catholic priests were members of Perez' expedition and kept daily accounts of their voyage. Fray Juan Crespi writes:

"We made out the land very well from the roadstead where we lay, a roadstead which has the shape of a C, and which the Captain named San Lorenzo. The land was low and heavily clothed with timber, though of what kind we could not distinguish."[1]

There has been some dispute among historians and anthropologists as to whether Perez anchored inside Nootka or was actually a few miles farther south near the Hesquiat Peninsula. Richard Inglis, head of ethnology at the Royal B.C. Museum, says that it is now generally accepted that the area described by Crespi and others on the Perez expedition, is the Estevan coastal plain, and that Perez most probably anchored off Hesquiat and was not at the entrance to Nootka Sound as was originally thought.[2] Nonetheless, on early navigational charts, what we now know as Nootka Sound was marked as "Surgidero de San Lorenzo" - the Roadstead of St. Lawrence[3] - and it was to this area that Spanish sailing ships later made their way.

As the *Santiago* neared shore, three canoes came out to meet the ship but turned back after failing to convince those on board not to land. Later that night, writes Crespi, "three canoes of larger size, with fifteen men in them, came out, and remained at some distance from the ship, their occupants crying out in a mournful tone." Joined by two more canoes, the Natives remained alongside until late that night, "about a musket shot's distance from the ship...talking one with another, and from time to time crying out."[4]

The next day, the Indians were confident enough to get a closer look:

"At daybreak we set about getting the long-boat into the water, in order to go ashore to plant the holy cross. While thus engaged we saw fifteen canoes leaving the land; in a short time they had come near to us, and we saw that there were about a hundred men, and some, though not many, women in them. They were given to understand that they might draw nearer without fear, and they came near and began to trade with what they had in their canoes, which consisted only of skins of otters and other animals unknown to us, and some hats made of reeds and painted like those seen at Point Santa Margarita,[5] except, we noticed, that in these the conical crown ends in a ball like a little pear,[6] and some cloths woven of a material very like hemp, and with a fringe of the same thread. Our people bought some skins and some cloths and hats in exchange for clothing, ribbons and shells which the men had picked up on the beach at Monterey and Carmelo, and we noted that these Indians had a great liking for the shells and ribbons... Some pieces of iron and of copper and of knives were seen in their possession."[7] According to the second priest, Fray Tomas de la Peña, the Indians preferred the knives and shells over any of the other trade items.[8]

Perez and his men spent that morning trading with the Indians, but they were prevented from going ashore by a sudden wind which came up from the west in the afternoon, threatening to run the *Santiago* aground. Quickly cutting anchor, Perez set out to deeper waters for safety, and then headed home to Mexico. The fact that he did not go ashore nor formally take possession of the land in the name of Spain, was later to be used by the British in their argument for England's prior claim to the west coast.

When Perez reached Nootka Sound in 1774, he was on his way south after having sailed as far north as the Queen Charlotte Islands. He was under orders to claim any and all of the Pacific coast lands in the name of Spain. As Warren L. Cook writes in *Flood Tide of Empire*, the Perez voyage was a scouting mission:

"He was prohibited from making any sort of settlement, no matter how easy or advantageous it might seem, but was to take note of likely sites so that they could be found with ease in case colonization plans resulted from his explorations. In places adequate for settlement, he should take possession, using the standard form attached to his instructions, and erect a large wooden cross supported by a cairn of stones hiding a glass bottle, stoppered with pitch, containing a copy of the act of possession signed by the commander, chaplain, and two pilots."[9] Further, if he met any Native inhabitants, he was to treat them with "amiability and kindness," and never use force against them unless necessary.

But Perez didn't take formal possession of either the Queen Charlotte Islands or Nootka Sound. In fact, no lands on the north Pacific coast were officially claimed until the following year when Spain sent a second expedition to the north. Under the command of Bruno de Hezeta, the *Santiago* and the *Sonora* set sail up the coast for what is now known as Alaska. The *Santiago* turned back, but the *Sonora* continued on, under the command of Bodega y Quadra, and eventually reached 58° north latitude. In a bay on the western side of Prince of Wales Island, a small party of men went ashore and claimed possession of the land for Spain, calling the place "Puerto de Bucareli" in honor of Mexico's viceroy. It is still called Bucareli Sound today.

Perez' visit marks the first contact between the Native inhabitants of the region and people from the European continent. For both parties, it was a meeting of the strange and the unfamiliar. The Indians, too, have a story about that first meeting. They say that their ancestors thought the vessel carried Qua-utz, a supernatural being of great powers. The following was told to José Moziño by the Indians when he arrived at Nootka in 1792, some 18 years after Perez:

"The sight of this ship at first filled the Natives with terror, and even now they testify that they were seized with fright from the moment they saw on the horizon the giant 'machine' which little by little approached their coasts," writes Moziño. "They believed that Qua-utz was coming to make a second visit, and were fearful that it was in order to punish the misdeeds of the people. As many as were able hid themselves in the mountains, others closed themselves up in their lodges, and the most daring took their canoes out to examine more closely the huge mass that had come out of the ocean. They approached it timorously, without sufficient courage to go aboard, until after awhile, attracted by the friendly signs by which the Spanish crew called them, they boarded the ship and inspected with wonder all the new and extraordinary objects that were presented to them."[10]

Moziño was a member of Bodega y Quadra's expedition to the northwest coast in 1792. A naturalist by profession, Moziño remained at Nootka for six months, learning the language and customs of the Native people. His observations on Nootka Indian culture have been translated into English by Iris Higbie Wilson and published in book form under the title *Noticias de Nutka*.

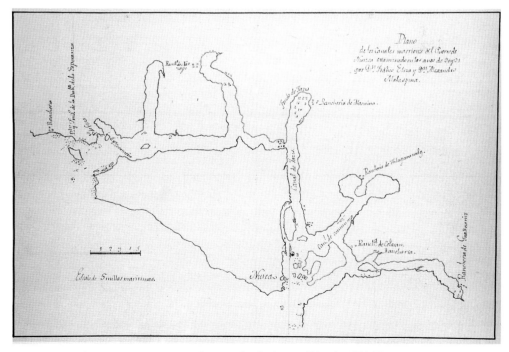

Spanish map of the Nootka Sound area, from Malaspina's expedition in 1790. From Plano de los canales interiores del puerto de Nutzca examinado en los anos de 90 y 91 por dn. Francisco Eliza y dn. Alexandro Malaspina.

Environment Canada, Parks Service

According to stories told by the Indians and passed on through the oral tradition, the arrival of the strangers was unexpected. Peter Webster, an Ahousaht elder living in Ahousaht on the west coast of Vancouver Island, tells a story about his people thinking that the ship was filled with the spirits of dead ancestors, partially explaining Fray Crespi's reference to the "mournful crying out" of the Natives. Peter Webster:

"I wouldn't say the first ship, but I do know that it was seen southwest side of Estevan Point. This Hesquiat seen something strange out in the open Pacific, looks like house poles out there. They went out in their canoe to see what it was. They saw these guy wires for each mast. The blocks look like skulls. Us old people would say an Indian word that means skull of a dead human, just the bones. And this is what they thought it was, dead people that was aboard that ship. And then the mast, yes the mast, somebody composed a song right away, while they were still on the ocean.

"The song says: 'I got my walls of a house floating on the water.' Since those ships were found floating on open Pacific, we started calling the white people *mamalni*, regardless of what nationality, even the white people that have never been on the water. In Europe I'd still call them *mamalni*. But *mamalni* means that you are living on the water and floating around, you have no land." [11]

At the time of Perez' expedition, the Spanish encounter at Nootka had little international significance. Spain's primary concern was to protect its territorial claim to the Pacific. While the Indians eagerly traded sea otter pelts and other items with Perez' crew, the Spanish showed little interest in exploiting a potentially lucrative fur trade. Crespi writes, almost dismissively, that the trade items consisted, among other things, "only of skins of otters and other animals unknown to us." A year later, the Hezeta and Quadra expedition completely bypassed Nootka Sound on its way to the Queen Charlotte Islands.

Indian village at Friendly Cove (Yuquot). Sketch by John Webber, 1778.

Captain James Cook, Portrait   Provincial Archives of B.C.

The Cook Expedition

The next recorded expedition to the region was led by Captain James Cook from Britain. Several hundred men aboard two vessels, the *Resolution* and the *Discovery,* arrived off the entrance to Nootka Sound in 1778, four years after Perez. Cook was under orders to search for the elusive North West Passage, a route that would link the Atlantic and Pacific Oceans. On board were scientific observers who were to make detailed records of the natural wildlife, landscape, and cultures at various stops along the way, paying careful attention to anything that might be of interest to navigation or commerce. Cook was also under orders to take possession of any lands he discovered in the name of the King of Britain.

Cook arrived off the west coast of Vancouver Island on March 29th, 1778. He sighted the coastline from some distance off shore, making a broad sweep of the area through his telescope. He was looking for a protected anchorage in order to repair one of his boats, the *Resolution,* which had been damaged during a storm at sea. From the position of the boat, the portion of coastline seen through the telescope resembled a large concave arc. In anticipation of finding a good harbor, Cook gave the name Hope Bay to the area bounded by what is now known as Breakers Point at the tip of Nootka Island in the south, and Brooks Peninsula in the north. Cook called it Woody Point, a name which didn't survive long; it was renamed Brooks Point in 1862. Before anchoring, Cook noted at least two main inlets, the most northerly one likely the entrance to Kyuquot Sound. But strong winds in the north persuaded him to make for the southern inlet, a decision that proved to be a turning point in the history of Nootka Sound.

What Perez named Surgidero de San Lorenzo, Cook called King George's Sound. We now know it as Nootka Sound. He spent a month in the sound, anchoring his boats, the *Resolution* and the *Discovery,* off Bligh Island, in a small protected cove since named Resolution Cove. During his stay at Nootka, Cook was preoccupied with preparing his ships for the difficult journey northward. He was anxious to repair the mast of the *Resolution* and resume his journey before the winter storms. Nonetheless, he spent the time constructively, setting up an observatory in order to record weather and marine navigational information, making surveys of the coastline, and trading with the Indians. A journal entry for Monday, April 30th, reads:

"A great many Canoes filled with the Natives were about the Ships all day, and a trade commenced betwixt us and them, which was carried on with the Strictest honisty on boath sides. Their articles were the Skins of various animals, such as Bears, Wolfs, Foxes, Dear, Rackoons, Polecats, Martins and in particular the Sea Beaver, the same as is found on the coast of Kamchtka.[12] Cloathing made of these skins and a nother sort made, either of the bark of a tree or some plant like hemp; Weapons, such as Bow and Arrow, Spears & ca Fish hooks and Instruments of various kinds, pieces of carved work and even human sculs and hands, and a variety of little articles too tedious to mention. For these things they took in exchange, Knives, chissels, pieces of iron & Tin, Nails, Buttons, or any kind of metal. Beads they were not fond of and cloth of all kinds they rejected."[13]

He also had time to survey the inner harbor of the sound. His first trip was informative if uneventful:

Monday, April 20, 1778: "I first went to the West point where I found a large Indian Village *[now known as Yuquot]* and before it a very Snug harbour *[Friendly Cove]* in which was from 9 to 4 fathom water and a bottom of fine Sand. The people of this Village who were numerous and to most of whom I was known, received me very curtiously, every one pressing me to go in to his house, or rather appartment for several families live under the same roof, and there spread a mat for me to sit down upon and shewed me every other mark of civility."[14]

From Friendly Cove, Cook toured the periphery of the sound. Passing the entrances to Kendrick Arm and Tahsis Inlet, he stopped only briefly to examine some empty house frames and fishing weirs near what is now known as Coopte, about a mile above the mouth of the Tahsis Inlet. Coopte was a local group village site which, over time, had become a seasonal fishing spot. Cook then crossed over the northern end of the sound to Tlupana Inlet.

"I now found what I had before conjectured, that the land under which the ships laid was an island *[since named Bligh Island]*,[15] and that there were many small ones laying scatered in the Sound on the West side of it *[the Spanish Pilot group]*. Opposite the North end of the large island on the Continent was an Indian Village at which I landed, the inhabitants were not so polite as those of the other I had visited; but this seemed in a great measure if not wholly owing to one Surly chief, who would not let me enter their houses, following me where ever I went and several

Captain Cook's ships **Resolution** *and* **Discovery** *in Nootka Sound, 1778. From a water colour by John Webber. Original in the National Maritime Museum, Greenwich.* Provincial Archives of B.C.

times made signs for me to be gone; the presents I made him did not induce him to alter his behaviour. Some young women, more polite than their surly Lordd, dress'd themselves in a hurry in their best cloaths, got together and sung us a song which was far from being harsh or disagreeable.[16] The day being now far spent, I proceeded for the Ships around the North end of the large island, meeting in my way several Canoes laden with Sardins which they had caught some where in the East corner of the Sound."[17]

The impact of Cook's visit on Nootka Sound wasn't fully realized until several years later, after the ships had returned to England and the official accounts of Cook's voyage had been published in 1784 and, more significantly, after news got out about the high prices paid for sea otter pelts in China. When Cook's expedition reached Canton in 1779, the crew received such high prices for their furs that they nearly mutinied, wanting to return to Nootka Sound for more furs rather than continue on to England. In fact, among the first British traders to set sail for Nootka were George Dixon and Nathanial Portlock, officers aboard Cook's expedition to the north coast.

The demand for sea otter pelts led to the opening of the Pacific coast. The publication of Cook's journals excited public interest. His marine charts and scientific observations paved the way for other explorers as well as for entrepreneurs who were interested in resource exploitation. Cook, however, didn't live to see the results of his findings. He was killed in the Hawaiian Islands in February, 1779, before his expedition ever reached England. His journals were published after his death. While the contribution he made to the body of human knowledge is of considerable academic importance, Cook's legacy lay not in his scientific observations, but rather, in his role in opening up the region to the rest of the world.

Trade and Commercial Developments

Nootka Sound's heyday was short and intense. During the brief, ten year period 1785 to 1795, Nootka Sound was the center of an active maritime fur trade and a major west coast anchorage for American, British, Spanish and even French ships. The first commercial trader to arrive was James Hanna in the *Harmon*. He reached Nootka Sound in August of 1785, and stayed in the area until the end of September, trading iron bars for furs. In Canton, China a few months later, his harvest of 560 sea otter pelts sold for more than 20,000 Spanish dollars.

Hanna was the first of several hundred traders to make their way to the west coast. In the beginning, the British led the trade; however, it was soon taken over by the Americans who dominated it during its peak. According to figures compiled by F.W. Howay, about 450 trading vessels were on the north Pacific coast during the period 1774 to 1820. More than half of those vessels sailed under the United States flag: 275, as compared to 93 British ships and 43 Spanish.[18]

The nature of the maritime fur trade was seasonal and transitory. Traders did not build permanent settlements, nor did they have any intention of remaining in the area for any great length of time. They came on ships, remained long enough to collect a profitable bundle of furs, and then departed. The Indians were responsible for hunting the sea otters, skinning them, and preparing them for market. In exchange, they received iron and other metals which were coveted as much for their prestige value as for their usefulness in making tools and other implements.

From the beginning, the trade was characterized by violence and abuse, starting with the first trader, James Hanna. The following story is based on Hanna's account and the report the Indians gave to the Spanish several years later. According to Hanna, Indians attacked his ship at Nootka but he was able to quell them "with considerable slaughter." The battle occurred after Hanna fired upon the

Indians for stealing a chisel.[19] Esteban José Martínez, commandant of the Spanish fort at Nootka in 1789, recounts a different story as told to him by the Indians. He says Captain Hanna went among the villages along the northeastern arm of the inlet "where he killed more than fifty Indians." Later, Maquinna visited the *Harmon*, "and when they had seated him near the binnacle, they sprinkled a little powder under his chair, giving him to understand that this was an honor which they showed to chiefs." But what Maquinna thought was colored sand was actually gunpowder. "Poor Macuina was raised from the deck by the explosion and had his buttocks scorched; he showed me the scars," writes Martínez.[20]

Martínez himself, for all his criticism of the British for their poor treatment of the Natives, was not much better. He had a reputation along the coast for an unruly temper which precipitated the shooting death of Callicum, the second highest-ranking chief at Yuquot. Callicum, angry with Martínez for capturing a British vessel and imprisoning its crew, approached Martínez' vessel in his canoe, berating him for his actions. "Irritated by such abusive language," writes Martínez, "I took a gun from among those which my men had carried over when they went to bring the sloop in, and fired it at him." But the gun misfired and another seaman, seeing what had happened, raised his gun and shot, killing Callicum.[21]

There were many other incidents of injustice and ill-treatment all along the coast by British, Spanish and American traders. The build-up of tensions between the Natives and the commercial traders came to a dramatic head in March, 1803, when Maquinna and his men slaughtered the captain and crew of the *Boston*. Only John R. Jewitt and John Thompson were spared. They lived as captives under the care of Maquinna for the next two years, during which time Jewitt kept a journal, recording his activities and observations.[22] Trading activity at Nootka had already been on the decline, and after the massacre of the *Boston,* ships steered clear of the area, stopping instead at Clayoquot or other places along the coast. Ironically, there is some speculation that one of the motives behind Maquinna's attack was to secure a load of furs for trade.[23]

Political Developments

Events in the region during the latter part of the 18th century were dominated by the political history of Spain and Britain. Driven by political and economic motives, Spain and Britain were interested in expanding their territorial powers, and Nootka Sound came to represent the "Pacific link" in that expansion. Marine surveyors, scientists, and explorers charted the coastline and gathered as much information as possible - information that would be useful in finding new trade routes, resources, and markets. Later, American traders would arrive and participate in the hunt for furs, but theirs were predominantly commercial and not political motives.

Politically, Nootka Sound was seen as a strategic port on the North Pacific coast. According to a proclamation by Pope Alexander VI in 1492 which divided the world between Spain and Portugal, the two great powers of that period, Spain was given all rights to the Pacific Ocean and any shores which it touched upon. The "other half" of the world was granted to Portugal. By the late 18th century, Spain's powers were waning and other countries, including Britain, Russia, and France, were expanding their political and economic territories.

Perceiving an immediate threat from the Russians who were moving down the coast from the north in pursuit of sea otter pelts and new lands to conquer, Spain hastened to build a fort and settlement at Friendly Cove in 1789. It was the only permanent base established by the Spanish north of San Francisco, and it differed from the usual forts in that its sole purpose was as a military base. Other Spanish forts were agriculturally-based or centered around Catholic missions. The fort at Nootka, however, was strategically placed to reinforce Spain's Pacific dominion.

The Russians weren't the only threat to Spain's sovereignty. In the search for the Northwest Passage, a much-desired shortcut linking the Atlantic to the Pacific, the British were also infringing on Spanish territory. Nootka Sound provided a safe port from which Spanish claims to the north Pacific could be protected.

The issue of sovereignty centered on rights to the west coast. The Spanish claimed prior discovery by Perez, and rights by divine law, as laid out in the Papal decree. Britain, however, argued that discovery alone didn't justify the rights to ownership. The land had to be occupied and developed, they said. Cook's month-long stay at Nootka, and John Meares' subsequent claim of having "purchased" land in Friendly Cove from Maquinna, were used as evidence of Britain's long-term commitment to the region. While Britain's interest was more obviously commercial than Spain's, it was no less political. Attracted by the profitable fur trade, Britain wanted territorial power over the area's rich resources, seeing the whole coast as having enormous potential for exploitation.

The Spanish Presence

The fort on the rocky shores of Nootka Sound was intended to be a permanent settlement. Spain's primary objective was to defend its claim to the coast and as such, the outpost at Friendly Cove was essentially a military base. There was little interest in colonizing or settling the lands, although large gardens were planted and some livestock was brought in to feed the soldiers manning the encampment. Spain was also actively involved in the fur trade but, unlike the British and the Americans, the Spanish trade was government-controlled. There were no commercial traders, and the trade was conducted through official channels.

Esteban José Martínez was sent to Nootka from San Blas, Mexico, to build the first settlement. He arrived May 5th, 1789, with orders to construct a rough building out of wood planks, "a great hut to serve as quarters for protection from the inclemency of the weather, a place of meeting for trading with the Indians, and an intrenchment for protection against their attacks, in case they should attempt any."[24] By erecting a building on the contentious site, Spain intended to establish its "right of the dominion of our sovereign in the port of Nootka and in the laterals of the coast."[25]

The Spanish fort at Yuquot, and the frigate Atrevida *in 1791. Sketch by Cardero.*   Provincial Archives of B.C.

Martínez, who had been second pilot on the Perez expedition, was already familiar with Nootka Sound, and wasted no time getting re-acquainted with the Indians he had met on his first visit. Their main chief was Macuina, now spelled Maquinna:

"While I was in Macuina's house, he showed me the shells which I had given him in 1774 when I came to this port with the frigate *Santiago*, under the command of the first pilot and brevet-ensign of frigate, Don Juan Perez, which corroborated all that I had said to the Englishman at mess," writes Martínez.[26]

Ten days after his arrival, Martínez began construction on the fort. The entry in his diary for Friday, May 15, 1789, reads:

"Observing that the best situation for the defense of this port is the point to the NE which forms the entrance, I gave orders to begin to place an embankment on the hill located on this point, where ten cannon could be mounted. I gave to this bastion the name of San Miguel."[27]

A few weeks later, standing on the beach of the small harbor which he called "Santa Cruz," situated at the entrance of the port of San Lorenzo de Nuca, Martínez formalized Spain's ownership of the coast. For Wednesday, June 24, 1789, Martínez writes:

"Here, with the usual ceremonies, I took possession of the port of San Lorenzo, its coast and adjacent islands, in the name of my sovereign, Don Carlos III (whom God protect!). As soon as the cross was set up, the voice of the holy evangel resounded by means of a sermon which the most reverend father-president Fray Severo Patero, delivered to all who were present... I had engraved on the cross the name of Our Lord Jesus Christ, that of our august Monarch, Don Carlos III, and the years in which I had been in this port, 1774 and the present year of '89."[28]

Unexpectedly, Martínez was ordered to abandon Nootka a few months after his arrival. Dismantling the garrison and entrusting the lands to Maquinna, he set sail for Mexico at the end of October, the reason for his return unknown: "Flores, the viceroy of Mexico, under whose direction the step was taken, seems to have been of a vacillating nature," says F.W. Howay in "The Spanish Settlement at Nootka." Flores' successor, however - the Conde de Revillagigedo - was determined to maintain Spain's hold on the coast. Consequently, in February, 1790, three vessels under the command of Francisco de Eliza were sent to Nootka, equipped with the necessary supplies to re-establish the fort and defend the settlement from foreign incursions.

"And now upon the shores of Friendly Cove arose a little Spanish village...The most imposing structure, occupying a prominent position almost in the centre of the horseshoe shore, was the dwelling of the commandante, Elisa, and later Quadra and Alava," writes Howay, "Clustered about were some sixteen houses: store-rooms for the supplies for the settlement and for war materials for the fort and the vessels, a hospital, a bakery, blacksmith's and carpenter's workshops, and residences for the officers and men. The church, too, with the priest's house and the church yard, stood in a conspicuous position." Howay notes that the settlement was supplied with water from a brick-lined well, and that luxurious gardens and pens for animals encircled the living quarters.[29]

Archibald Menzies, a botanist on board Captain George Vancouver's expedition to the Pacific in 1792, was not impressed with Spain's initial attempts to protect the coast. Built on the rocky San Miguel Islands, the fort, "if it might be called such," says Menzies in an entry for August 28, 1792, "Was no other than two Guns mounted on a small Platform on the outer Point of the Cove, with

Spanish settlement at Friendly Cove, circa 1792. Artist unknown.　　　　Provincial Archives of B.C.

a Flag Staff on which the Spanish colours were hoisted & a small guard mounted to give the appearance of a place of defence.[30]

His observations of the Spanish settlement attached to the fort were more favorable. Menzies accompanied Vancouver ashore in order to pay their respects to Bodega y Quadra who was at that time Governor and Commandant of the settlement. "We found him on shore at a decent house two story high, built of Planks with a Balcony in the front of the Upper Story after the manner of the Spanish Houses. One end of the ground floor was occupied as a Guard Room, & the other as a Kitchen & Servants' Hall, while the Upper Story was divided into small apartments & occupied by the Governor & his Officers, who were separated by a large Hall in the middle where they commonly dined."[31]

"After leaving the Governor's we took a walk round the place & found several other Houses erected here by the Spaniards as Barracks, Store Houses & an Hospital on the Scite of the Old Village formerly occupied by Maquinna the Chief of the District & his Tribe, there were also several spots fenced in, well cropped with the different European Garden stuffs, which grew here very luxuriantly..."[32]

By Menzies' account, the Spanish settlement was active and firmly established. As well as fresh vegetables "...There was a well-stockd poultry yard, & Goats Sheep & Black Cattle were feeding round the Village. Blacksmiths were seen busily engaged in one place & Carpenters in another, so that the different occupations of Building & repairing Vessels & Houses were at once going forward."[33]

The British

British expeditions to the west coast were financed by groups of merchants who were quick to capitalize on the lucrative market for furs. Outfitted with trade goods - copper, iron, blankets, and other items - and enough supplies to last several months, these expeditions did not represent the British government. In fact, they often sailed under foreign flags in order to escape Spain's restrictions against British ships on the west coast, and to avoid the monopoly of Britain's government-endorsed trading companies.

John Meares commanded several such expeditions to the North Pacific. He made his first trip in 1786 aboard the *Nootka*. Returning in 1788 on the *Felice*, Meares was responsible for building a small trading post on land he says he purchased from Maquinna and constructed the first sailing ship ever to be built on the west coast.

In an entry in his journal dated Sunday, May 25, 1788, Meares says Maquinna "...had not only most readily consented to grant us a spot of ground in his territory, whereon a house might be built for the accommodation of the people we intended to leave there, but had promised us also his assistance in forwarding our works, and his protection of the party who were destined to remain at Nootka during our absence.

"In return for this kindness, and to ensure a continuance of it, the chief was presented with a pair of pistols, which he had regarded with an eye of solicitation ever since our arrival."[34] Later, when the dispute between Spain and Britain came to a head, Meares told the courts that he had purchased the whole of King George's Sound and not merely the parcel of land upon which his trading post stood.

It's important to note here that Meares did not speak the Native language, and Maquinna was not fluent in English. Given the language barrier, as well as the cultural differences, it would appear that Meares' account of the land deal was somewhat embellished. We do not have a record of Maquinna's side of the story, but I think it's safe to say that his understanding of the transaction may have been quite different.

Another view of the Spanish settlement at Nootka. Meares' trading post is shown at far right.

Construction of the trading post began a few weeks after Meares' arrival at Nootka and was completed in less than a week. Meares' entry for May 28, 1788:

"The house was sufficiently spacious to contain all the party intended to be left in the Sound. On the ground-floor there was ample room for the coopers, sail makers and other artizans to work in bad weather: a large room was also set apart for the stores and provisions, and the armourer's shop was attached to one end of the building and communicated with it. The upper story was divided into an eating room and chambers for the party. On the whole, our house, though it was not built to satisfy a lover of architectural beauty, was admirably well calculated for the purpose to which it was destined, and appeared to be a structure of uncommon magnificence to the Natives of King George's Sound.

"A strong breast-work was thrown up round the house, enclosing a considerable area of ground, which, with one piece of cannon, placed in such a manner as to command the cove and village of Nootka, formed a fortification sufficient to secure the party from any intrusion."[35]

There is some dispute as to just how extensive the establishment was, although Meares himself was impressed when he returned to Nootka a month later, after a trip down the coast. "The situation and circumstances in which we found our little colony at our return, very evidently proved their diligence, as well as attention to the orders left with them for their conduct during our absence," he writes in July, 1788, "The house had been rendered perfectly secure from any attack of the Natives, though they should have employed their whole force against it. A palisade of strong stakes, with a well-formed fence of thick bushes, had rendered our ground, in a great measure, impregnable. Various other improvements, of less consequence, had been made...which, altogether, gave the place an appearance of a little dock-yard, and not only engrossed the attention, but excited the astonishment of the Nootkan people."[36]

According to one of the first officers of Meares' ship, the *Felice*, the house "consisted of three bed-chambers, with a mess-room for the officers, and proper apartments for the men; these were elevated about five feet from the ground, the under part serving as warehouses: That, exclusive of this house, there were several out-houses and sheds, built for the convenience of the artificers to work in."[37]

Reports from the Americans, Captains Gray and Ingraham, suggest the settlement was much less elaborate. "On the arrival of the *Columbia* in the year 1788, there was a house, or rather a hut, consisting of rough posts, covered with boards made by the Indians; but this Capt. Douglas pulled to pieces, prior to his sailing for the Sandwich Islands, the same year. The boards he took on board the *Iphigenia*, the roof he gave to Capt. Kendrick which was cut up and burnt as fire wood on board the *Columbia*: so that on the arrival of Don E. J. Martínez there was no vestige of any house remaining."[38]

The trading post was built on what became known as Meares' Corner, a small section of land at the northeast end of Friendly Cove which was secluded from the remainder of the beach by a rock outcropping. Historically, that small plot of land has remained British: when Reverend Brabant wanted to establish a church at Friendly Cove in the 1880s, he was given permission to build on the site of Meares' trading post. In 1899, a store and trading post belonging to Stockman and Dawley from Clayoquot were built on that same site, making use of the still-standing rectory.

While at Nootka, Meares' party built a small sailing ship, the *Northwest America*, which was launched with much fanfare on September 20th, 1788. On hand to witness the event were Maquinna, Callicum - the second highest-ranking chief of Nootka - and a large number of their people, the crew from an American vessel, the *Lady Washington*, newly arrived from Boston, and the Chinese carpenters Meares had brought with him from China to build the ship.

"The vessel was then waiting to quit the stocks; and to give all due honour to such an important scene, we adopted, as far as was in our power, the ceremony of other dockyards. -As soon as the tide was at its proper height, the English ensign was displayed on shore at the house, and on board the new vessel, which at the proper moment, was named the *North West America*, as being the first bottom ever built and launched in this part of the globe...."[39]

In the spring of 1789, Meares organized a third expedition to the North Pacific, this time with the intention of establishing a permanent factory on the west coast, a "solid establishment, and not one that is to be abandoned at pleasure," he tells James Colnett, captain of the *Argonaut* and commander of the expedition. His objective was to develop a permanent trading post as well as to provide a facility for building, repairing, and outfitting vessels. Once the first permanent post, or factory, had been established, Colnett was to survey the coast for other sites which would be ideal for the development of additional posts.[40]

The Nootka Crisis

Meanwhile, the actions of Esteban José Martínez during his brief stay on the coast in the summer of 1789 put an abrupt end to Meares' plans for Nootka, and precipitated what has become known as the Nootka Crisis or Nootka Controversy. Soon after his arrival at Nootka, Martínez seized several British vessels, including the *Argonaut*, and took Captain James Colnett prisoner of war, charging him with violating Spanish sovereignty. Two of the ships were eventually released and told not to return. The *Princess Royal* ignored the warning and was promptly recaptured and sent to Mexico along with the *Argonaut* and another ship, the *Fair American*. The *Northwest America* was rechristened the *Santa Gertrudis* and used by the Spanish to explore the coastline between Nootka and the Strait of Juan de Fuca.

Martínez' actions brought the conflict between Spain and Britain to a head, poising the two countries on the brink of war. Several attempts at resolving the dispute were made but it wasn't until 1795 that the fight was finally over. In the first settlement, the Nootka Convention of 1790, Spain agreed to open up the west coast to both Spanish and British traders, and to restore the captured British ships to their owners, along with damages amounting to $210,000.

The original Nootka Convention also stated that all lands owned by the British were to be returned to them: a point which caused some controversy. The Spanish argued that the only British territory was the small section of Friendly Cove where Meares had built his trading post. The British, however, claimed Meares had purchased the whole of Nootka Sound from Maquinna.[41]

The Spanish insult to the British flag at Nootka Sound, 1792.

Provincial Archives of B.C.

In 1792, Captain George Vancouver was sent as Britain's emissary to negotiate the terms of settlement with Bodega y Quadra, then commandant in charge of the Spanish fort at Nootka. Although the two were on friendly terms, they could not come to an agreement on behalf of their respective countries. Vancouver, heady with the success of his circumnavigation of Vancouver Island, promised to name the island "Vancouver and Quadra's Island" in honor of the two men's friendship. Later, the name was shortened to Vancouver Island, and Quadra's name was given to a small island in Johnstone Strait, across from Campbell River.

On January 11, 1794 Spain and Britain signed the third and final Nootka Convention. The following year, Spain dismantled its garrison at Nootka and retreated south. Britain, once it had achieved territorial rights to the west coast, turned its attention inland, to the establishment of a land-based fur trade. Overland expeditions had been gradually moving west from the Rockies, and had reached the interior of what has now become British Columbia.

Today, little concrete evidence remains of the Spanish and British presence. A plaque, erected by the Washington State Historical Society, in 1914, and a granite cairn, built by the National Parks and Historic Sites Branch of Canada, in 1924, commemorate that short but momentous period.

A Well-Recorded Period

Much has been written about the early European presence on the west coast. It is, in fact, the most well-documented period in the history of the Nootka Sound region, thanks to the careful records kept by Spanish and British explorers, and American traders. Navigation charts, journals, daily ship logs, and scientific observations kept by ships' captains, scientists, and priests provide us with a wealth of information. Many include sketches of local Indian life and natural wildlife and vegetation.

A number of important records have survived, the most well-known being the accounts of Captain James Cook's voyages to the North and South Pacific Oceans, Captain George Vancouver's trip around Vancouver Island, and John Jewitt's popularized tale of his two years spent as a captive of Chief Maquinna and the Mowachaht people. A more extensive list is included in the bibliography.

While the British documents are readily available, the Spanish records, no less profuse, have been less accessible. Only in recent years have they become available to the public. For one, Spain had a secrecy rule on its documents, ensuring that they were for the Queen's (or King's) eyes only, secret and confidential. Many of those documents have been translated into English and copies of transcripts are located in the Provincial Archives in Victoria, including the journals of Estevan Martínez and Alejandro Malaspina. Others, as in the case of Tomas de Suria and José Moziño, have been reprinted in journals or published in book form.

These first-hand accounts are fascinating to read. They contain information on the local animal-life, vegetation, climate, and physical geography of the places explored, and detailed descriptions of Native Indian life at the time. Anthropologists consult them for their ethnographic material. Modern historians use them to piece together events which played an important role in world history. Several contemporary authors dealing specifically with those events are Warren L. Cook, F.W. Howay, Derek Pethick, and Hilary Stewart, to name a few.

An important outcome of this period in the history of the Nootka Sound region, and what's important about these early accounts, is that they are the first written records on the northwest coast Native Indian culture. The men who kept those records were ships' officers and scientists, trained in the skills of observation and recording, whose ultimate task was to collect information. And, while their lack of understanding and acceptance of northwest coast Native culture may have distorted their interpretation of that information, it has nonetheless proved invaluable to researchers and Indian people today.

Decline of the Fur Trade

By the early 1800s, the maritime fur trade had declined, leaving behind a few marine charts of the coastline, depleted sea otter populations, and an irrevocably altered Native Indian culture. Interest shifted away from the coast to a land-based fur trade which was moving in from the east, and which changed the whole nature of the business. Permanent posts were built, and trade activity became more centralized and stable. Unlike the maritime trade, the land-based operation promoted settlement and colonization, a key factor in Britain's plans for the new colonies of Vancouver Island and the mainland.

With the decline of the maritime fur trade, Nootka Sound faded into obscurity. Exploration and discovery gave way to exploitation and colonization. Motivated by economic gain, the predominantly American fur traders used the Indians to obtain as many sea otter pelts as possible. When the supply was exhausted, the Americans too left the coast in search of a more profitable resource.

The years of association with the Europeans had a profound effect on the region's first inhabitants. The flourishing

A granite cairn, built by the National Parks and Historic Sites Branch of Canada in 1924, commemorates the brief but momentous period of the Spanish and British claims on Nootka Sound.

Royal B.C. Museum, Ethnology Division.

fur trade was a major boon to what had been, before contact, a fairly stable and consistent economic base. Once outside contact was made and a new economic pattern established, it was impossible to return completely to the old ways of life. For one, and as with the introduction of any new technology in any society, trade items such as iron and other metals, woven cloth, tools, and guns had entered the culture, thereby altering traditional hunting and food-gathering practices, and changing the nature of such key social institutions as the potlatch. Disease and warfare had decimated Native populations. Village sites were abandoned as people relocated nearer to the center of trading activity at the entrance to the major sounds: Clayoquot, Nootka, and, to a lesser degree, Kyuquot. In short, the Indians—and Nootka Sound—had entered into the modern industrial world.

Notes

[1] George Butler Griffen ed., *Documents from the Sutro Collection*, Publications of the Historical Society of Southern California, (Los Angeles: 1891), p. 201.

[2] Conversation with Richard Inglis, head of ethnology, Royal B.C. Museum, (Victoria: August 1990).

[3] Captain James Cook, *The Voyage of the Resolution and Discovery, 1776-1780*, ed. J.C. Beaglehole, (Cambridge: 1967), p. 63.

[4] Griffen, p. 202.

[5] Point Santa Margarita was the name given by the Spanish to a point of land on the Queen Charlotte Islands, in Henry R. Wagner, *The Cartography of the Northwest Coast of America to the Year 1800* (Amsterdam: 1968).

[6] Popularly known as "Maquinna hats" after the high-ranking chief of the Mowachaht people at Yuquot. See Hilary Stewart's annotated version of John Jewitt's narrative *The Adventures and Sufferings of John R. Jewitt, Captive of Maquinna* (Vancouver: 1987), p. 78, where she notes that this type of hat was worn only by whaling chiefs.

[7] Griffen, pp. 202-203.

[8] Ibid., p. 132.

[9] Warren L. Cook, *Flood Tide of Empire: Spain and the Pacific Northwest, 1543-1819* (New Haven: 1973), p. 58.

[10] José Mariano Moziño, *Noticias de Nutka: An account of Nootka Sound in 1792* (Toronto: 1970), p. 66.

[11] In *nu-tka: The History and Survival of Nootkan Culture*, ed. Barbara I. Efrat and W.J. Langlois, (Victoria: 1978), pp. 59-60. It is clear from this account that, according to the oral traditions of the Natives, the *Santiago* anchored off the Hesquiat Peninsula. Richard Inglis, head of ethnology at the Royal British Columbia Museum, says those accounts have been confirmed (Conversation, Victoria: 1990).

[12] The "sea beaver" was in fact the sea otter, known for its thick silky pelt.

[13] Captain James Cook, pp. 296-297.

[14] Ibid., pp. 303-304.

[15] Named after Vice Admiral William Bligh, commander of the *H.M.S. Resolution* on this, Cook's third and final voyage. See John T. Walbran, *British Columbia Coast Names* (Vancouver: 1971), pp. 53-54.

[16] Cook was most likely at the village of Tlupana-nutl, a rival chief of Maquinna.

[17] Captain James Cook, pp. 303-305.

[18] F. W. Howay, "A List of Trading Vessels in the Maritime Fur Trade," in Warren L. Cook, *Flood Tide of Empire* (New Haven: 1973), p. 551.

[19] Warren L. Cook, p. 101.

[20] Esteban José Martínez, *Diary of the Voyage of Don Esteban Josef Marinez to the Port of San Lorenzo de Nuca in 1789*, tr. William Schurz, unpubl. ms. Provincial Archives of B.C. (Victoria), p. 207.

[21] Ibid., p. 144.

[22] John R. Jewitt, *The Adventures and Sufferings of John R. Jewitt*, ed. Hilary Stewart, (Vancouver: 1987), pp. 21-22.

[23] Ibid., p. 21 for Hilary Stewart's summary of some of the reasons for Maquinna's attack on the *Boston*.

[24] Martínez, p. 4.

[25] Ibid., p. 5.

[26] Ibid., p. 81.

[27] Ibid., p. 91.

[28] Ibid., pp. 112-113.

[29] F.W. Howay, "The Spanish Settlement at Nootka," *Washington Historical Quarterly*, Vol. 8, No. 3 (July 1917), pp. 167-168.

[30] Archibald Menzies, *Menzies Journal of Vancouver's Voyage: I: 1790-1792*, Provincial Archives of B.C., (Victoria), p. 365.

[31] Ibid., p. 370.

[32] Ibid., p. 371.

[33] Ibid., p. 372.

[34] John Meares, *Voyages made in the years 1788 and 1789 from China to the North West Coast of America* (Amsterdam: 1967), p. 114.

[35] Ibid., pp. 115-116.

[36] Ibid., p. 185.

[37] Captain George Vancouver, *A voyage of discovery...1791-1795* (London: 1984), p. 679. Testimony given by Mr. Robert Duffin to Captain George Vancouver.

[38] Warren L. Cook, p. 140. From Gray and Ingraham to Bodega in Provincial Archives of B.C. report, Victoria: 1913 (1914), pp. 15-17.

[39] Meares, pp. 222-223.

[40] Meares, Appendix No. 2, p. E.

[41] Derek Pethick, *The Nootka Connection: Europe and the Northwest Coast 1790-1795* (Vancouver: 1980), p. 23.

CHAPTER 4   **EUROPEAN SETTLEMENT**

The early European settlement of Nootka and Kyuquot Sounds took place gradually and on a small scale. The region was largely ignored during the initial period of colonization in the late 1800s. Remote, difficult of access, and sparsely populated, it was not a priority for the government, nor did it hold any interest for commercial developers.

Settlement activity centered around the major trading and shipping centers of Fort Victoria, Fort Langley, and New Westminster. Vancouver Island had been given to the Hudson's Bay Company as a crown grant, in 1849, for a nominal rent of seven shillings a year. In return, the Company was responsible for establishing settlements and developing industries. Anxious to attract settlers to the region and interested in diversifying its own economic base, Hudson's Bay Company concentrated on affairs close to home.

Later, marine transportation routes along the inside passage linked the northern trading posts with the main centers in the south, opening up the east coast of Vancouver Island. The sheltered waterways and more favorable terrain, coupled with regular transportation, were key factors in establishing settlements in the Cowichan Valley, Comox, and the northern end of the island.

On the remote west coast, the maritime connection continued to dominate well into the middle of the twentieth century. The rough coastline and rugged terrain were not conducive to families who were looking for land to cultivate and settle on. In the mid-1800s, trading schooners visited the area several times a year, and Indians traded salmon, furs, and fish oil - sometimes for cash, but usually for food supplies, hunting gear, or tools. Between the mid-1850s and into the 1880s, there was a brisk trade in dogfish and shark liver oil. The oil was in high demand in the Washington State lumber industry, where it was used in huge quantities in the woods to grease the logging skids, and in the sawmills to lubricate the machinery. The oil was extracted from the dogfish by the Indians themselves before being sold or traded to the west coast traders, who in turn sold it to the Hudson's Bay Company.

Seal furs were also in demand, and a thriving sealing industry soon developed, attracting both American and Canadian traders. The most notable are Captains Spring and McKay who formed a partnership in 1858, establishing several small trading posts along the west coast of the island, including stores at Nootka and Kyuquot. In 1868, they entered the sealing industry in full force, following the seal herds as they made their way north, up the coast from California to their breeding grounds in the Bering Sea. Captain Spring and the vessel *Favorite* was the first to successfully use Indian hunters in the sealing trade.[1] The schooners called in at the sounds to pick up the Indian men and their canoes before heading out to the hunting grounds where they would remain for several months at a time. The Indian hunters supplied all their own gear and were paid $2. per skin as compared to the $3. per skin paid to white hunters.[2] Out of that, they were expected to pay for their room and board while at sea.

Sealing lasted until 1911 when a treaty was signed protecting the herds from extinction. During its heyday, upwards of a hundred boats were involved in the industry, more than half of them based out of Victoria.

The Land Connection

One of the first official expeditions into the interior lands of the Nootka Sound region was in July, 1852, when Hamilton Moffatt, a Hudson's Bay Company surveyor, was sent on a scouting trip overland from Woss Lake to Tlupana Inlet and then by canoe to Friendly Cove. His trip took him on trails used by the Indians for trade and communication between the west and east coasts of the island.[3]

The government's push for colonization and settlement eventually led to the survey and subdivision of Nootka and Kyuquot Sounds. Surveyors were sent out to record and map the region in order to make it available for lease, purchase, or pre-emption. Surveyors were also expected to assess the land's agricultural and industrial potential. Next to farming, which the government saw as an ideal way of attracting stable families, raw resources were considered to be a high priority, for they attracted commerical investors. Early government reports concerning the west coast refer to it's abundant timber, and land that was potentially rich in minerals.

The development of transportation routes was a major factor in opening up the island to settlers. For many years, there was public pressure to extend the Esquimalt and Nanaimo Railway which, in the 1880s, ended at Wellington, southeast of Nanaimo. Survey crews were sent out to determine the most suitable route. In 1887, Henry Fry made an exploratory trip from Woss Lake down the Woss and Tahsis Rivers. He set out in mid-September, discovering what he describes as "easy" terrain. A journal entry for September 17, 1887, reads as follows:

"Following this river downstream, through a wide and fertile valley, for seven miles, we reached a large lake, called by the Indians 'Muchalat Lake'.... Two miles north of this lake lies a very high mountain, the summit of which I climbed to obtain a view of the surrounding country, and looking *[northeast]* saw a large and well-defined valley, through which I could see the British Columbia Coast range of mountains. Nothing of any height lay between myself and the East Coast of Vancouver...

"Left the east end or outlet of Muchalat Lake, following down stream I met two Indians, of the Muchalat tribe, in canoe, who informed me that I was 12 miles from the coast; that a large stream from the north came into this river one mile below, and another from the east, about six miles downstream; on the latter, they assured me, was a trail by which the Comox Indians frequently came across."[4]

Fry reported that construction of a railroad down through Muchalat Lake and the Gold River Valley would be relatively light and easy work with about eight miles of heavy work near the lake itself. He also noted that the terrain from Woss Lake down through the Tahsis River Valley was not suitable for railroad construction "for although a road might possibly be built," he said, "very heavy grade would have to be made on a steep rock side-hill, or two miles of rock tunnel built to pass the divide between Woss Lake and the headwaters of the Tahsis River." Fry concludes that a proposed railway line passing Buttle Lake and across to the Muchalat River valley would find no obstacles in its path.[5]

In his recommendations to the Legislative Assembly, Fry's boss, civil engineer J.H. Gray, submitted two proposals for the railway extension. The first was for a northern route which would follow the east coast to Menzies Bay, north of Campbell River, and then inland along the Salmon River and the White River, crossing the headwaters of the Adam River and proceeding down the Davie River to Woss and then along the Nimpkish Valley to Fort Rupert.

The second proposed route was through the interior of the island, up the Campbell River past Buttle Lake and along the Elk River Valley to the Gold River, up through Muchalat Lake and the Woss Valley to Fort Rupert. Gray recommended the Muchalat Lake route as having more favorable terrain and being less costly for railroad construction.[6]

If the railway extension had been built, it would have opened up the west coast, with the head of Muchalat Arm the potential site of a major harbor. The proposal wasn't immediately rejected. According to the Land Registry in Port Alberni, the Esquimalt and Nanaimo Railway pre-empted several hundred acres along the proposed route. And there seems to have been a flurry of activity in land speculation. Several pre-emptions were taken in the Muchalat Inlet area, including mineral claims at Head Bay by then-Governor James Dunsmuir and timber leases by prominent pioneer lumberman W.P. Sayward. Small-scale mining yielded some iron ore, but whether the timber leases were actually worked is difficult to determine. There is some indication that some logging did occur, but not to any great extent. Generally, the region remained undeveloped during this early period.[7]

Homesteading

In the early 1900s, homesteaders, prospectors, and trappers began trickling into the region, drawn to the frontier by the promise of plenty of land and a new life. In 1912, Nootka Island was surveyed, sub-divided into 90 lots, and promoted as

Karl Leiner's property on the Leiner River near Tahsis, circa 1924. John and Peter Perry purchased the homestead in 1926. John Perry photo.

Tahsis Archives.

farmland. At the same time, a complete townsite was laid out at Friendly Cove, indicating there were plans, at one time, to build a major settlement, plans that did not reach fruition. Several plots were purchased during that same year, most notably by William Ross Lord, who later formed the Nootka Packing Company, and W.T. Dawley, a prominent storekeeper and trader from Clayoquot who had established a second trading post at Friendly Cove in 1899.

A few years later, the provincial government embarked on a campaign to actively encourage settlement in the area:

"Upon the south and west shores are many sandy beaches, but the remainder of the shoreline is generally rugged," notes a government pamphlet for prospective homesteaders. "The beaches are open to the Pacific and, except in summer, boat landing is hazardous. Land suitable for settlement is mostly on the south and west within about two miles of the shore. Friendly Cove is the steamship landing, and Nootka post and telegraph offices and store is located here, adjoining the Indian village. A trail leads westward through an area cut up with rough rocky knolls and

Perry brothers' homestead on the Leiner River near Tahsis, circa 1930.
John Perry photo.   Tahsis Archives.

John Perry cleaning salmon at the homestead he shared with his brother, Pete, on the Leiner River.
Pete Perry photo.   Tahsis Archives.

ridges and containing numerous small lakes for six miles to Beano Creek, westward of which there is a considerable area of flat land, much more or less swampy, but easily drained. There are numerous creeks. A coarse grass grows in the swampy area which affords fair pasturage. Soil is of a gravelly or clayey nature, peaty in the swampy part. In the creek bottoms, generally small, is dark sandy loam. Timber is principally scrubby hemlock and cedar, with a fringe of spruce along the shore. Cost of clearing varies from $150. to $300. an acre. Settlers have good gardens and some raise cattle and poultry successfully. Climate is mild. Precipitation is from 90 to 100 inches a year, about 75 per cent falling from November to January and in April. Snowfall is light, seldom exceeding a few inches."[8]

There were quite a few land pre-emptions and purchases during the first part of the 1900s. Many were acquired in 1912, but were soon abandoned and reverted to the Crown within a few years. It's doubtful whether many of those who applied for land in the region ever set foot on the ground they owned, let alone worked it. But, while most of the land remained untouched, there were several pockets where homesteaders carved a place for themselves and managed to tough it out.

In the southwest corner of Nootka Island, near Beano Creek and Bajo Point, a small community of Latvian immigrants struggled to make a living from the land, clearing the trees, planting gardens and fruit trees, even raising cattle and chickens. To the north, in a small bay across from Centre Island, a family from England built a fairly large house on a slope overlooking Esperanza Inlet where they lived for more than twenty years. Their beautiful, landscaped garden with trails winding through the woods and benches to take advantage of the natural beauty attracted visitors from around the region. All that remains today is an intricately-built rock wall, and three graves beneath the trees.

Centre Island, situated in the entrance to Esperanza Inlet, was home to an enterprising family of five. They raised foxes, tried their hand at cranberry farming, and planted fruit trees and a garden. Elsewhere, at the head of the Tahsis Inlet, along the mouth of the Leiner River, lived John and Pete Perry on a homestead they'd bought from Karl Leiner who had been there since 1912. The Perry brothers are the oldest surviving residents of the region, having arrived in 1921 to homestead on Nootka Island. They soon moved to the Leiner River where they lived until the 1950s, moving from there to Seabreeze, just around the corner from the Tahsis Narrows. In 1963, the Perry brothers moved to Oliver for health reasons. Pete died a few months

Pete Perry and friend, prospector Billy Poole. Poole was one of the first settlers in the region. John Perry photo. Tahsis Archives.

later and, soon after, John was married for the first time, at the age of 81. Now 96, John continues to lead an active life.

The homesteaders who stayed were strong and independent, preferring a life of hard work and solitude in the wilderness to an easier life in more populated areas. John and Pete Perry; Karl Leiner; Billy Poole; the Centre Island group. It was a hard life, but one which no one seems to complain about. It was not enough to clear a piece of ground and expect to survive solely by raising chickens and planting a garden. Homesteaders lived by doing a little bit of everything: trapping in the winter and fishing in the summer, both commercially and for personal use. Furs were sold to the fur buyer who travelled up the coast on the *Princess Maquinna.* Prospecting was another common activity, although it was done mostly during free time, since it didn't contribute directly to food on the table or money in the pocket.

For a brief period, fox farms proved to be financially successful and adaptable to the region. Silver fox furs were in high demand by the upper class in New York and England. They were raised in pens on Centre Island, Catala Island, and the Leiner River homesteads. But a slump in the market eventually brought the prices down and it became unfeasible to continue operating.

Marble Quarried for Export

In Hisnit Inlet, marble was quarried and milled for about eight years. The marble was first reported, in 1893, by three prospectors who had staked a claim on Deserted Creek. According to the annual report of the Minister of Mines:

"Some fine samples of white and gray marble came in from Deserted Cove, Nootka Sound. This deposit is said to be of great extent, and is situated at the water's edge, with every facility for shipping."[9]

In 1907, the claim was taken over by John Mortimer who later turned it over to Nootka Marble Quarries Ltd., a company which had incorporated on November 20, 1906. By 1909, a mill had been installed and marble was being quarried and

Blocks of marble await shipment from quarry operated by A.W. McCurdy.   Provincial Archives of B.C.

shipped out to Victoria, Vancouver, and Seattle. John T. Walbran, writing in 1909, calls the marble quarries "the principle industry" of Nootka Sound:

"The Quarries are situated on an excellent harbor near the centre of the Sound. A marble mill has been erected here and during the past year excellent examples of monumental work in blue marble, and large blue marble slabs have been manufactured and sold..."[10]

Walbran also refers to the open pit iron mines owned by James Dunsmuir, Lieutenant-Governor of the province. The iron mines were located further up Tlupana Inlet, at Head Bay. Both the iron mine and the marble quarries closed in 1914, at the outbreak of World War I.

Fish Processing Provides Economic Boon

Throughout the history of the region, fish has played a primary role, both as food source and as economic activity. For the Indians, salmon was a dietary staple and the west coast people had the most advanced fishing technology on the continent. Later, Native Indians cured salmon for trade to the west coast schooners, which visited the area in the mid-1800s. Early homesteaders also depended on salmon as a major source of protein, supplementing a diet of elk, deer, and wildfowl with fresh fish. But it wasn't until the beginning of the 20th century that the region first became involved in the commercial fishing industry.

Commercial fish processing in British Columbia began as early as 1829, when the Hudson's Bay Company began curing salmon for export at Fort Langley. Cleaned, filleted salmon was salted and packed in barrels for export to markets in Hawaii and later, California. In one sixteen-day period in 1830, 15,000 salmon were salted down in 200 barrels. In 1846, 460 barrels were reportedly sold for export at $9. a barrel.[11] Other salmon salteries were operated at Port Renfrew from 1851 to 1872, and in Nanaimo in 1853.[12]

The fish processing industry was one of the first to capitalize on Nootka Sound's natural resources on a large, industrial scale. The first cannery to be built in the area was at Nootka, and started out as a saltery. It was built in 1897, a peak year for the province's salmon canning industry, according to John Forester in his book, *British Columbia's Commercial Fishing History*. Salmon were running in "vast numbers," and canners put up over a million cases, their highest pack ever at that time. The first plant at Nootka was built by West Coast Packing Company, apparently to take advantage of the heavy salmon runs. It only operated for one season. Later, in 1916, another cannery was built at Nootka. Located about one mile north of Friendly Cove, in a small bay called Boca del Infierno, the plant was owned and operated by the Nootka Packing Company. It canned salmon and pilchards, and processed fish oil and fish meal.

Canneries and fish plants on the west coast of the island were marginal operations. There were fewer plants and they produced smaller packs than elsewhere in the province. The main processing activity was concentrated on the mainland, around the Fraser River in the south and the Skeena River in the north. These were areas where the largest runs occurred as fish made their way up the major rivers and inlets to spawn. Plants in these locations were also closer to markets and transportation routes.

Salteries

Prior to the establishment of canneries and reduction plants, several Japanese-owned salteries were built on the west coast of the island. Herring and later chum salmon were dry-salted and shipped out to markets in China and Japan. According to the Annual Report of the Minister of Fisheries for 1905-07, the salteries were exporting fish as early as 1902. By 1934, eleven salteries were operating on the westcoast.[13] At least three of them were located in the Nootka Sound region.

Information about the Japanese saltery business is sketchy. The markets were overseas and of apparently little interest to the local fishing industry. Herring and chum salmon were not being used in domestic production at the time, and so the Japanese salteries didn't pose an economic threat. The saltery operations, themselves, required little in the way of machinery and capital. They were temporary structures which, once abandoned, were quickly taken over by the forest. What few records remain indicate there were salteries at Ceepeecee and Saltery Bay on Esperanza Inlet, and at Nootka. The Nootka saltery may have been the plant built by W. Ross Lord in 1897 which operated for only a year before closing down. Salteries at Ceepeecee and Saltery Bay couldn't have operated any later than 1926, when the first reduction plants were built at Hecate and Ceepeecee.

The Japanese-owned salteries began closing down in the years following 1935. Overseas markets were being affected by the Sino-Japan war, and in British Columbia, there was increasing hostility over the Japanese presence in the fishing industry. The government began restricting the number of licenses granted to Japanese fishermen and saltery owners, thus forcing many salteries to close down.

Nootka Cannery

A description of Nootka in *Wrigley's British Columbia Directory for 1918* reads: "A post office and fishing village on Nootka Island, west coast of Vancouver Island, in Alberni Provincial Electoral District, 125 miles from Port Alberni. It is reached by C.P.R. WestCoast steamers from Victoria. Has telegraph office. Population 73 (75)? Local resources: fish canning, lumbering, mining."

Among those listed in the directory are W.R. Lord, cannery manager, W.T. Dawley, general store (branch of Clayoquot), H.M. Smith, lighthousekeeper, the Reverend Father E. Soby, Roman Catholic priest, Tony Stanovich, captain of a fishboat, Karl Leiner, trapping and farming, and William Poole, mixed farming and prospector. Several homesteaders, including George and A.J. Ossinger, George Beck, and S. Newton, are also listed as being engaged in mixed farming, ranching, poultry-raising, and fruit-farming.

Nootka Cannery, located about a mile north of Friendly Cove, in Boca del Infierno Bay, became a main center of activity during the 1930s and 40s. It boasted a post office, telegraph and general store, and was a main stop on the steamship run.
John Perry photo.   Royal B.C. Museum, Ethnology Division.

The main attraction, however, was the fish plant, and Nootka soon developed into a major service center for the region, serving the homesteaders, fishermen, trappers, and Indians who lived at the southern end of Nootka Sound. The company operated a general store and also ran the post office and telegraph. During the summers, steamships carried visitors and sightseers up the coast. Indian women - basket weavers - displayed their wares on the dock and later, in the 1920s, John Perry, who had developed a passion for photography, sold his postcard photos of local scenes to tourists aboard the *Princess Maquinna*.

Located about one mile north of Friendly Cove in Boca del Infierno, Nootka Cannery was built by the Nootka Packing Company, a subsidiary of Everett Packing Company Ltd. in Washington. According to Cicely Lyons in *Salmon: Our Heritage*, William R. Lord persuaded the Everett firm to register a company in B.C. and build a cannery on the site of a saltery he had established earlier.[14] The new company was incorporated August 23, 1916. Land registry records show Lord as having purchased several lots in the Nootka Townsite that same year. The following June, in 1917, he applied for a twenty-one year lease on a three-acre parcel nearby and began construction on the cannery. The lease was granted in March, 1918.[15]

Nootka Packing Company was the first to can pilchards in Canada. It later added a reduction plant to its cannery operation, enabling it to process fish oil and fish meal. J.J. Pettrich replaced W.R. Lord as president and general manager, in 1926. At some point between 1930 and 1931, Nootka purchased the Langara Fishing and Packing Co. plant near Masset on the Queen Charlotte Islands. A few years later, in 1937, the company severed its ties with the Everett Packing Company by re-organizing as Nootka Packing Co. (1937) Ltd. In 1940, Nootka joined with the Banfield Co. in Tofino to form Nootka-Banfield Company Ltd. Based in Vancouver, the new company operated the plant at Nootka in conjunction with its Port Albion cannery near Tofino. Nootka-Banfield was purchased by the Canadian Fishing Company, in 1945.

Nootka Cannery, looking south.   Royal B. C. Museum, Ethnology Division.

Wives and children of the staff at Nootka Cannery. Photo by John Perry was taken between 1925 and 1930.   Tahsis Archives.

Jack Munro worked at the Nootka plant for several seasons in the 1930s, starting out in the cannery and later, moving up to storekeeper, postman, and bookkeeper. His first job was in the summer of 1934. It was the Depression, and the only places that seemed to be hiring were the logging camps and fish canneries along the coast.

"My first recollection of Nootka when I arrived there - apart from the docks - was the thousands of empty forty-five gallon oil drums. Empty," he said, "All dirty, all old. Secondhand. And they were all on their sides and they were stacked up against the wall, as high as the building so the tops of them were in the ends of the building, under the eaves. Right from the dock up. And they were about three or four deep. There was thousands of them, these forty-five gallon drums."[16]

One of Jack's first jobs was pulling fish out of the tanks which was "the dirtiest job of the place," he said, "Wet and filthy." He did that for two shifts and was then promoted to top-oil man when the chemist didn't show up.

"Pilchards are very very fat. Oh, tremendously fat," Jack said, "They would reduce them, squeeze the oil out of them, put the oil in tanks, and then cool it. Then the styrene, the fat, would settle. And the top oil is the stuff that was left on the top... And although pilchard oil is used for all kinds of cooking fats, the top oil, the best oil, was used in paint-making. Can you believe that? I had to check the tanks, measure them, get them cooled down, get this oil. And then I had to pump the oil off the top of the tank into these drums."

But first he had to clean the drums out. "That was done with lye. Steam and lye. And they had everything in them. Oil of all sorts and kinds - diesel oil, gasoline, linseed oil - that was the worst kind to clean. And you had to sterilize the inside of these tanks that you take this top oil off. That was the first job I got and that was the job I did all of that season."

During the peak season, the crew often worked twelve-hour shifts. "We were paid seventy dollars a month for eight hours a day, six days a week, if there was no

The Princess Maquinna, *docked at Nootka Cannery. John Perry photo.*

fish," said Jack, "And out of that we paid twenty-five dollars a month for board. If there was fish, you had to work ten hours and however much longer it was. The plant ran twenty-four hours a day so in effect there was two, twelve-hour shifts. Of which ten hours was straight time and two hours was overtime at thirty-five cents an hour. So the thirty-five cents - that was seventy cents you made - paid your board. So, if you had fish everyday, you could clear seventy dollars a month. Clear. There was no taxes then."

In addition to the salmon cannery and fish reduction plant, there was a small fleet of fishboats and packers, although Jack says the company bought most of its fish from independent boats up the coast.

"We'd start canning about the beginning of June, in a small way. And it was all trolled salmon. We'd buy from the Kyuquot Trollers' Co-op and from other fish buyers up there. There wasn't too much fish around, and if they couldn't get enough to run all the way to Seattle with it or all the way to Vancouver with it, they would sell it to us."

The cannery and reduction plant were separate operations and generally hired their own crews. In the reduction plant: "If you were running all out, you might have three fish pullers, then it went from there to the pressman - one man there. Then to the dryer - there was one dryer man, there was one oil man. There was two men on the sacking machine, sacking the meal. Then there would be two or three truckers, depending on how far they had to truck this. Because it all had to be cooled," said Jack, "They had a tremendous warehouse, and you had to set all the sacks up on end, with air round about them. The floor, of course, was almost grilled so the cold air could come up to cool this stuff because if you put them together they'd go on fire. The meal would. Spontaneous combustion. Then, after they cooled down - after about a week - then they were stacked and piled. The Nootka Packing Company never had a fire claim in all the years they operated."

Fish processing companies hired mainly Native Indian and oriental laborers to work in the canneries and fish plants. At the time, it was popularly believed that

"Indian Camp" at Nootka Cannery. Native workers and their families came from villages all around the sound to work at the fish plant during the summer and fall.   Royal B.C. Museum, Ethnology Division.

Chinese and Indian women were more skillful at wielding a filleting knife than were white workers. More to the point, the companies paid low wages for long hard hours under primitive working and living conditions. One unenlightened canner, testifying to the Royal Commission on Chinese and Japanese Immigration in 1902, pointed out that the Chinese were "less trouble and less expense than the whites. They are content with rough accommodation at the cannery. If you employ white people, you have to put up substantial buildings with every modern appliance, only to be occupied six weeks in the year." [17]

Until 1940, canneries hired Chinese and Japanese women under what was called the "Chinese contract system." The companies dealt with an agent who was responsible for getting a crew together and supplying their provisions. The agent was paid so much per case, out of which he paid his crew.

"The Chinese contractor - now, he handled all the labor in the cannery," said Jack, "In the reduction plant, it was all white men, or white men and Indians. Why, I don't know, but that was the way it was. In the cannery, your technical men, your machine men, were white, but there was only four or five of them, depending on all the things you did. And the rest were Indian, except the contract labor was operated, in the case of the Nootka Packing Company, by what you call a Chinese labor contractor: Mah Sing, who was quite a character. And he had Chinese men and Japanese women. And Indians, of course, men and women."

Mah Sing contracted to provide the labor for all of Nootka Packing Co.'s operations. "He hired the Chinese, he hired the Indians, he hired whoever was necessary," said Jack, "All except the white men. The white men were on the payroll, the company payroll, and it was a fairly small payroll. And Mah Sing was paid so much a case of the amount of fish that was canned. And out of that, he had to make his profit and pay his crews and the rest of it. And we supplied him with a house."

At Nootka, the Chinese quarters consisted of a large, two-storey communal house with built-in bunks along the sides, a one-storey annex, a toilet, and a pig pen. Cooking was done on two brick "Chinese furnaces" with cast iron pots, and an electric range.[18]

The Japanese crew was housed in two single-storey bunkhouses, two people to a room. They also had a small storage shed and a separate bath house, equipped with a large wooden tub and hot and cold running water.[19]

During the fishing season, Indians from the neighboring villages would move in to Nootka, bringing their families with them. The men unloaded fish, worked in the reduction plant, or hired on the boats as crew members while the women were employed in the cannery, cleaning fish and packing it into cans. They lived in a small settlement behind the main cannery community. A 1939 appraisal shows seven wood-frame 'community houses' for Native Indians, ranging in size from three rooms to eight rooms. There was also a separate, three-room house built for Captain Jack and his family. Captain Jack was a hereditary chief of the Mowachahts at Friendly Cove.[20]

Separate single-family houses were built for the manager and other plant staff. They were usually three or four rooms, had their own indoor plumbing, and their own kitchen facilities. The manager's house was small but well-furnished, and included, among other things, a brass double bed, an oak dining table and sideboard ("Sheraton" pattern), and a brass chandelier. The showpieces in the management houses were porcelain flush toilets and enamelled iron bathtubs and sinks. Everyone else made do with wooden tubs and toilet seats.[21]

The buildings were of plain shiplap construction, set on cedar posts over the water, and connected by boardwalks. Miles of wooden sidewalks led from the dock to the main plant and up to the houses and outbuildings scattered along the shore.

The plant itself consisted of a cannery, a fish house, a reduction facility, several warehouses, a blacksmith shop, and a carpentry shop. Although the fish processing business was labor-intensive, it also required a great deal of modern equipment. And Nootka had the latest: pilchard cleaning machines, an 'Iron Chink', 6-knife 'cutters,' can-filling machines, a California Cooker and Oil Press, salters, grinders, dryers, a labeller machine, and an Automatic Scale and Sacking Machine. There was even a tomato ketchup mixer for preparing the sauce for canned herring and pilchard.

Pilchards Swarm to the West Coast

What prompted the growth of the fish processing industry in the Nootka and Kyuquot Sounds was the pilchard: a small, sardine-like fish, extremely rich in oil, and found in large schools off the Pacific coast. A ton of fish typically yielded 45 gallons of oil which was used in food manufacturing as a base for margarine and cooking oils, in cosmetics, and in high grade paints. The oil was extracted through a reduction process which utilized all parts of the fish. High-pressure steam cookers reduced the flesh to a soft pulp which was then passed through a press to separate the liquid from the fish meal. The liquid was then boiled and left to settle so that the oil could be skimmed from the top and put into barrels for export. The remaining

Pilchards were delivered to fish plants in large scows, and had to be shovelled out by hand.   Provincial Archives of B.C.

meal was dried in high-temperature dryers and shipped out in sacks. The meal was used as an ingredient in animal feed for poultry, cattle, and hogs.

The first pilchards to be canned occurred in 1917, when Nootka Cannery put up a small pack on an experimental basis. Canadian consumers didn't seem to find them all that palatable - "too salty" and "fishy" were the common responses - but there was a market for canned pilchards in California and Great Britain, and B.C. processors continued to put up a pack annually, until 1948.

Unusually large schools of pilchards first appeared off the west coast of B.C. in 1925, prompting most of the canneries to build fish reduction plants for the processing of fish oil and fish meal. On the west coast alone, between Barkley Sound and Kyuquot Sound, fifteen reduction plants were built in an 18-month period from 1925 to 1927.[22] These included the construction of plants at Hecate, Ceepeecee, Port Eliza, Espinosa Arm, and Chamiss Bay. "The west coast pilchard grounds were alive with fish, seiners, tenders, and scows," says Forester.[23]

During the first few seasons, the pilchards swarmed in the inlets and bays just inside the entrances of the sounds. They were taken mainly by small purse seiners, working close to shore, and delivered to nearby reduction plants. Ted Cox, a former pilchard fisherman, says the boats they used then were much smaller than today's purse seiners.

"All we had were those little boats with their gasoline engines... Didn't matter that the boats were so small. In the early twenties, Village Island *[Effingham Island in Barkley Sound]* was about as far out as anybody went. There was always a big swell out there that could scare the best of them. And who needed to face that? They were catching pilchards right in the channel, just three, four hundred yards off the reduction plant... they were so plentiful you didn't have to go far."

Scowload of pilchards waiting to be unloaded at a reduction plant.
Royal B.C. Museum, Ethnology Division.

"In those days, pilchards all went into scows. We didn't put them below. The tender towed the scow and the little boats made the set. If you had a good catch and were drying up the net you couldn't pull up the net and bring it in (it was so heavy with fish)... In the twenties, everyone had to get in on the pilchards."[24]

A few years later, the fish changed their migration patterns. They moved farther out to sea and were sometimes thirty to forty miles off shore. Large seine boats and packers took over from the small purse seiners, averaging hauls of 2500 tons per season. Without the small-boat fleet to serve them, the small, outlying reduction plants at Queen's Cove and Espinosa closed down. Both Hecate and Ceepeecee became auxiliary operations, processing overloads from the larger, more central plants in Port Alberni and Clayoquot Sound.

The huge runs of pilchards dwindled in the mid-1940s, and eventually stopped altogether. The 1947-48 fishing season was the last big pilchard run on the west coast of Vancouver Island. Scientists suggest that shifting currents of warm ocean water were partly responsible for bringing the pilchards as far north as the B.C. coast in the first place. Their subsequent disappearance, although somewhat of a mystery, was probably caused by cooling seawater temperatures and heavy fishing.[25] Many of the smaller reduction plants closed down after the initial boom. Other plants continued to process fish oil and meal, using herring, eulachon, salmon offal, and dogfish instead of pilchards.

Hecate

A reduction plant was built at Hecate, in 1926, by Gosse-Millerd Packing Company. Two years later, Gosse-Millerd amalgamated with B.C. Packers and a cannery was added to their fish meal and oil operations. Hecate operated for about five years during the height of the pilchard runs, although the cannery operated for only one season, 1926. In 1931, there was a slump in the fishing industry, and B.C. Packers' decided to close the plant down as part of its overall plans to consolidate and centralize its fish processing operations. Hecate remained inoperative for several years, although a skeleton maintenance crew and caretaker remained on site to look after the buildings and equipment.

The Hecate plant was remodelled in 1936 and re-opened as an auxiliary fish meal and oil plant for B.C. Packers, run out of their Kildonan plant, in Port Alberni. According to production reports, the Hecate reduction operation processed pilchards and herring from 1936 until 1945, when the pilchards disappeared. It continued

Fish plant at Hecate, B.C. on the northern end of Nootka Island, operated for several years. First owned by Gosse-Millerd Packing Company, it was later taken over by B.C. Packers.   Provincial Archives of B.C.

operating for several more years, using herring instead of pilchards. A crew of about 26 or 28 was required to run the plant on a twenty-four hour basis.

By 1950, Hecate was permanently closed down. Four years later, in July 1954, the plant was demolished. Some of the bunkhouse buildings were sold to the Nootka Mission for use as a Children's Bible camp. The machinery and equipment was dismantled and transported for use by other B.C. Packers' operations on the west coast.

Hecate is now the site of a logging camp for Doman's Logging. All that remains of the cannery and reduction plant are two huge concrete block pilings in the small bay, and some wooden planks, rotting under a thick layer of alder, seagrass, and wild strawberries. On one side of the bay, where once were the bunkhouses and boardwalks of the worker's settlement, is now a hand-built cedar home belonging to Tom McCrae, a former mayor of Tahsis, and his wife, Maxine.

Ceepeecee

In 1927, Maclean's magazine called Ceepeecee "the largest pilchard reduction plant on the west coast of Vancouver Island."[26] It was built by Canadian Packing Corporation Ltd., in 1926, to take advantage of the unusually large runs of pilchards. But the company only operated the plant for a few seasons. In 1930, Nelson Brothers Fisheries took over operations of Ceepeecee and eventually purchased it, in 1934. A few years later, in 1938, they added a cannery which processed mainly pilchard and herring for overseas markets during World War II.

Ceepeecee's name is derived from spelling out the initials of Canadian Packing Corporation, C.P.C., the company which built the reduction plant. The name stuck, even though Nelson Brothers Fisheries owned and operated the plant for more than 25 years. Although Canadian Packing Corporation was a B.C. company, the majority of its shares were held by California Packing Corporation, an American

Ceepeecee in Esperanza Inlet was featured in Maclean's magazine as the largest pilchard reduction plant on the west coast of Vancouver Island. Ceepeecee stands for Canadian Packing Corporation, the company that built the plant in 1926. Provincial Archives of B.C.

company based in San Francisco. In 1934, when Nelson Brothers purchased Ceepeecee, they also took over stock held by the California firm.

Ralph Hansen first went up to Ceepeecee in 1933, to work as a bull cook in the mess house. He was thirteen years old. His first two seasons were spent learning how to cook and washing dishes: "There was a crew of twenty-five people," he said, "I know. I washed all the dishes." During the fishing season, the reduction plant was running 24 hours a day:

"You get up at five in the morning to get the stove going. We had coal," Ralph said, "Then the cook would get up and start making breakfast. There were two shifts, by the way, in the reduction plant. And so you fed one shift, they went to work, then the other shift came up. About twelve men each, roughly."[27]

Jobs were scarce in those days. It was the Depression, and you took what you could get. And at Ceepeecee what you could get was 25 cents an hour for 12-hour shifts - no overtime - and you paid a dollar-a-day for board. "When the shift was over," said Ralph, "We'd go down after we'd had our supper meal, morning meal, whatever it was shift you were on, and we'd spend an hour or two stacking the meal in the warehouse, just stacking it. And there it would wait until the steamer came in."

But it was the smell of the reduction plant that most people remember. It was horrible at first, said Hansen, but eventually you got used to it:

"What got me, the *Norah* and the *Maquinna* used to come in - they used to be five days apart in the summertime - and there were tourists aboard, you know. And the tourists would come along, and we'd be loading, and they'd hold their noses! We wouldn't even notice it! But then, when you'd come back to town here in the fall, you'd have clean clothes on - fresh-washed and everything else - and go on a streetcar. If it was warm, people would kind of look at you sideways. Because the smell was in your pores, and you didn't know it."

Living conditions at Ceepeecee were rough. Only men were hired to work at the reduction plant, many of them Finnish and Swedish, who did not speak English. They lived in wood-frame bunkhouses with no insulation, poor wiring, and a pot-bellied stove for heat. Later, Indians, Chinese, and Japanese were employed to work in the cannery, and they moved up with their families. The Chinese workers lived in what was called the 'China house,' and the Indians lived in several shacks next to the cannery, on the other side of the small cove.

Del Lutes was the manager at Ceepeecee. Ralph says he was "quite a character" from back east: "New Brunswick or somewhere. He had a rough voice, a rough exterior, and a heart as soft as butter... Oh, he used to yell and scream. He was quite well known, even down here *[Vancouver]* because he came down here as manager of the plant in later years. Back then, you did something wrong and—."

Del had lots of ideas and didn't hesitate to put them into practice. "We had a store up there," Ralph said, "Without the boss's knowledge, I believe, Del built a store up at Zeballos. And they lost money on it, lost their shirt on it. I think it was Seth Witton, a fellow by the name of Seth Witton, who took it over eventually. And Del, he even put up a telephone line between Zeballos and Ceepeecee. I had to go and trouble-shoot the thing. It was just a single, galvanized wire, tacked to trees, with an earth return. Trees used to fall down on it and I'd have to go along the beach there with a boat and try and find it and repair the breaks."

The telephone line, which was installed around 1939, was Del's own private telephone system. "He was the only guy who could do any talking," said Ralph.

Ceepeecee was also the main service center for people living on logging camps and homesteads up the inlets and in the small bays around the Esperanza Inlet area. It was a

Visitors to the cook's garden at Ceepeecee were impressed with the abundance of fresh vegetables. Elvera Ericson photo.

major steamship landing on the regular CPR run up the coast, with both the *Princess Maquinna* and the *Princess Norah* stopping to deliver passengers, freight, and mail. On the return journey, the boats called in to pick up sacks of pilchard meal for delivery to Victoria. The post office, a first aid station, and a fairly good store were also operated out of Ceepeecee. Next to Port Alberni to the south, and Port Alice to the north, the tiny settlement on Esperanza Inlet was the closest thing to a town that one could find.

Fisheries statistics show that Ceepeecee was one of 24 fish processing plants still operating on the B.C. coast in 1950, and the only plant left in Nootka and Kyuquot Sounds. The following year, it was closed down. Nelson Brothers continued to use it as a fish buying and packing station for a few weeks during the fall chum salmon fishery, and there was some speculation they would re-open the plant when the fishing improved. But in July, 1954, Ceepeecee was destroyed by a fire which appeared to be caused by sparks from some welding being done in the plant. One of the first things to burn, said Hansen, was the wooden pipeline carrying water down from the lake. And without water, the fire couldn't be put out. "It just gradually went up the line there, up the plank sidewalk, and the store and the post office went, and the messhouse went." The cannery and reduction plant were demolished, and only a few houses on the shore were spared.

With the decline of the fishing industry, the Imperial Oil station located next door to Ceepeecee also closed down. The site was eventually purchased by John and Pete Perry who were homesteading on the Leiner River at the head of Tahsis Inlet. John says Gordon Gibson's logging operations in the area forced them to find a more suitable location. The two brothers lived at the old Imperial Oil station - now called Seabreeze - until the 1960s, when they moved to drier climes in the Okanagan Valley.[28]

Nelson Brothers continued to hold onto the Ceepeecee property until 1968, when its leases expired. Meanwhile, a few of the bunkhouses and bungalows were sold, in 1961, to various logging companies who floated them off to be used in their camps around the area. Later, when Nelson Brothers relinquished its leases, caretaker Ralph Trelvik took over part of the property. He had been operating a small marine boat ways at Ceepeecee for several years and wanted to continue.

The boat ways are still operating. Trelvik left in 1976 - he was 75 years old and the boat ways had become too much work for him. Otto Bettell and Art Hansen took over. Bettell, a fisherman from Quatsino, was mostly a "silent partner," according to Art's wife, Margaret. Hansen did most of the work. He, Margaret, and their three children had been living at Ceepeecee on their floathouse since about 1962. Mrs. Hansen says they originally moved to Ceepeecee because it was a "convenient place" to tie up. But they ended up getting involved with Trelvik - helping him out when his generator broke down, giving him a hand with the boat ways. Mrs. Hansen ran the machine that hauled the boats out of the water, an old Fairbanks Morris engine:

"You'll have to take a recording of that," she said, "It sounds funny. It goes 'putt-putt-putt-putt-putt,' and then there's dead silence for quite some time, and you figure the machine has quit, and then a loud bang and away she goes again!"[29]

Art Hansen died in 1981. At the time of this writing Margaret, who now lives with her daughter in Tahsis, is still part-owner of the boat ways with Frank and Lucille Collins.

Espinosa Reduction Plant

Another fish reduction plant which operated in Nootka Sound during this period was Canfisco's plant at Espinosa Arm. Built in 1928 by Canadian Fishing Company Ltd., the plant began operating the following season, processing fish oil and fish meal until its closure, in 1937-38.

Like other reduction plants, the Espinosa operation was built on pilings over the water. Buildings were of typical shiplap construction and made from rough lumber. Insurance appraisals for 1928 and 1931 list a kitchen, messroom, and bunkhouse equipped for 24 men; a store and office; four houses; and even a laboratory.[30]

There were other reduction plants in the region. According to the Land Registry records for the Nootka District, located in Port Alberni, Anglo-B.C. Packing Company was granted a 21 year lease on land in Espinosa Arm. And in Queen's Cove, Island Packing Company Ltd. acquired a 20 year lease for a fishing station, cannery, and fish reduction plant. The lease was later turned over to a California company based in San Francisco. It is not known whether fish processing plants were actually built at these two locations, although we do know that Canfisco later operated a trolling station at Queen's Cove.

The commercial fish processing industry in Nootka Sound was controlled by outside interests. New, more efficient technology in the way of fishing gear and refrigeration units allowed boats to go out farther for longer periods of time, while packers transported their fish from the fishing grounds into the plants. The industry consolidated. Small independent operations were bought out, forced to close, or amalgamated with the larger companies. Plants in remote locations, such as Nootka and Kyuquot Sounds, were closed down as operations became increasingly central-ized in the lower mainland area. Today, B.C. Packers and Canadian Fishing

Company are the two largest fish processing companies in B.C.. Between them, they control nearly all of the canneries, reduction plants, and fishing fleets on the west coast.

First Aid Station

In the 1930s, the population of the region more than doubled, and with it grew the need for medical services. There were people living on homesteads at God's Pocket, Flynn's Cove, Centre Island, Daffodil Bay, the Leiner River, and the southern end of Nootka Island, and in Indian villages at Nuchatlitz, Queen's Cove, and Friendly Cove. Fish plants at Hecate, Ceepeecee, Nootka, and Espinosa Arm were operating at full capacity during the spring and summer fishing seasons. And logging camps on floats were scattered up and down the inlets, logging the sidehills.

The region was remote and the work dangerous. The nearest doctor was a hundred miles away at Tofino and the nearest hospitals were at Port Alice and Port Alberni. For several years, the only medical help of any kind available in the region was the first aid station at Ceepeecee, a tiny, two-room building containing an examination table and a couple of cots. It was built across from the reduction plant and was reached by a short trail from the docks. The fish companies and one or two logging outfits contributed money to its operation.

In attendance was P.B. Ashbridge, who George Nicholson says received his training in the Royal Army Medical Corps. He and his wife, Anne, "treated practically every injury from a fractured skull to a sprained ankle," and even did their fair share of pulling teeth, says Nicholson in *Vancouver Island's West Coast*.[31] Those who were seriously sick or badly injured were taken by fishboat or steamer to the hospital in Port Alice or Port Alberni.

Mr. Ashbridge left Ceepeecee, in 1933, to become the Indian Agent and a magistrate at Port Alberni. He was replaced by Mrs. Ian Davies, a trained nurse. At the time, Mrs. Davies and her husband were running the Imperial Oil station across the bay from Ceepeecee. She continued to operate the first aid center until 1937, when a hospital was built nearby at Esperanza.

Nootka Mission General Hospital

A well-known figure on the coast, in the 1930s, was Percy Wills. Percy was active as a missionary working for the Vancouver Island Branch of the Shantymen's Christian Association, an outreach missionary group in Victoria whose mandate was to serve people living in isolated parts of the island. Through his efforts, the group had established a mobile marine mission to spread the word of God on the island's remote west coast. Using, first, a converted fishboat, the *Otter Point* and, later, the *Messengers II* and *III*, Wills travelled up the outer coast, calling in at every logging camp, fish cannery, Indian village, and homestead between Barkley Sound and Quatsino. While his main concern was for the spiritual well-being of the island's residents, he also saw a strong need for medical care. By 1937, he had established a new health care facility at Esperanza.

Percy lured Dr. Herman McLean to Vancouver Island to help build what became known as the Nootka Mission General Hospital. Dr. McLean and his family were living in Alberta at the time, and according to Dr. McLean's wife, Marion, the west coast was not where they had originally planned to go. She says she couldn't believe it when her husband received a letter from Percy, asking for help with a hospital on the west coast of the island:

"You know my reaction? I thought, I just didn't want a thing to do with the west coast! That's the last bit of news that I ever wanted to hear," she said, "I was

Nootka Mission General Hospital, circa 1940, served the Nootka and Kyuquot Sound region for more than 35 years.

willing to go to the foreign fields, to Africa - But - the west coast of Vancouver Island!"[32]

Yes, the west coast of Vancouver Island. Dr. McLean arrived in the summer of 1937. Impressed by the Shantymen's work, he accompanied Percy up the coast in the *Messenger II*, seeing for himself the desperate need for medical aid. He decided God wanted him to be on the west coast, said Mrs. McLean, and chose Esperanza Inlet as the place to build a hospital. Percy selected the site: he found a fairly level piece of land on the north side of Hecate Channel, west of Ceepeecee and directly across from B.C. Packers' reduction plant. It boasted water from a clear mountain stream and, best of all, a southern exposure which caught every last bit of sunshine possible - an important consideration during the short days of winter.[33]

Dr. McLean and Percy spent the summer building the hospital. The foreman of the sawmill across the channel in McBride Bay donated lumber to the project, and men from the mill and from the fish plant at Hecate volunteered their time and labor in exchange for the doctor's promise to pay for their meals at the summer's end. By fall, the building was completed, and on November 1st, the doctor treated his first patient, a logger with a swollen gland.[34]

Mrs. McLean arrived in Nootka Sound that same month. She came up on the *Princess Maquinna* with five children in tow, the oldest was 12 years old and the youngest had just been born that summer. It was winter - "One of the worst times to travel," she said - and their house at Esperanza wasn't completed yet. They spent their first few weeks on the coast in the tiny hotel at Nootka Cannery before finally moving to what would become their home for the next 36 years.

The first few years were spent struggling to build up the new hospital and mission. Local residents, people from the logging camps, fish plants, and sawmill formed an association to oversee the hospital's operation. They held their first meeting on January 21, 1938, where, according to the minutes of the meeting, "Owing to the evening being very bad, the attendance was not large." However, there were representatives from Zeballos, McBride Bay, Ceepeecee and others. One

Nootka Mission General Hospital at Esperanza as it looked in 1985. The hospital closed down in 1973, but continued operating as a mission for the Shantymen.   Laurie Jones photo.

of the main items of business was to establish a list of priorities, among them the construction of a modern, 10-bed facility with the latest equipment, a good boat, a radio phone, and a facility in Zeballos.[35]

Their dreams were soon to be realized. By the end of 1938, the original hospital building - a two-room structure built of rough lumber - had been expanded from three beds to seven and a much-needed X-ray machine had been acquired. A schoolhouse and living quarters for the staff were built, and a telephone line which ran from Ceepeecee to Zeballos gave the hospital access to the outside world.

All this and more on volunteer labor and donated materials. At the first annual general meeting held in January, 1939, thanks were given to members who had helped get the hospital started, including Harold and Aina Swanson, Budge and Alice Young, and Bert Hammond and his wife, all from the sawmill at McBride Bay; Nootka Packing Company; Olson's Logging; and the Spud Valley and Rey Oro gold mines at Zeballos. The minutes for that meeting also include a special thanks to their neighbors, Mr. and Mrs. Walter Smith who owned the Esperanza Hotel, for their "courtesy and co-operation," particularly in supplying the hospital with electricity and running water.[36]

But Dr. McLean wouldn't be satisfied with anything less than first class facilities. At the annual general meeting of the Hospital Society, he told the group that he wanted something more for his outpost hospital and mission at Esperanza:

"Our vision for 1939 is a hospital and equipment second to none, a library, lounge room, a day school, and a bible school. Everything and anything that will be of service to our friends in the mines, logging camps, and fish plants...."[37]

One month later, his prayers were answered. An anonymous benefactor had donated several thousand dollars worth of Alberta bonds to the Nootka Mission General Hospital. The cash value was $23,000, more than enough to build and equip the kind of hospital facility Dr. McLean and Shantyman Percy Wills had dreamed of for so long.[38] Work began immediately under the supervision of a local contractor,

Mr. Llewellyn. The large, two-storey building with surgeries, examining rooms, patient wards, meeting rooms, and a library was open and ready for business by 1940.

There were no government grants or medical assistance programs in those days, only donations from grateful patients and supporters of the Shantymen's Christian Association. The Nootka Mission General Hospital was staffed by nurses and doctors who believed in the missionary work. The hours were long and hard, and they received little in the way of remuneration. In 1940, the salary was set at $10. a month "to cover needs other than room and board," although Dr. McLean expressed his disappointment that money had become an issue to the staff. [39]

Early on in the history of the hospital, the association, at the urging of Dr. McLean, had adopted a policy of administering to the spiritual as well as the physical side of life.[40] Missionary work, prayers, and devotionals were combined with the everyday practice of medicine, to heal the sick and injured, and to spread the gospel. Nurses, who had two hours off each day and one day a week free to tend to personal affairs, were expected to spend half of that free time in prayer. Perhaps the most memorable aspect of the Esperanza hospital was the use of prayer. Dr. McLean's daughter, Shirley Sutherland, who used to assist her father in the operating room, recalls one particular incident:

"I remember once there was a Mrs. Billy that was very, very sick. We were in the O.R. *[operating room]*, and she was bleeding a lot, and she stopped breathing. She was like a ghost, you know. We thought she'd died. I think we stopped and prayed - Dad didn't know what else to do. Mother was at home, and she had just finished having prayer time, time with the Lord. She was washing dishes or something, and it came to her that she should really pray for us in the O.R... She was so impressed that she should pray for us, so she stopped and prayed. That was the time that we were actually having trouble with Mrs. Billy. And she started to breathe again."[41]

The doctor and staff at Esperanza served the entire region. Travelling by boat and seaplane, they made regular visits to the outlying settlements, holding medical clinics in Kyuquot, Zeballos, Tahsis, Gold River, and Friendly Cove. They initiated a children's bible school, operating it first out of the abandoned bunkhouses of the Hecate reduction plant, and later moving to Ferrer Point, an old army encampment on the western tip of Nootka Island. Many residents recall with pleasure childhood summers spent swimming and boating at Camp Ferrer.

Living on the remote and isolated west coast in the 1930s and 40s was to experience a different way of life, one that didn't include the same kinds of amenities found in more populated areas. School was done by correspondence, and Mrs. McLean turned her bedroom into a classroom by putting up a plank shelf for her children to use as a desk. Later a tiny, one-room schoolhouse was built and a correspondence teacher paid regular visits to help them through the courses. The older McLean children eventually went out to school in Zeballos. But what Shirley remembers most about growing up in Esperanza is the isolation and the hard work. She said that there weren't many children around in those days:

"One of my main entertainments was going over and visiting the patients. At least they gave me somebody else to talk to. There weren't always that many new people around, and just to see something different, talk to somebody new that had come in. But then, we worked. I worked from the time I was twelve in the hospital."

For the McLeans, the day began at six to the sounds of the doctor singing "Heavenly Sunshine," at the top of his lungs, while he got the woodstove going and the rest of the household up. Once breakfast was over, Dr. McLean was off for a full day at the hospital or one of the outreach clinics. As for the rest of the family, much of the time was spent doing chores. Everything was done by hand, requiring a certain amount of effort and co-operation. Laundry is a particular case in point. Without a washing machine, everything had to be done on a wash board. But Mrs. McLean said she had learned a little trick that saved her an awful lot of work:

"Put your clothes, all your white clothes, in the boiler. You can put the soap in with it, and maybe a little bit of blueing, just a little bit, and put that on the stove, cold, and bring those right up, slowly, to a boil. And do you know? I did it that way for months upon months, and the clothes always kept just as white and just beautiful." The wet clothes were hung on racks which were suspended above the stove. In the winter, said Shirley, we had clothes hanging all over the place.

The Nootka Mission Hospital was forced to close in 1973, when the provincial government built a ten-bed facility in Tahsis. Dr. McLean and his wife moved to Victoria. The doctor died two years later, leaving behind an impressive legacy to the spiritual and physical well-being of the people living in Nootka and Kyuquot Sounds.

In 1987, for the first time since leaving, Mrs. McLean, then 83 years old, returned to visit her old home. The occasion was a reunion in honor of Esperanza's fiftieth anniversary. The three-day celebration brought together many of the doctors and nurses and old friends who had worked on behalf of the hospital. Mrs. McLean died three months later, at her home in Victoria, British Columbia.

The little settlement at Esperanza remains. The hospital is still standing and Esperanza is still a spiritual retreat and mission for the Shantymen: an idyllic setting, with its gently sloping lawns and the wind whispering through the branches of the giant hemlock trees towering above the buildings.

Esperanza Hotel

At about the same time as the hospital was being built at Esperanza, a hotel was going up on an adjacent lot. It boasted several rooms, hot showers for the fishermen, a pub and restaurant, and two huge stone fireplaces. The hotel was a popular place for locals, particularly on Friday and Saturday nights.

"It was something to do," said Elvera Ericson, "There wasn't anything else there. There were no movies around. It was just the only thing there was to do. Gather at the hotel, and there was a beer parlor there, and Eric and his accordion, and Tommy English and his little squeezebox. Between the two of them, they provided some music for dancing."[42]

Esperanza Hotel, circa 1939. Built in 1938, the hotel was destroyed by fire in 1960.   Provincial Archives of B.C.

Relaxing on the steps of the Esperanza Hotel, circa 1940.

Elvera Ericson photo.

Four generations of the Moore family who owned and operated the Esperanza Hotel at the time of the fire. John Perry photo.

Tahsis Archives.

Elvera's husband, Eric, ran an A-frame logging outfit in the Tahsis and Esperanza Inlet area. "We did have a lot of fun there, as I remember," said Eric, "There wasn't all that much room to dance in the living room there, in front of the fireplace. So, whoever was playing had to get up and sit on a chair, on a table, to get out of the road, you see...Anyway, I was sitting there playing - playing 'Life in the Finland Woods' - and I had to pull it quite hard because it had a different tone where you push and you pull, you see. And I forgot all about this thing, and I kept on pulling away, and everybody's dancing so happy, and plop! the thing busted in two!"[43]

Margaret Sharcott, author of *Place of Many Winds*, a collection of stories about Kyuquot Sound, recalls the Esperanza Hotel with fondness. She stayed there while waiting to have her baby in the hospital. "My large room upstairs in the two-storey hotel was delightfully cool after the over-heated room where I had spent the previous night," she writes. "A fragrance combined of salt water and evergreen trees wafted through the casement windows which opened wide over a green lawn bordered with red dahlias... There were six guest rooms all panelled in dark-stained plywood. Downstairs, heavy hand-hewn beams supported the ceilings. Fireplaces of natural grey stone warmed the lounge and the beer parlor."[44]

Less than three months after Margaret Sharcott's visit, the hotel caught fire and burned to the ground. Art and Margaret Hansen just happened to be passing by at the time. It was Christmas Eve, 1960.

"We stopped in, and they couldn't get their water pump started," said Margaret, "Which was typical, I guess. My husband tried to start it for them, but they couldn't get it going. Anyway, Myrtle Moore, she had her ninety-year-old mother staying with them, and my husband got her out of the hotel, clutching a girlie calendar! I guess she grabbed the first thing that she could lay her hands on. George Moore came out with a frozen turkey under his arm. Yes, it burned down. It's too bad, because the bar had a huge stone fireplace in it. A huge thing that would take six, seven foot logs. Just beautiful."[45]

Shortly after the fire, the Shantymen's Missionary Society acquired the property and built a new community centre on the foundations of the old hotel.

Notes

[1] Lewis and Dryden, *Lewis and Dryden's Marine History of the Pacific Northwest*, ed. E.W. Wright, (New York: Spring,1961), p. 426.

[2] According to Richard Inglis, prices did go up to as high as $12. per skin, depending on the quality of the pelt, the demand for furs, and the policies of individual captains.

[3] J. Despard Pemberton, *Facts and Figures Relating to Vancouver Island and British Columbia* (London: 1860), pp. 143-147.

[4] Legislative Assembly, *Sessional Papers* (Victoria: 1888), p. 173.

[5] Ibid., p. 174.

[6] Ibid., p. 174.

[7] Brian P. White, *The Settlement of Nootka Sound*, unpubl. M.A. thesis, Simon Fraser University, (Burnaby: 1972), p. 25.

[8] Bureau of Provincial Information 1902-1921, Bulletin No. 14, Province of British Columbia, (Victoria: 1921), p. 14.

[9] Legislative Assembly, *Sessional Papers* (Victoria: 1894), p. 1080. Report of the Minister of Mines for 1893.

[10] *Victoria Daily Colonist*, November 14, 1909.

[11] Cicely Lyons, *Salmon: Our Heritage* (Vancouver: 1969), p.50

[12] Ibid., pp. 65 and 70.

[13] Joseph E. Forester and Anne D. Forester, *British Columbia's Commercial Fishing History* (Saanichton: 1975), p. 155.

[14] Lyons, p. 314.

[15] Land Registry, *Nootka District* (Port Alberni), Lot 173.

[16] Interview, Jack and Jean Munro (West Vancouver: August 20, 1988).

[17] Forester, p. 125.

[18] Universal Appraisel Co. Ltd., *Fire insurance plans, Nootka Packing Co. Ltd.*, 1939 and 1943. Special Collections, University of B.C. Main Library, Vancouver, pp. 451-460.

[19] Ibid., pp. 438-449.

[20] Ibid., pp. 462-465A.

[21] Ibid., pp. 400-401.

[22] Forester, p. 67.

[23] Ibid., p. 69.

[24] Ibid., pp. 69-70.

[25] Ibid., p. 69.

[26] *Maclean's Magazine*, "Humble pilchard becomes a blueblood," January 1, 1927, pp. 15, 49-50.

[27] Interview, Ralph Hansen (Steveston: August 18, 1988).

[28] Interview, John Perry (Tahsis: March 7, 1988).

[29] Interview, Margaret Hansen (Tahsis: July 12, 1988).

[30] Universal Appraisel Co. Ltd., *Fire insurance plans, Espinosa*, Special Collections, University of B.C. Main Library, Vancouver.

[31] George Nicholson, *Vancouver Island's West Coast: 1762-1962* (Victoria: 1962), p. 243.

[32] Interview, Marion McLean and Shirley (McLean) Sutherland (Esperanza: August 3, 1987).

[33] W. Phillip Keller, *Splendour From the Sea* (Chicago: 1963).

[34] Ibid., p. 99.

[35] Nootka District General Hospital Association, *Minute book*, in Millicent Lindo papers, 1938-1967, Provincial Archives of B.C., Victoria.

[36] Ibid.

[37] Ibid., January 1939.

[38] Ibid.

[39] Ibid., June 3, 1940.

[40] Ibid., March 6, 1938.

[41] Interview, Marion McLean and Shirley (McLean) Sutherland, 1987.

[42] Interview, Elvera and Eric Ericson (Sointula: February 15, 1988).

[43] Ibid.

[44] Margaret Sharcott, *A Place of Many Winds* (Toronto: 1960), p. 233.

[45] Interview, Margaret Hansen, 1988.

CHAPTER 5   ZEBALLOS BOOMTOWN

As the canneries and pilchard plants began closing down along Esperanza Inlet, the focus of economic activity shifted. And, while fishing continued to play an important role in the economic development of the region, mining became the centre of attention. Surprisingly rich veins of gold were discovered in the hills along the Zeballos River Valley and, by 1937, hundreds of mineral claims had been staked, covering nearly every square inch of land in the Zeballos and Nomash River watersheds. A year later, three mills were in operation and 400 men were employed at 30 different properties which were actively engaged in prospecting, development work, and production.[1] By 1939, a substantial community had been built on the flat delta at the head of Zeballos Inlet, boasting an electric light plant, three hotels, several stores, a bank, a school, a weekly newspaper and even a Board of Trade. Records show the population at that time was about 1,000.[2]

Zeballos became known as British Columbia's "wonder camp." According to the mining industry's leading newspaper, *Western Canada Mining News*, Zeballos was the first large tract of virgin mining ground to be discovered in the province since the turn of the century, and it was more important than any other camp in "exciting the imagination" of Eastern Canadian investors.[3] Howard T. Mitchell, writing in *The Financial News*, noted that the resurgence of prospecting on the west coast of the island made the area "the most interesting mining territory in Western Canada."[4] During the peak period of operation, from 1938 to 1942, thirteen mines produced a total of 178,740 ounces of gold valued at over $13 million.

The flurry of excitement generated by the Zeballos goldfields, and its sudden rise to public attention, came as no surprise to people who knew the area. Prospectors had been actively working up the Zeballos River Valley for many years, and in 1908, the first recorded gold was taken from the mouth of the Zeballos River by Tom J. Marks, a fisherman from Kyuquot.

At the time, the primary technique employed was placer mining - panning the river and creek bottoms, or using a sluice box, to sift through the mud and gravel for raw gold. It was the simplest and easiest way to extract gold, requiring a minimum amount of equipment and labor. Several placer claims were registered during the 1920s, but unfortunately, due to a lack of records, we are unable to determine the extent to which the placer claims were developed.[5]

By 1929, forty mineral claims had been staked in the Valley. Among them was the Tagore group, the first lode gold property to be discovered. Staked by J. West and A. Ostman, in 1924, the initial find was one-and-a-half miles from tidewater up the Zeballos River. The property was prospected intensively in 1925 and again, in 1929, when A.B. Trites, a prominent Canadian mining developer, optioned the site from Harry Malmberg and a Mr. Nordstrom, prospectors from Quatsino. According to the mining records, Malmberg shipped out several sacks of high grade ore in 1929, reported to have assayed at 20 ounces of gold to the ton.

View of Zeballos townsite, circa 1939, showing the commercial district on what was called 'The Beach'.

But the results must not have seemed sufficiently lucrative. Trites let his option lapse, and the property lay idle for several years. Then, in 1932, Conrad Wolfe, another prominent mining developer, acquired the property and actively began developing the prospect. Hiring Malmberg, Nordstrom and four associates, Wolfe drove a tunnel into the hillside just above the river bank. But Wolfe was forced to return to the U.S. before completing his work and, once again, the property was left idle.

Early Prospectors

Although the Tagore property didn't prove profitable, Wolfe's efforts none-theless offered encouragement to prospectors working in the area. The men Wolfe hired to work on the mine remained after he left, prospecting and staking other claims. That core group of prospectors were Scandinavian fishermen from Quatsino, Cape Scott, Kyuquot, and the Brooks Peninsula. They fished in the summers and trapped in the winters, scraping together enough money to finance a grubstake for prospecting during the off-seasons. This first group consisted of brothers Harry and Axel Malmberg, Andy and John Donaldson, Nels Overson, Sam Knutsen, the Ildstad brothers - Roy, Alfred, Thomas, Schuyler, and William - Joe Doyle, Alex Mac-Donald, Herb Kevis, and Andy Morod.

A second group arrived on the *Princess Maquinna* from Port Alberni, lured by the prospect of striking it rich. Alfred Bird, a Welshman, and Charles Smith from Nova Scotia, met in Alberni and came up as partners. Other prospectors included Albert Bloom and Alec Stewart. According to one newspaper story, the area required "a type of indigenous, self-supporting miner who could swing a single jack *[hammer]* and load a hole *[with dynamite]* and who could earn the money at salmon trolling to make a prospecting and mining grubstake."[6]

It wasn't until after 1932 that the Zeballos goldfields really took off. Prospect-ing began in earnest that year, with surprisingly positive results. Surprising, because the west coast of the island had, historically, been considered a high risk area, despite what mining reports called its "obvious mineral wealth." The area was known for narrow veins which petered out quickly and didn't follow a straight course. The abrupt twists and turns through the rock made it difficult to mine. Critics, skeptical of the long-term potential of Zeballos, pointed to the failure of mines at the beginning of the century in the Alberni and Barkley Sound area:

"At that time, the west coast of Vancouver Island geologically had a bad name," said Jack Crosson. " 'There's no gold on Vancouver Island,' is what they said. They made up their minds there was no gold. So, these prospectors had to prove that there was. So the only way they could prove it was to send sample tonnage shipments - a ton of ore. Then these mining companies would pay attention to that. But a couple of samples - they wouldn't. Because the geology was against it... And you can go out - even right now, you can go out and find little pockets of native gold in different peaks. But that doesn't make a mine. You've got to have volume. You've got to have length and strength."[7]

Jack Crosson made his first visit to Zeballos, in 1934, as part of the Dominion Government Hydrographic Survey expedition. During the survey of Zeballos Inlet, Jack and a few other crew members went ashore for their noon meal, landing on the beach in front of a cabin belonging to Alfred Bird. It was the only building on the beach at that time.

"During our meal, he came out of the cabin and asked us what we were doing, and we told him," said Jack. "So then we asked him what he was doing. He told us he was trapping and prospecting. And naturally, the first question we asked him is did you

Packing supplies up to the mines.
Photo courtesy of Kathleen and Bruce Davies.

find anything rich? So he went back in the cabin and brought out a big piece of ore which he'd burned in the stove all the previous evening, and a pestle and a crucible, and he ground the ore up in front of us. And went right on the saltwater beach there and panned it out, and the bottom of the pan was just covered with gold. So that's when I got the gold fever."

Jack continued with the survey crew for the next two years, but every cheque went into the bank to build up a grubstake. When he had enough money put aside, he quit his job as a surveyor and in October, 1936, returned to Zeballos where he signed on as a carpenter with Alex MacDonald, a prospector who had staked several claims in the Gold Valley.

"By the time I got there, things were starting to boom up there. The Privateer had been discovered, and Spud Valley, and the Donaldson brothers - they all had good shipments, you see."

Not only prospectors, but the mining industry as a whole had begun to consider Zeballos a potential area for development. A government report by H.C. Gunning, released in 1932, recommended that active prospecting be carried out.[8] On its heels came an announcement from the Honorable Wesley Gordon, federal Minister of Mines, that the area showed "outstanding promise."[9]

Sparked by the encouraging reports, interest in the area deepened when the price of gold rose to

$17.02 an ounce for coarse placer gold, and $20.01 an ounce for fine lode gold. It was the first increase in the price of gold in thirty years. A year later, the price rose again, to $28. and $34. an ounce, respectively.

Another report, this time by Dr. Merle F. Bancroft, released in 1937 but based on survey work done in 1935, led to increased activity. "Men flocked to the district by every boat and came in by air to join in the rush to stake claims."[10] Prospectors, speculators and investors, lured by the possibility of making the big strike, turned their attention to Zeballos. By 1936, prospectors had managed to ship out enough high grade ore to convince even the most conservative of companies that Zeballos was worth developing.

Rich Veins

The first of what was to become one of the most important gold-bearing quartz veins was discovered during the period 1932 to 1934. In the summer of 1932, Alfred Bird discovered rich gold quartz float while panning in Spud Creek, leading to the staking of the Gold Peak and White Star groups of claims, as well as the Privateer, destined to become the richest-producing mine in the Valley.

By February 1934, the Bloom and Donaldson veins plus several others had been staked: Gold Peak was staked, in 1932, by John and Andy Donaldson; White Star was staked the following year, also by the Donaldsons; and the Privateer was staked in 1932 by Alfred Bird.

At the time of staking, the Donaldson vein looked the most promising. A 90-foot cut in the hillside was opened and the Donaldsons became the first shippers of high grade ore, receiving a return of 150 ounces of gold from the open cut.

"The ore was sorted, sacked, backpacked to Zeballos River, canoed to Tagore, and backpacked again around Zeballos canyon, then taken in motor-boat to Ceepeecee and thence shipped by freight to Trail, B.C."[11] By the end of June, 1935, approximately fifteen tons of ore were shipped to Trail from the White Star claim of the Gold Peak group. One newspaper wrote that "Bloom, Bird, and Smith were the first to attempt the hazardous and exciting business of running gold ore in a small boat through the white water of the swift Zeballos River."[12] That "hazardous and exciting" business cost at least one life. On November 3rd, 1934, one of the original partners in the mine, Mike Francis, was killed while hand lining a boat loaded with ore through the rapids of the Zeballos River.

"They were using the lefthand side of the valley and crossing the main Zeballos River at the fork of Spud Creek and Zeballos in a canoe," says Jack Crosson. "They built a big raft, a log raft, and put the ore on the middle of the log raft and towed it themselves down to Ceepeecee and shoved it on the *Maquinna* to Trail, to the smelters."

It was hard work, and the journey to tidewater was arduous and difficult. "The property was about six miles from tidewater and for the first few years the only means of communication between the mine and the beach was

Taking rock and ore out of a prospect and "sacking" it in preparation for hauling it down the mountain.
Photo courtesy of Kathleen and Bruce Davies.

over bear and elk trails along the river bank," writes George Nicholson in his book, *Vancouver Island's West Coast*. "Trees had to be felled to make footbridges over the small streams and gulches, deadfalls crossed, the river waded in two places and ladders scaled up the steeper cliffs."[13]

Determined to convince distant investors that the veins were worth bringing into production, prospectors undertook the huge task of developing their own properties. Bird and his associates concentrated on the Gold Peak property, neglecting the Privateer site which remained largely undeveloped for the first few months. Other important claims were also staked during this initial period: Herb Kevis and Charles Henry located the Van Isle group, in 1933, and began shipping out high grade ore in 1935. Sam Knutsen located the Goldfield group, in 1935, and Alex MacDonald staked the Lone Star (Rey Oro), in 1934.

Jack Crosson worked on the Rey Oro mine with Alex MacDonald. Alex had sold the claim to Edward G. Brown, so he and Jack worked for wages. The going rate at the time was $5 a day:

"We used to have to pack everything up. Pack our grub up for ten days - actually eight days, because it always took a day to go up and a day to come back down," said Jack. "Grub for eight days, then all our nails and wedges and hammers and everything else went up, you see."

"One of the first packs I had was a case of dynamite and some caps," he said. It had been snowing all day, so when he went back up the mountain with his load, the trail was covered with about eight inches of snow. "So there I was with this backpack of dynamite and caps, and I had to walk across these icy snowy logs, and it was freezing before I got there. I tell you, I wasn't very happy about it. My knees were shaking. But eventually, I got used to it." Packers carried between fifty to sixty pounds per load, and made one trip a day up the mountain for 10 cents a pound.

The cabins built up at the mines were no more than one- and two-room shacks. "No mining inspector would allow people to live in those things," said Jack, "But because they were prospectors, they were excluded from safety measures and all that, you see."

"When we were building up on the mountains, everything came right out of the woods, all cedar shakes and everything. We had to make every piece of board we used. Cut a cedar tree down, split it into quarters, and use the shake frow to make the boards."[14]

"There was nothing else to do but get up and work. It was tough all the time, because in the winter there was not much daylight left, you know. So you worked from daylight to dark. Then you spent so much time in your cabin - the cabins were just shelters, you know. And you had a stub of a candle to eat with, to light the cabin up. And there was no such thing as reading a book, because you couldn't afford the candles."

Entrance to Privateer Mine, showing ladder up the steep hillside.
Provincial Archives of B.C.

Later, Jack worked on a property with Andy Morod and Andy's partner, Murphy. Andy had found a showing about 3,000 feet up, called the Barnacle. According to Jack, Andy had been given some money from the Department of Mines for trailwork and had asked Jack to help build the trail. "Every time we come to one of these canyon things, we'd fall a log, roll it down - that's quite a lot of work for three men to do all that. We had to use rope to get the log over the canyon, and once we got it there and made it secure, then we had to get on it and flatten it to walk on it. We all had caulks on, caulk boots *[pronounced 'cork']*, and if you used it enough the caulks themselves will make a trail. Then we put handrails on. We had to make about three or four of them I guess *[log bridges]*. Then, Andy had already built a ladder, it must have been 60 feet high - to get to this Barnacle showing."

It took six weeks to build a trail that was finally good enough to pack in on. Then, they started mining. It was all done by hand. "We'd mine a sack of ore first - oh, a hundred pounds it was - and give it to Murphy - Murphy was older than I was - and start him off back down the trail. Then Andy and I would carry on and mine out another sack each. Sometimes we had enough time to mine a third sack, which would be the fourth for the day, and have that ready for Murphy in the morning."

It was three thousand feet from the cabin to the mine, "straight up and down," said Jack, "You just simply couldn't hurry. You just had to take one step at a time. Well, what we did, being human beings, we got greedy at the end, you see." They were three days ahead of schedule, for when the packhorses were due to pick up the sacks of ore. "So Andy says, 'Well, we won't waste these three days. If you're agreeable, we'll keep mining right up to the last day. But you and I'll have to make two trips a day.' So Murphy would come up and get his. Then Andy and I would follow with our two sacks - one each - and by that time, Murphy would have the noon meal cooked, and we'd just eat, and go back up, three thousand feet, come back

Another view of an entrance to a mine. Ladders were often the only means of making it up steep, rocky sections to the mines.   Royal B.C. Museum, Ethnology Division.

down with the second one. So instead of shipping two ton, we shipped two and a half ton, I guess. And the packhorses took it alright."

At that time, prospectors were "high grading" veins which had been opened up from the surface. "We were only taking the best stuff," said Jack, "Just taking stuff that we could see free gold in. We'd drill a hole with our steel. And it broke up quite easily, so we only put in about half a stick of dynamite. That would take us all morning." Then, they blasted the rock and broke up the big pieces with a sledgehammer to fit in the sturdy canvas sacks for shipping out to the smelter.

Rich Strike

Meanwhile, another group of prospectors had begun work on the Van Isle claim which had been staked, in 1933, by Herb Kevis and Charles Henry. They were part of the original group of fishermen from Quatsino who had come down to work on the Tagore claim. In 1935, Kevis and Ray Pitre were grubstaked by D.S. Tait, a lawyer from Victoria, to start work on high-grading the Van Isle. The first shipments were sent to a smelter in Tacoma. The returns, although good, barely covered their costs. The grade of ore wasn't as high as they wanted, and needed, to make a profit. The Van Isle property, located on the east side of the Zeballos Valley, was reached by a short branch road off the main Zeballos road, 3-and-a-half miles from the townsite.

Many mines used pack horses to carry the bags of ore down to the beach, where the ore was loaded onto the Princess Maquinna *for shipment to the smelters.* Photo courtesy of Kathleen and Bruce Davies.

Late in 1936, the prospectors suspended work on the Van Isle and moved over to the Privateer property. Alfred Bird and his associates, the original stakers, were busy with the White Star and Gold Peak claims. In a move they would later come to regret, they sold their Privateer claims to David S. Tait, Ray A. Pitre, and associates Joseph and Louis Pedneault, Herbert Kevis, Chester Canning, and John J. Frumento.

"They got out their first shipment, about two-and-a-half tons, three weeks work, and it brought a cheque from the smelter of $2,600," reports *The Mining News,* "The ore from that narrow vein assayed from 30 to 45 ounces of gold to the ton for several shipments. British Columbia mining interests then began to sit up and take notice, and so the Privateer mine, begun with what might have been called a small and possibly erratic vein, is now able already to gaze on a potential net profit of a million dollars."[15]

The first shipment of 4800 pounds of ore was made at the beginning of 1937. "It was a terrible task," writes McKelvie, "Those who took part in that work still shudder at the remembrance of it. The ore was sacked and was carried on the backs of men down the narrow trail, slippery trail, through the mud and over the windfalls to Zeballos River."[16] By mining standards, it was a small shipment, but it yielded a large return. They had an answer from the smelter in March: the ore had a value of .54 cents a pound - $2,600. in all. McKelvie:

"And with that cheque came the knowledge that their wildest hopes were realized. They had a mine - a real, rich mine - and it could be made to pay from the outset."

Corporate Investment

"Zeballos has been called a rich man's gold strike," wrote Maude Studholme in the *Geographical Survey,* after a trip to the area in 1938. In the past, the great gold rushes had been for "visible gold" which was easily obtained through panning or sluicing and required as few as one or two men to work the claim. Zeballos was different. "The gold is there, but it is hidden in the womb of the hills and must be delivered by scientific methods," said Studholme, "Man is not enough."[18]

The orefields were so rich with ore that, initially, it was comparatively easy to find and extract. Any individual could develop the find to a point where its productivity could be established. Once established, however, heavy machinery and large capital investments were needed to turn the raw goldfields into producing mines.

Developments moved onto a larger scale, one that prospectors with limited resources couldn't compete with. They could only hope to ship two tons of ore after two to three months of back-breaking labor. Mining companies, on the other hand, could install rock-crushing mills which could handle 75 tons of ore a day.

The rich strike at Privateer and the consistently good returns from other prospects which were shipping out high grade ore, prompted a flood of investment in the area. Most prospectors sold their claims to mining companies. Some retired while others remained in the area, sinking the money from the sale of one claim into developing new claims. "One prospector I can think of right away, he must have made three fortunes in the short time I was there," said Marjorie Frumento who first went to Zeballos in the early spring of 1938. "Just went to town, blew it all, and came back. Struck it rich and made another fortune. A fortune at that time was maybe sixty or eighty thousand dollars, that was a real fortune then. Went to town - was gone a few months - went on a big bender, and would come back broke and start over again. There were lots of prospectors did things like that."[19]

Not every mine paid off and not everyone made a fortune. When Jack Crosson worked with Andy Morod on the Barnacle, they made just enough to cover expenses, plus a little on the side. "We shipped our ore to Tacoma - Andy did. And at that time the American dollar was worth a dollar ten or eleven, something like that. We made enough on the foreign exchange to pay for the packhorses. I forget what I got out of it - two hundred dollars, something like that. We all did. Of course, out of that Andy took the expenses - the groceries and dynamite and all that."

"The mining companies were the only ones that made the money," Jack continued, "It's the same old story. The prospector very seldom gets anything. You see, the psychology of a prospector is you go up there and find something big. So the companies and the bigshots, they know its big. But they know he can't do nothing about it. So, they get it for whatever price. They finally starve the old prospector out and he's getting disheartened and dejected, so he says okay, give me my ten thousand dollars."

Some prospectors became embittered while they watched their claims - sold for less than 50 thousand dollars - turn into mines worth more than a million dollars. The dispute over the Privateer property is one such story:

"See, Bloom, Smith, and Bird, they sold the Privateer I think it was for 45 thousand dollars, you see. Total. That's what they got for it. Well, the company got millions out of it," said Jack, "You see, Bird and Smith didn't realize the value of their mine, until they got into that fracas with Roy Ildstad. Then Bird went up and he could see that great big beautiful gold vein. But in the meantime, prior to that, Ildstad knew it was there, and he got hold of Ray Pitre who was mining the Man-of-War group of claims, and told him...showed him big hunks of free gold. Well, of course Ray got interested in it... So then Ray went to Zeballos and phoned Tait - D.S. Tait in Victoria - and said 'Get the Privateer, buy the Privateer. Never mind this bloody Man-of-War, we're getting nothing out of that except hard work.'"

So Tait bought the group of claims and the Ildstad brothers wound up with a hundred thousand dollars, mostly in shares, said Jack.

Bird and the others were bitter. "'Christ, if I'd only hung on, if I'd only hung on.' See, where those boys made their mistake, if they'd all stuck together, they'd have had a whole sidehill. But they went in as a group, then they broke off into individual groups. Then these individual groups started to have - well, they'd have disagreements among themselves like, you see. They were close-knit when they came down *[from Quatsino]*, but as soon as you put gold in front of them, then human nature takes over. And it's only human nature that 'I want more than you have.' And that's the way it went. There was litigation all over," said Jack.

Charlie Smith took his share of the sale of the Privateer and returned to Nova Scotia where he married, bought a farm, and retired. Andrew Donaldson retired to Vancouver. John Donaldson went salmon fishing. Les R. Brown built Zeballos' first hotel, sold it for a profit, and retired to a farm in the Fraser Valley. Alfred Bird moved to Tofino. Ray Pitre became a wealthy man and settled in Duncan where he started up a manufacturing firm.

One tragedy from that period was Alfred Bloom's suicide. "He got his share of the money from the Privateer, plus he sold Zeballos Gold Peak. And he went down to Vancouver for three months or so," said Jack. Then he returned to Zeballos. Jack was his partner at the time, but he was out prospecting when Bloom returned. "Bloom went back to that shack, got dressed - put his collar and tie on - then laid down on the floor and shot himself right through the heart."

"He got lonely," Jack said, "He'd cut a poem out of a magazine, and the poem went 'Is it worthwhile? When the skies are dark and gray and everybody is away, is it worthwhile?'... And he had cut that out of the magazine, wherever he got it from, and he had put it up against the can of honey. And on this side there was a letter that my folks had sent to me with my name and address on it, and another one the same with Alex MacDonald's, on either side of the can. Then he laid down and shot himself. You have to make up your own mind why he did it."

Expansion

With the financial backing of the large companies, the mines boomed and the town of Zeballos flourished. Privateer, with its rich vein and Victoria investments, led the way. The Pedneault brothers, Joseph and Louis, sold out their logging interests in Sooke and invested $25,000. in the company, agreeing to furnish trucks and other road-building equipment in exchange for shares in the mine.[20] On June 5, 1937, a tractor and angledozer were landed at the head of Zeballos Inlet, and a road was pushed through to the Privateer Mine. Later that same year, construction began on a network of roads paid for by the federal and provincial governments.

The financial backing of corporate investors led to expansion. Above, a new rock-crushing mill on its way up to one of the mines.   Photo courtesy of Kathleen and Bruce Davies.

Mining Methods

Ore was mined and shipped out in several forms. *High grading* was the usual method used when a mine was first being developed. Rich outcroppings of quartz which were laced with free gold, visible to the eye, were hand-picked, sacked, and shipped out to the smelter as soon as a few hundred bags were ready. This method ensured quick returns in order to finance further development of the property. The remaining ore was stockpiled until a mill was built.

Once mills had been installed, the rock was crushed on site and the gold was separated out to be melted down, poured into brick molds, and shipped out as *gold bullion*. The remaining residue was an *ore concentrate*, a substance which, having "the appearance of wet black mud and being exceedingly heavy, is bagged in small but strong sacks."[21] Both high-grade and concentrates were shipped to the smelter in Tacoma by Price-Waterhouse Steamship Companies.

The gold bullion bricks were shipped by mail - via the *Princess Maquinna* and later, Ginger Coote Airways - to the Dominion Government Assay Office in Vancouver and from there to the Federal Mint in Ottawa. According to Nicholson, the bricks weighed, on average, any where from ten to sixty-five pounds apiece, requiring as much as $40. postage for an average 60-pound gold brick. Each brick was wrapped and stitched in strong canvas and tied securely with wire.[22]

"As many as half-a-dozen bricks would sometimes be mailed in one day and as the post office department doesn't provide it's country postmasters with safes and my own was to small to receive them, they were usually placed under my bed," Nicholson writes, "However, when my wife and I went to a dance or show, we always found them there on our return."[23]

Spud Valley

The first rock-crushing mill in Zeballos was installed on the Goldfields (Spud Valley) property, in 1935. It was a small prospecting mill with a 2-ton capacity (Stevenson, 1950, says the mill had a 10-ton capacity). "Knutsen backpacked that mill, weighing 253 pounds, all the way to the Goldfields camp over a mountain trail that was little more than a series of fresh blaze marks in the wilderness," writes Mitchell, "It took him two days to travel the six miles from the point on the flats where he first shouldered the load: A fact that deserves a place in history!"[24]

Spud Valley was originally staked as the Goldfields property by Sam Knutsen in June 1935. Knutsen sold it to A.B. Trites a year later for $50,000, payable over a five year period.

The 50-ton mill started up November 25, 1938 and the first bullion was shipped out in January, 1939. They were recovering about $40,000 a month from the mill. "In Spud Valley, the general nature of the ore is so rich that the operating policy has been to pack out the waste and send the rest to the ore dump, rather than the reverse," reported *The Mining News* in 1938.[25]

Shortly after the first gold brick was poured, A.B. Trites sold the mine to a group of Seattle and B.C. businessmen for $800,000 - $400,000 in cash with the remainder to be paid from production. According to the *Western Canada Mining News,* it was "one of the biggest cash deals that Canadian mining has seen in many weeks."[26] The property Sam Knutsen had sold for $50,000, in 1936, had increased considerably in value.

Rey Oro

Rey Oro, the first mine to bring a major mill into production, produced the first gold bullion brick in Zeballos. The 15-ton mill arrived on the *Princess Maquinna* in late July, 1938, and was hauled up to the mine by packhorses over a trail which had barely been completed. The first brick was poured August 27th, 1938.

The property was staked by Alex MacDonald, in 1934, but it was brought into production by Rey Oro Mines Ltd. under the management of E.G. Brown. Brown later built Zeballos' first hotel, the Pioneer Hotel, with money he made from the mine.

Rey Oro truck on main street, Zeballos.　　　　Photo courtesy of Kathleen and Bruce Davies.

Some of the men behind the Privateer Mine.   Photo courtesy of Kathleen and Bruce Davies.

Privateer

Of all the mines in production at Zeballos, the Privateer was the most successful and well-known. During the eight-year period between 1934 to 1942, Zeballos' total production of gold bricks and concentrates was $13 million. Of that, just over half came out of Privateer.

Entrance to Privateer Mine before the first big strike was made.   Provincial Archives of B.C.

An eastern newspaper said it was "probably the richest mine in Canada."[27] One shipment of quartz to the Tacoma smelter contained the highest percentage of gold on record there and was valued between $35,000 to $140,000 a ton.

"From one section of the upper tunnel came several big carbide cans of ore which smelter officials said they were reluctant to melt down," wrote Mitchell, "It was the richest ore and the most extensively impregnated with free gold that the Tacoma smelter had ever received."[28]

McKelvie called it the "romance of the Privateer." The property was first staked in 1932-33, but it wasn't until 1936 that the rich vein, staked by Roy Ildstad, was found. By that time, Bird and his partners had sold their interest in the Privateer

Celebrating the first gold bricks poured at the Privateer Mine in Zeballos, 1938. Photo by Bruce McKelvie.

Provincial Archives of B.C.

for $45,000 (see story above). Tait and his associates purchased the property in December, 1936, gambling on the mine's richness by putting up their own money to finance the work.

The gamble paid off. By the end of March, 1939, shipments of high grade ore and bullion had yielded one million dollars' worth of gold and Privateer had settled down to a steady production of well over $100,000 per month: $75,000 of that was pure profit.[29]

The 75-ton amalgamation-cyanide mill arrived in July, 1938. Fred Peet was one of the engineers sent to install it. Peet worked for Shoemacher and Burnham, the company hired by Connell Mining to design and install the new mill and plant. "The Privateer Mine, being so rich, had a high-grader's dry," Peet says, "This is a building where the miners strip naked when coming from the mine and are checked to be sure that no gold is being taken illegally from the workings."[30]

Sometime during the first few days of the mill's operation, Peet checked to see why so much high grade was being lost into the lower grade ore. "It was instantly

Gold bricks packed for mailing.   Photo courtesy of Kathleen and Bruce Davies.

apparent the reason the jigs were not functioning correctly," he says, "The collecting sumps were so full of gold, they could hold no more. The gold was overflowing the jigs and going directly into the cyanide circuit. In all my life I have never seen such a collection of raw gold as I saw in those Denver Jig sumps at Privateer Mine."[31]

The first gold brick out of Privateer was poured on October 18th, 1938 with much fanfare and celebration. The *Princess Norah* was chartered for a special trip up the coast to bring dignitaries, government officials, and other guests to witness the event. After a tour of the mine and a ceremonious pouring of the gold bullion, there was a luncheon at the mine and a dance that evening in the community hall.

Crushing mill at Privateer Mine.   Provincial Archives of B.C.

In 1939, Privateer joined with Dentonia Mines Ltd. to bring the adjoining Prident property into production. Dentonia had been shipping high-grade to the smelters in Tacoma, but after the deal with Privateer, a tramway was built between the two properties and ore from Prident was milled at Privateer.

Mount Zeballos, Central Zeballos, Homeward

The principal mines and mills, in order of production, were Privateer, Spud Valley, Mount Zeballos, Central Zeballos (Reno), White Star, and Rey Oro. The first to install mills were Rey Oro, Spud Valley, and Privateer. Mount Zeballos, Central Zeballos, and Homeward Mines soon followed.

Mount Zeballos was staked, in 1938, by S.H. Davis and H. Kinvig. Later, Conwest Exploration acquired a 50 per cent interest in the newly-formed Mount Zeballos Gold Mines Co. and put up the money to construct a mill. An amalgamation-flotation mill with a 55-ton-a-day capacity was installed in 1939.

At Central Zeballos, under the terms of a takeover by Reno Gold, a 50-ton amalgamation-flotation mill was built in January, 1940. The mill operated until the mine closed in the fall of 1942. It re-opened in early 1946 but closed down again in the summer of 1947.

Homeward, the sixth and last mine to install a mill, was staked as the Golden Horn by H.E. Smith in the summer of 1937. Some surface work was done by Pioneer Gold Mines Ltd. before Homeward Mines acquired the property in 1939. An amalgamation-flotation mill with a 50-ton capacity was built in 1941, and ran from June, 1941 until the mine closed down in February, 1942.

Mining Communities

By 1938, between 375 to 400 men were steadily employed on about thirty properties in Zeballos, the bulk of them concentrating on the six major producers.[32]

Mining community at Privateer Mine. Privateer and Spud Valley had the largest settlements, boasting stores, bowling alleys and community halls.

Provincial Archives of B.C.

Once mills were installed and steady production was underway, small communities housing miners and their families began to spring up on the steep hillsides around the mines. The largest settlements were at Privateer and Spud Valley, and boasted stores, bowling alleys, movie houses, community halls, and their own schools. The business and commercial district for the area was located on the flat delta at the head of the inlet where the steamships docked and the seaplanes came in.

"The mines all had their own halls and communities. But there was a lot of coming and going in between," said Jesse Crabbe, one of Zeballos' early residents. "We'd go up there and do their dances, and they'd come down to ours. And everything that went in or went out had to come down through the Beach, which is what we called where we were, you see."[33]

At Spud Valley, Marjorie Frumento's parents built a pool hall, grocery store, and small cafe where Marjorie's mom would make lunches and serve coffee and doughnuts to the miners. "It was something to do," Marjorie said, "There was nothing for the men to do in lunch hours and after work."

As of December, 1939, eleven houses had been built near Spud Valley and in September, 1940, three more are reported to have been built.[34] During that same period, construction began on a community hall for the tiny settlement. A weekly report from the mine manager in February, 1940, notes that 80 members had already signed up to join the community club.[35]

The community hall was completed the first week of March, 1940, and an opening dance was held on March 16th. By April, the mine manager reported that the new building was a great success. "Interest is so keen in social and sport activities that little time is left for troublemakers," he wrote.[36] In the fall of 1940, a "picture projection room" and additional bowling alleys were built, and school began in a new schoolhouse which had just been completed.[37]

Community at Privateer Mine thrived until the mine closed down during World War II.

Provincial Archives of B.C.

Near Privateer Mines, Jack Crosson recalls that in the fall of 1937, spring of 1938, "quite a community" was built on what was called "Privateer Flats," a level stretch of land near the Zeballos River and just down the hill from the mine. It wasn't the best spot to build, he said, because it flooded during heavy rains.

Jack met Argyle and Giles as they were starting to build their store. He told them that, before they did anything else, they should cut five-foot posts and build their house on posts to protect it from floods. They didn't believe him at first. "I took them to the alder tree and they could see the height of last year's flood there by all the little pine needles around in a circle," Jack said. So, they took his advice and built their store on posts. "By golly, a flood come, you know, and the water came right under their floor joists, but not in. They had worked all night, putting all the flour and sugar on the counters and on the top shelves, but nothing came in the building."

Charlie Hill, the first mayor of Zeballos, says French Henry and Slim Beale ran a rooming house cum hotel at Privateer where they had pool tables and sold liquor. French Henry later moved down to the Beach where he bought a haberdashery. Slim Beale eventually bought the *Chamiss Queen* and operated the booze boat between Zeballos and Tahsis.

Charlie says one of the problems with the mining settlements was that miners, not loggers, built the houses. "They went up to Spud Valley and they built a lot of homes...But they built them on hemlock posts. And hemlock posts in this country don't last too long. They had lots of cedar, but they never thought of using it."[38]

The Beach

"There is no business like mining to transform some obscure spot in the wilderness into a hive of industrial activity and to put a little-known name suddenly on every tongue," wrote Howard Mitchell in the mid-1930s.[39]

Housing construction boomed almost overnight during the height of the Zeballos gold boom. Above, wooden planks served as both road and sidewalk.   Provincial Archives of B.C.

He was referring to Zeballos. In the beginning, Zeballos was no more than a rough clearing at the head of an inlet with a handful of prospectors' shacks clustered along the shore. "It has one street, of planks, laid trackwise for motor trucks, a huddle of shacks, a slough in which scows and barges are anchored at the back doors of the houses, and the street and settlement are just a slit in the dank and dripping forest of spruce, fir, hemlock, and cedar trees on the flat at the mouth of the Zeballos River. The street is locally known as Rotten Row..."[40]

Almost overnight, the flat delta at the mouth of the Zeballos River burgeoned into a substantial community teeming with activity. Marjorie Frumento and her parents arrived in Zeballos in March, 1938. "There were tents everywhere," she said, "All along the road there were tents." Marjorie's father had been up a few months earlier and had built a little shack for them to live in until they could find something more permanent. "Just four walls and a little woodstove in it. That's where we stayed for awhile. But there were little shacks like that all over the place. Everybody was coming in and building them because the hotels - they were so full they were renting every space for sleeping bags," Marjorie said, "Like, all upstairs in the hotels, about every four feet there was a space. For fifty cents, you could get space to put this sleeping bag down. There was no way you'd ever get a room anywhere."

People were flocking in by boat and plane. "It was growing so fast," said Marjorie, "There were so many people coming in every boat-day, it grew really quickly. And soon as they could build places - they'd get lumber in and build something and then the next boat, their family would all be in."

The town was officially born on December 6th, 1937 when 90 subdivided townsite lots went on the auction block. The lots ranged in price from $50 to $200 apiece.[41] Three months later, fifty houses had sprung up. "From the conclusion of the townsite sale the days of Zeballos have been filled with the ring of hammers, the groans of saws, the pounding of pile drivers, the banging of lumber being unloaded and the chugging of truck and tractor engines."[42] Houses, stores and hotels were springing up "like magic," wrote one reporter. "One man was in such a hurry to build that he put up his house on the wrong lot and had to move the house."[43]

View of the townsite under construction.   Provincial Archives of B.C.

In April, 1938, two hotels were in operation, there were three restaurants, a large general store and a second smaller one, two pool halls, an "imposing club building," and a post office run by postmaster George Nicholson. "Six months ago the postmaster could put the mail for Zeballos in his back pocket when taking it from the boat," wrote the *Daily Colonist*. That had changed by 1938 when one typical consignment was 26 mail bags, mostly filled with ore samples.

By the spring of 1939, conditions had changed even more. The town had grown from a "scattered straggling collection of shacks" housing 300 people, to a comparatively substantial town of 1100. In addition to the above, the town boasted a government wharf, a third hotel, a school, a hospital, a movie theatre, a Roman Catholic Church, and a weekly newspaper.[44]

Zeballos began to think in terms of the future. "The community is more than a temporary trading center; it is a settlement that expects to grow. Its residents are planning for permanency, and for that reason the buildings are better built than is usual in a mushroom town. Rough as they are, the buildings are on substantial foundations and there is evidence of an interest in workmanship and thoroughness in spite of the speed in construction."[45]

General stores, a hardware store, a drygoods store, and a drugstore were established. There was even a haberdashery and a local bakery. A radiotelephone was installed. Then came the Bank of Commerce, a brokerage office, an insurance agency, the Red Cross Hospital, a fire department, and a jailhouse. The Community Hall was officially opened with a Halloween dance in 1938, and two weeks later, the first movies were shown in the hall.

Boomtown

Marjorie Frumento's father had been working at the mill in Powell River when he heard about the gold rush in Zeballos. "The place was booming and everybody was going there from all over," said Marjorie, "He just thought he'd like to get in on something. At first, he took some cows up because there was no fresh milk there. He pastured them over on the flats beyond the river, and he went over every day with

Flooding was a major problem in the Zeballos townsite at the beach. In the 1960s, the village undertook extensive work in rerouting the river and building dikes to combat the problem.

Photo courtesy of Kathleen and Bruce Davies.

a rowboat and cut hay and so on. But that only lasted a short time," she said, "Because one of the cafes, I guess they got wind of no pasteurization and decided the milk should be pasteurized. So Dad went up to Spud Valley and built a pool hall and grocery store and little coffee shop."

Marjorie had just turned sixteen when she went to Zeballos. When her parents moved to Spud Valley, Marjorie stayed behind at the Beach where she worked as a radiotelephone operator for Northwest Tel.

"There's no comparison between a mill town and a gold booming town," she said, "There's no comparison. There's just - an excitement. And, a mill town - well, the mill is running and everybody's going to work steady hours. But a mining town! I mean, you're always waiting for the prospectors to come in with stories of their trips, and to see if they struck it rich. And they're bringing all their bags of nuggets and that in to send out to be assayed. And you're waiting for all the big news when it comes back. There's just an air of excitement all the time, somehow."

Zeballos was known in the region as a 'good time town.' There were three hotels, each with a bar, several gambling clubs and pool halls, a bordello, and, until a liquor store was built, a number of bootleggers.

Charlie Hill arrived in Zeballos in November, 1941, on his way to work in one of the mines. "I flew in November the first, and got off the plane, and there's guys standing around the dock, you know. I walked up - it's about fifteen hundred feet to the beer parlor - and I think I had two hundred drinks offered to me before I got to the hotel. Guys with them bottles hanging out of their pockets," Charlie said, "So, I couldn't think of any holiday, you know. And I says 'What are you guys celebrating here?' 'Oh,' he said, 'We just opened up the liquor store today.' Nothing moved for about three days."

Wes Coburn was a commercial fisherman on the westcoast during the 1930s and 40s. He remembers stopping in at Zeballos to go to the beer parlor. "It used to get kind of exciting at times you know," he said, "Saturday nights they wouldn't sell bottled beer. Because of the fighting. A bottle of beer, full or empty, is quite a weapon. Especially if you knock the blame thing on the table. It's as good as a knife. You could make doughnuts out of them."[46]

Wes said that the loggers and the miners used to split up into different factions. "In the mining camps, if you had a bunch sitting at a table drinking beer, and someone said 'Turn your glass upside down,' do you know what that meant? You had a fight on your hands, just that quick," he said, "That meant you were the

Coping with flooding and muddy streets was one of the drawbacks to life in Zeballos during the gold rush era.

Photo courtesy of Kathleen and Bruce Davies.

Post Office and home of Major George Nicholson, a prominent figure in Zeballos' business community. Major Nicholson was Postmaster, Government Agent and Mining Inspector during the period 1938 - 1953. He wrote Vancouver Island's West Coast.　　　　Royal B.C. Museum, Ethnology Division.

Zeballos, circa 1946.　　　　Provincial Archives of B.C.

best man at the table. Oh no, that wasn't only here in Zeballos. That was in the whole set up. Turn your glass upside down or you had a fight."

Zeballos was perhaps best known for its bordello or "goat ranch" as some of the locals referred to it. It was run by a woman named Audrey Monet, from Montreal. "Everybody was glad it was there," said Marjorie, "Because I doubt if it would have been safe for any girls to be around if it hadn't been there... There were hardly any women then, and hundreds of prospectors - it was a good thing to have."

Ann Hill, Charlie's wife, called it the "halfway house," because it was located a mile or two out of town on the road to the mines, midway between the mining camps and the townsite. "She ran a great place," said Ann, "It was spotless, it was beautifully kept. I saw it afterward when it was empty, and you could still smell lysol in each room...She was a marvelous lady."[47]

According to Jack Crosson, Audrey got permission from Del Lutes, the manager at Ceepeecee, to build her bordello on property across the river from the Tagore Mine, of which Lutes was part-owner. "They built it right on the ground, you know, and of course that winter the first flood come along and floated it," Jack said, "They took the seine boats from Nelson Brothers Packers up the hill on a truck, and then launched them on the water the other side of the hill, and rowed over and got the girls out through the windows."

The bordello did a thriving business, and some say the women took more gold from Zeballos than was shipped from the mines.

Zeballos' heyday as a gold mining town lasted for five years. A brief flash across the world stage, intense, but short-lived. The mines began closing down in 1942. Labor shortages brought on by World War II, and a lower grade of ore, made it unprofitable for the companies to keep operating. In 1942, conditions at the mines became serious. "The mill tonnage has been maintained at nearly the capacity of the ball mill," reports the manager for Spud Valley, "But the labor shortage is becoming more acute, and the grade of the ore is such that not much profit can be made on a smaller tonnage."[48]

Spud Valley closed down at the end of June, 1942. Other mines had already closed and the remainder soon followed. And when the mines went, so did the town.

"In nineteen-forty-two," said Wes Coburn, "You could fire a blame gun down the road here and wouldn't hit anybody."

The gold mines re-opened for a brief period after the war, but then closed for good, in 1948. The cost of labor had risen and the price of gold remained fixed by government order at $35. an ounce. Again, it was unprofitable for the companies to continue operating.

The town nearly died at that point. Residents had hung on through the war,

"Sharon's Shop" is one of the few buildings remaining from the gold boom era. Several other buildings from the same period are boarded up.   Tahsis Archives.

clinging to the slim hope that the mines would reopen. With that hope shattered, the abandoned buildings and deserted streets took on a sense of permanent despair. "You could walk the full length of the town and you'd never see a soul," says Bruce Davies who grew up in Zeballos.[49]

Logging

The will to survive was strong and the town's residents refused to give up, despite a population that had dropped from a boom-town high of 1,100 to less than 40. Instead, they turned to logging and fishing as their economic mainstays. Manning Timber Co. had operated a small sawmill in Zeballos during the gold rush period and, after the war, it acquired licenses in the Zeballos and Nomash River Valleys. Together with the government liquor store, Manning Timber provided Zeballos with a somewhat fragile economic base during this unstable period.

Several A-frame logging outfits, including Gordon Gibson and Earl O'Malley, were also working in the area. The Gibson Brothers, subsidized by the federal government to supply black spruce for the making of Mosquito air bombers, began logging up the Zeballos River Valley and Little Zeballos. Both areas had prime spruce stands:

"They only took the very very best," said Bruce Davies, "The very best. If they felled a tree and once they got it on the ground they found it wasn't just what they wanted, they left it."

After the war, in 1949, several lumber companies acquired timber leases around the Zeballos area, including Manning, Nootka Timber Co. Ltd., Roy Darville, and East Asiatic Co.. Vic O'Hara and Gibson were also operating in the area during this time.

Meanwhile, the town's residents continued to strengthen their community, establishing ongoing institutions and services. In 1952, the town was incorporated as a village municipality and Charlie Hill was elected mayor. "They organized the place, you know," said Charlie, "We had an interim committee...And in six months we had to have an election. So the guy that was chairman, he didn't want it. Nobody else wanted it, and they all looked at me. 'Well,' I said, 'Let's call it off. No need to organize this outfit, we're well-organized as it is.' But 'No,' they said. So I said 'Okay, you go ahead and we'll have an election.' So we had an election. Well, when you're the only name on there, you can't lose," Charlie said, "So I was on there for pretty near four years, I guess."

Zeballos Iron Ore Mine

Mining returned to Zeballos in 1959, briefly injecting the town with new life and energy. High grade iron ore, located on a mountainside about three to five miles from tidewater, was developed for export by Zeballos Iron Ore Mines Ltd. The company spent $3 million to bring the property into production, building a wharf and bulk-loading facility near the townsite. Up at the minesite, a tramway and crushing mill were installed and houses were built for the miners. The first load of ore was shipped out on May 25, 1962. It was the first shipment in a five-year contract to supply Japanese smelters and refineries with iron ore.

Zeballos Iron Ore Mines closed down in 1969. During its peak period of production, it employed about 200 men, and produced a total of 761,470 tons of iron concentrate. Other iron ore mines in the area during that same period included the Kla-anch Iron Mine near Nimpkish and the Argonaut Mine in the Campbell River-Quinsam area. Copper was also being mined at Buttle Lake (Westmin), Port Hardy (Island Copper), and Port Alice (Coast Copper, Yreka, and the Merry Widow).

Tahsis Company Ltd.

With the closure of the iron mine, Zeballos' existence was once again threatened. This time, the town's survival hinged on Tahsis Company's application to extend its Tree Farm License to include about 24 square miles of timber in the Zeballos-Artlish River system. If granted the timber, the company promised to extend its logging road north into the new area and be cutting within the year. Zeballos would become the company's main logging base.

"Their plan looks like our only hope," said Stan Jones in a newspaper interview during that period. At the time, Stan was mayor of the tiny village. "This town has been kept going through the years more by stubbornness than anything else, but unless we get another industry, this time will probably be the end of us."[50]

The company also promised to connect its logging road to the existing CanFor [Canadian Forest Products Ltd.] road, thereby providing Zeballos with its first overland link to other communities on the island. "I will be the first to admit that the plan helps us as well as Zeballos," said company president Jack Christensen, "But let's look at this a little deeper. There's no use letting the town die... We're a west coast company," he said, "And the more communities in the area, the better it is for us. We find it much better to have our men and families together and Zeballos would offer us that opportunity."[51]

Tahsis Company was granted its application for an extension. Its plans included the construction of a pulp mill and new townsite at Gold River, an expansion

Fair Harbor on Kyuquot Sound (below and right) was Tahsis Company's main logging division until 1969 when the division was moved to Zeballos. The Fair Harbor camp was closed and workers and their families moved into Zeballos. Photo by George Allen Aerial Photos Ltd., 1960.

Tahsis Archives.

George Allen Aerial Photos Ltd.

of logging into the Zeballos watershed, and a joint agreement between Tahsis Company and Canadian Forest Products to build a 12-mile stretch of road completing the link between Zeballos and the main highway at Nimpkish.

Logging operations started up on October 22, 1969. The new road opened the following year in September, 1970. Telephones were installed in 1975. Nonetheless, according to one resident, the population of Zeballos was at a low of about 35.[52] Zeballos still had a long way to go.

Zeballos Today

Today, Zeballos has come full circle and stands on the threshold of a future which may once again include gold. Active exploration of the old Spud Valley and Privateer properties has produced some encouraging results, enough to convince speculators to continue with exploratory drilling. McAdam Resources, one of the companies now working in the area, is seriously considering re-opening the mine at Spud Valley. One of the advantages of an old minesite is that a lot of the prospecting work has already been done.

"If you have a piece of ground out in the middle of nowhere, and you go out and stake it, and then try and find a mine on it, your chances of finding a mine are about a thousand to one," said Dave Cawood, the Project Geologist for McAdam Resources.[53]

John Crowhurst, the mayor of Zeballos in 1988, is convinced Zeballos has a future. He says it goes back to the reason the village was started in the first place: that same reason is why it's going to continue. "Zeballos isn't going to go away," he said. "It's still the three basic resources being utilized here. Fishing, mining, and logging. The mining to a lesser degree, and the logging more, at this point in time."[54]

Crowhurst and the Village Council want to see their village's history as a gold rush town preserved in some tangible form. One way has been to establish by-laws which help to retain the 'look' of the old mining town. "When we look at doing some sort of project in the village - like, we've contemplated putting in sidewalks - you've got to sit down and think, 'How would they have done it in 1938?' We don't want to lose the look of the community," said John, "This is why we've asked any new business that's come in here and set up - like the new store, for instance - to put on a false front. When we built the firehall, we put a false front on it. It just carries on the theme of the original idea. So anything that this council does, as best we can, we carry that theme out."

Zeballos, today, is a tiny community of some 150 people, mainly loggers and their families employed by Canadian Pacific Forest Products. Logging continues to be the main economic force, although mining and aquaculture have recently begun to establish themselves as potentially strong secondary industries.

The 'look' of the gold mining town remains: a gravel road leads up from the dock through town, past abandoned stores with their false fronts, past old wooden houses now homes to loggers, past the original Pioneer Hotel, renamed the Zeballos Hotel, up the canyon and into the hills where the mines once were and where they are coming to life once again.

Notes

1   John Stevenson, *Geology and mineral deposits of Zeballos mining camp, B.C.* (Victoria: 1950), p. 13.

2   *Victoria Daily Colonist*, by B.A. McKelvie, (Victoria: November 6, 1938).

3   *Western Canada Mining News*, "A history of the golden romance of Zeballos," by H. Hilliard, April 25, 1939.

4   *The Financial News*, "Prospectors, young and old, covering 140-mile zone on west coast of Vancouver Island," by Howard T. Mitchell, n.d.

5   Ben Hines, *Pick, Pan, and Pack: A History of Mining in the Alberni Mining Division* (Port Alberni: 1976), p. 52.

6   *Vancouver Province,* "Adventure and history are mined in Zeballos," by Howard T. Mitchell, (Vancouver: nd.).

7   Interview, Jack Crosson (Sooke: June 21, 1988).

8   *Victoria Daily Colonist,* (April 3, 1938).

9   *Victoria Daily Colonist,* McKelvie, (November 6, 1938).

10 *Victoria Daily Colonist,* "Faith in island mining is maintained by consistent reports on Zeballos area," by B.A. McKelvie. (Victoria: August 28, 1938).

11 Ibid., p. 14.

12 *Vancouver Province,* "Adventure and history are mined in Zeballos," by Howard T. Mitchell, (Vancouver: nd.).

[13] George Nicholson, *Vancouver Island's West Coast* (Victoria: 1962), p. 303.

[14] A shake frow is a cleaving tool with a heavy blade set at right angles to the handle. It is used to split wood into shakes or planks.

[15] *Western Canada Mining News,* "History and romance of Zeballos revealed," by A.D. Sykes, (February 10, 1938).

[16] *Victoria Daily Colonist,* McKelvie, (November 6, 1938).

[17] *Victoria Daily Colonist,* McKelvie, (August 28, 1938).

[18] Maude Studholme, "The Latest Gold Rush," *The Canadian Geographical Journal*, Vol. 19: No. 2, (August 1939),p. 136.

[19] Interview, Marjorie Frumento (Campbell River: January 25, 1988).

[20] Nicholson, p. 307.

[21] *Victoria Daily Colonist*, "Five tons of gold under a bed," by George Nicholson, (Victoria: February 7, 1954).

[22] *Victoria Daily Colonist*, "Zeballos Gold," by George Nicholson, (Victoria: July 28, 1968).

[23] *Victoria Daily Colonist*, Nicholson, (February 7, 1954).

[24] *Vancouver Province,* Mitchell, n.d.

[25] *Western Canada Mining News,* Sykes, (February 10, 1938).

[26] *Western Canada Mining News,* (April 25, 1939).

[27] *Victoria Daily Colonist*, McKelvie, (August 28, 1938).

[28] *Vancouver Province,* Mitchell, n.d.

[29] *Western Canada Mining News,* April 25, 1939.

[30] *Victoria Daily Colonist*, "Zeballos gold," by Fred Peet, (Victoria: April 24, 1977).

[31] Ibid.

[32] Merle F. Bancroft, *Zeballos Mining District and Vicinity,* Geological Survey, Paper 40-12, (Ottawa: 1940).

[33] Interview, Jesse Crabbe (Courtenay: June 19, 1989).

[34] Spud Valley Mines, Reports.

[35] Ibid., February 16, 1940.

[36] Ibid., April 24, 1940.

[37] Ibid., September 4, 1940.

[38] Interview, Charlie and Ann Hill (Nanaimo: November 9, 1987).

[39] *Vancouver Province,* Mitchell, n.d.

[40] Ibid.

[41] Land Registry, Nootka District, Port Alberni.

[42] *Victoria Daily Colonist,* (April 3, 1938).

[43] *Victoria Daily Times,* "Gold boom town," by Leslie Fox, (Victoria: March 5, 1938).

[44] *Western Canada Mining News*, (April 25, 1939).

[45] *Victoria Daily Colonist,* (April 3, 1938).

[46] Interview, Wes Coburn (Zeballos: January 28, 1988).

[47] Interview, Charlie and Ann Hill (Nanaimo: November 9, 1987).

[48] Spud Valley Reports, April 16, 1942.

[49] Interview, Bruce Davies (Zeballos: January 28, 1988).

[50] *Vancouver Province,* (July 27, 1968).

[51] Ibid.

[52] *Victoria Daily Colonist,* September 20, 1970. Quote from Wally Thomas, Zeballos resident.

[53] Interview, Dave and Maya Cawood (Zeballos: January 30, 1988).

[54] Interview, John Crowhurst (Zeballos: December 17, 1987).

CHAPTER 6   WESTCOAST LOGGING—EARLY BEGINNINGS

While the present-day communities of Gold River, Tahsis, and Zeballos owe their existence to the forest industry, the region's dependence on a single large corporation is a relatively recent phenomonen. Less than a hundred years ago, logging had virtually no impact on the long-term development of the area. In the 1930s and 40s, the policy of committing large tracts of timber to single companies had not yet been established. At that time, the majority of timber along the coast was divided into individual parcels and put up for bid at public auction. Independent logging outfits either bid on the timber themselves, hoping to sell it on the open market, or would contract out to a sawmill or pulp mill with timber licenses of its own.

In Nootka and Kyuquot Sounds, these small blocks of timber, mainly located along the water's edge or up river valleys, were logged by a handful of independent operators, most of whom were not interested in establishing a permanent base in the region. They used floating A-frame rigs to take the timber from the sidehills, shipping their logs south to mills in Port Alberni and Victoria. When the timber had been removed from one claim, they moved on to the next.

"It's the simplest way of logging there is," said Eric Ericson, an A-frame logger and former resident of the Tahsis area, "If you have good timber, it's almost a sure thing that you make ends meet. The overhead was much smaller than it is now when you have to build miles and miles of road. Expensive equipment and everything. All you needed then was a float with an A-frame on it, and a donkey, and four or five men, a bit of timber, and away you go, you see.

A-frame logging operation on Tahsis Inlet. Floatcamp in the background.   Photo by Laura Anderson.

A cold-decker was used to swing logs into a pile before moving them down the hillside to the water.

Photo by Laura Anderson.

"You logged right off the sidehills, right down to the water. And sometimes, if the timber was too far back, then you'd run a cold-decker up there - a smaller machine to pile *[the logs]* up - and another machine down below on the A-frame would swing *[them]* in to the water... And then you corral the logs down in the water there, and make them into booms or rafts, and tow them down to the mill."[1]

The first timber license in Tahsis Inlet was issued, in 1905, to the Sutton Lumber Company for a block of timber near Sandpoint, and another on Nootka Island, across from the Tsowwin River. The company, which operated a sawmill in Ucluelet, was a subsidiary of the American-based Seattle Cedar Company.[2] Sutton also held several other licenses for large tracts of timber at the head of Hisnit Inlet, along the Kleeptee River near Williamson Passage, and along Hoiss Creek in Tlupana Arm.

Although the company's total holdings in the region amounted to 7,443 acres, there are no records available indicating that their claims were ever logged. According to Brian White's study of the settlement patterns of Nootka Sound, the majority of the timber licenses granted to large companies prior to the 1930s were speculative in nature.[3] Most were holding onto the land in anticipation that the Esquimalt and Nanaimo Railway would be pushed through from Nanaimo to the north end of the island, thereby opening up the west coast. The railway's "northern extension" never materialized, and speculators, which included Sayward Mills, then Governor James Dunsmuir, and even the E & NR itself, soon lost interest in the area. Outstanding timber licenses either reverted back to the Crown or were sold to other companies.

Active logging emerged some years later when small logging shows ventured into the region to take advantage of the virtually untapped timber resources. Earl O'Malley had one of the first A-frame operations in the Tahsis Inlet. According to Laura Anderson, he had a camp near Nootka as early as 1932. At that time, Laura's husband, Gunnar, worked for O'Malley building Davis rafts, a type of log boom used to tow logs to market. Laura lived on the floatcamp from 1936 until 1941. She said Gunnar used to tell stories about how, in 1932, some of the crew from O'Malley's camp would go out in motorboats to meet the rumrunners just off the entrance to Nootka Sound. "The *Malahat* was one of the ships that was a rum runner," she said, "The ships used to be out twelve miles, and they used to go out there and pick up the cargo. Some of them got caught, some not."[4]

By 1936, O'Malley had established another camp at Chamiss Bay in Kyuquot Sound and had moved his Nootka operation to Sandpoint, midway up the east side of the Tahsis Inlet. When Nootka Wood Products started up a sawmill in McBride Bay, O'Malley was one of the first to supply them with timber. His wife was a Whalen, said Laura, and the Whalen family was involved in establishing the mill.

The McBride Bay Sawmill, circa 1937. Photo by John Perry.   Royal B.C. Museum, Ethnology Division.

McBride Bay Sawmill

The sawmill at McBride Bay, in Esperanza Inlet, was built in 1937 by Nootka Wood Products Ltd., a British company based in England. According to the Land Registry records, Nootka Wood Products acquired the land in December, 1926 from Arthur D. McBride, a fishpacker, but they didn't begin building the mill until ten years later. At the time, there was apparently a reduction plant at McBride Bay. Few records remain about its operation, although a journal kept by the manager of Canfisco's plant at Espinosa notes that he went to McBride's to borrow some equipment for the reduction plant.[5]

The sawmill at McBride Bay was built on pilings over the water. June 5, 1937. Photo by A.B. Young.   Courtesy of Bud and Alice Young.

In January, 1937, Bud Young went up to McBride Bay to help build the mill. He said it was an ideal set-up:

"There was a reduction plant which had a large boiler and a steam engine... This was ideal, because they wanted a steam engine... There was a large company house, there was about eight or nine bunkhouses - they were double storey, you know - and a cookhouse-dining room."[6]

The mill was originally called the Port Tasis sawmill. "They were going to put it into Port Tasis, in the Tahsis Channel," said Bud, "That's where they surveyed. There's a large flat piece of ground in there, and deep water for ocean freighters... They had a contest and somebody called it Port Tasis." The name stuck, even though the company eventually decided against the Tahsis site, a decision which, in hindsight and in view of subsequent developments, may have been an unfortunate one.

The mill was built almost completely on pilings over the water. Even today, more than fifty years later, you can see the remains of thousands of feet of wood planking covering the shoreline and buried deep in the forest. There was very little room for other buildings: houses for management and staff were built on a tiny islet at the entrance to the bay, and a few families built their own homes in a tiny bay a short distance from the mill. The little settlement was reached by a narrow wooden boardwalk; the island homes were linked to the main plant by a wooden "swinging bridge."

A Swedish gangsaw, pictured above, was installed at the McBride Bay Sawmill in June, 1937. Photo by A.B. Young.
Photo courtesy of Bud and Alice Young.

A unique feature of the mill was its use of waste wood to fuel the plant. "One of the investors of the mill was Crossley Brothers," said Bud, "And they manufactured producer-gas engines. Now, the producer-gas engine is an engine that utilizes the waste - the bark waste - and it uses about one-sixteenth of the fuel that a steam engine would use. They supplied the engine. They were the leading manufacturer of producer-gas engines."

Producer-gas engines extracted the creosote, tar, and resin from the wood. But then: "They had no use for it," Bud said, "They had to build settling tanks for it. So there was this lake of tar... It could be used for road-building, but of course there were no roads up there."

During construction, the mill employed close to a hundred men. Later, when the mill was in operation, the crew dropped to about twenty-five. "The mill's capacity was three million board feet a month," said Bud, "We had to have an empty freighter there every month to take all the wood." And when the ships came in, the whole crew pitched in to load them up. "We even had to shut the mill down and then everybody had to help load to get the place

Budge Young and his wife, Alice, in their home at McBride Bay, 1937. Budge and Alice spent their first year of marriage at McBride Bay.
Photo courtesy of Bud and Alice Young.

clear, otherwise they would fill up the yard so quick with lumber."

The mill operated for eighteen months and then closed down due to unstable market conditions. While it was going, it provided the small logging outfits in the area with a market for their timber. Instead of having to tow their logs down the treacherous west coast to mills in Port Alberni and Victoria, they were able to sell them locally.

Olson's Logging

Towing camp from one logging show to another, circa 1931. This picture of Erik Olson's logging camp was taken on the inside passage.

Olson's A-frame rig in Tahsis Inlet, circa 1941. Davis raft at left is nearly ready to be shipped out to market.

Photos courtesy of Elvera Ericson.

Another small logging operator in the area at the time was Erik Olson who, in 1937, moved his camp from the east coast of the island, around Cape Scott, to Tahsis. Eric Ericson was Olson's son-in-law. "He was finished where he was working on Sonora Island," said Eric. "He was trying to find something else to do for his outfit. And Nootka Wood Products at that time was looking for a contractor to come up and log in there, you see. So he met them and made a deal that he was going to be the one to log for them, to supply the mill that they were building then in McBride Bay."

In those days, moving camps from inlet to inlet along the sheltered inside passages was a common occurrence. "You went in to log a claim. Say you only had a certain amount of timber to take out," said Eric, "And that was all done, so you went to look for some more, and then you had to move, you see, to another bay or wherever. It was the natural thing to do...

"Usually you had a fair-sized boat that could hook onto your floats... A seine boat, or a tugboat if you had your own. Just hook onto it and away you'd go, on the end of a towline. Wake up next morning and you're in a completely different place. If you were logging a small show you could be moving practically every year, you see. Or more, even, if you had little tiny bits of timber to take out."

Less common and certainly more difficult was moving a whole operation down the outer coast of the Vancouver Island where heavy seas and high winds could break up a float in a few hours. It was a bit unusual, said Eric, but the Nootka Wood Products offer was too good to pass up. Olson had run out of contracts on the east coast, and the timber in Tahsis was "practically guaranteed." He brought the camp with him so that he wouldn't have to start completely from scratch while setting up his logging operation.

So, in the spring of 1939, Olson tied his floats together, hitched them to the back of a tugboat, and towed the whole camp - bunkhouses, cookhouse, machinery, and all - around the northern tip of Vancouver Island, down the outside coast to Esperanza Inlet and up to Tahsis. By the time he reached the sheltered waters of Esperanza, the camp had been "boxed around pretty good," said Eric. Several buildings were completely destroyed and the first few weeks were spent rebuilding the camp and setting up his equipment.

Eric Ericson worked for Olson's Logging Company in the 1930s and early 1940s. It was his first job in B.C.: he had come to Canada from Sweden, in 1930, and ended up on the west coast because it was similar to his homeland. At the time,

Olson's Logging Camp at Tahsis, circa 1938, from a postcard photo taken by John Perry.
Photo courtesy of Elvera Ericson.

Olson was logging near Ocean Falls on the northern mainland coast before moving down to the inside passage, where he logged for the Powell River Company until 1938, running a "winter show" at Knight's Inlet and a "summer show" on Sonora Island.

It was while he was working for Olson, in Knight's Inlet, that Eric Ericson met Olson's daughter, Elvera. They were married in December 1936. Their first home was a tiny, two-room shack on floats. "I used to have to watch my chance when the men were out in the woods to use the outhouse, or to go and take a shower in the washhouse," said Elvera, "So as I say, it was a little primitive."

In the fall of 1939, the Ericsons joined Olson in Tahsis. Their old house had taken a beating coming around Cape Scott, so Eric fixed it up and moved it onto its own float. "We were quite independent, with our own outhouse and everything, you see," he said. Equipped with a flush toilet, the outhouse was pretty modern by logging camp standards. It was actually an old-fashioned "water-closet," said Elvera. The tank was mounted near the ceiling and was activated by pulling a string. "Real fancy," she said, "Real fancy."

Most of the A-frame shows were relatively small by today's logging practices. They generally employed twenty- to thirty-man crews consisting of a handful of machine operators, a few fallers, and the "rigging crews," or loggers. According to the Ericsons and Laura Anderson, the Olson and O'Malley camps were somewhat larger and had better living conditions than most floatcamps at that time. At the height of logging activity in Tahsis Inlet, both operations were running three or four machines and employed about 80 men each. Elvera says her father's new cookhouse, built after the original one was lost coming around Cape Scott, was one of the best on the coast. "The new big cookhouse," she said, "That was built on the beach and transferred onto

House on floats belonging to Gunnar and Laura Anderson, circa 1938.
Photo by Laura Anderson.

a float when they built the new float for it. It was huge. I think the cookhouse was supposed to seat over a hundred men. Up to a hundred and twenty, if need be. But I think there was eighty at the most."

Jack Gibson of Gibson Brothers Ltd. which later purchased Olson's Logging Company, went up to Tahsis, in 1942, to look at the camp which was then shut down and sitting idle near the head of the inlet. "I remember being very impressed with the quality of the floating camp," he said, "Camps in those days were pretty haywire. But this had a good bunkhouse, fairly well painted, a beautiful dining hall with living quarters above it. I remember seeing a full-length bathtub up there, which was something rather unusual for a logging camp."[7]

Floatcamps

"Haywire" was a term commonly used to refer to small logging outfits on the coast, meaning you made do with what you had. Floatcamps were not intended for permanency. Bunkhouses and the few two-room shacks for married men and their families were constructed out of rough cedar planks and put onto floats for easy mobility. The floats were lashed together and secured to a beach by a system of stiff legs (logs) and cable.

Interior views at Laura Anderson's floathouse, showing plain, shiplap construction and wood floors.

Photos by Laura Anderson.

"It was a fairly easy life as far as living on the floatcamp was concerned," said Eric, "The wood was easy to get and the garbage was no problem, and wherever you wanted to go you just took your home with you and tied it up somewheres else in a little bay. It was no hardship, really... As long as you had a good boat, you see. So you weren't altogether stuck."

Water came from hoses fed from nearby creeks. The only problems were when temperatures dropped to freezing, said Eric, and after a bad rain, when the creeks became so swollen and full of churned-up silt and leaves that the water was undrinkable. Other than those minor inconveniences, life on the floats seemed to be simple and uncomplicated when compared to the fast-paced modern world of microwave ovens and computers, rush hour traffic, and line-ups at the check-out stands in grocery stores.

There were only a few women living on the camps in the '30s and '40s. Logging was an industry dominated by men, with a lifestyle unsuited to raising a family. But a few women preferred to live on the floats with their husbands rather than spend months at a stretch living without them. Elvera Ericson was one of those women. She says she didn't find the life lonely or isolating. The women she met during that period have remained close friends, despite the years that have passed.

"We used to meet so many interesting people, travelling on the coast," she said, "Or even just living on the coast. Where, sitting in a house in the city, you met two or three of your neighbors, and that's all you met."

Laura Anderson was another woman who accompanied her husband to the isolated coast. She and Gunnar met aboard the *Princess Norah:* she was taking a holiday, he was on his way back to work at O'Malley's camp near Nootka. They were married in Port Alice in 1936, returning to O'Malley's camp in Sandpoint where they had their own little house and float. For the next three years, Laura spent the spring, summer, and fall seasons at O'Malley's, in Tahsis Inlet, leaving only during the winter months when "it was pretty rough up there," she said.

While on the coast, Laura took her Kodak Brownie camera everywhere, taking photographs of the floatcamp, her house, the logging operation, anything she could think of. Her collection, covering a period of several years from the mid-1930s to the early 1940s, is a rare glimpse of everyday life on the coast. Many of her photographs are published for the first time in this book.

Like Laura Anderson and most of the other women who lived on the floats, Elvera Ericson did what she could to make life on the coast more pleasurable. She grew flowers in the spring, hauling the rich topsoil in from the shore to fill the planters - wooden 'Carnation Milk' boxes, the remains of an old dugout canoe that Eric salvaged from the bush - anything that was made of wood and could hold soil would do. Then, "If it was a nice day and I got my two-room house tidied up, I'd put my daughter under my arm and we'd pop in the skiff and row ashore," she said. She would often go on excursions with some of the other women from the logging camps. Packing a picnic lunch and bundling up the children, they'd explore the little bays and beaches along the inlet, or hike up the creeks into the woods and along the hills overlooking the inlet. Occasionally, they visited John and Pete Perry on their homestead up the Leiner River, or stopped in at Esperanza to visit the hotel and hospital.

Although the canneries in Esperanza Inlet were running full steam during the summers, there wasn't much interaction between the fishing settlements and the logging camps. From time to time, one of the canneries would hold a dance and invite everyone from miles around. And one year, Ceepeecee organized regular movie showings on Friday or Saturday nights. There wasn't a lot of free time for socializing, said Eric. When there was, it took the form of

For children, wearing a lifejacket was an everyday part of life on the floats. Pictured above: Mimi Ericson, Eric and Elvera's daughter.

Photo courtesy of Elvera Ericson.

Rigging a raft of logs for shipment to market, circa 1938.
Photo by Laura Anderson.

visits and the occasional evening at the pub in the Esperanza Hotel where Eric would haul out his accordion, someone else a guitar or harmonica, and the rug would get rolled back for dancing.

Life on the floats also had its unnerving aspects, not the least of which was raising children. Lifejackets were standard gear for youngsters, but sometimes even that precaution wasn't enough. Elvera remembers one incident that gave her nightmares for years after. The Ericsons had a daughter, Mimi, who "wasn't afraid of anything," said Elvera. "Like the time she was playing with another little girl, Mona. I'd get her dressed in the morning, and get her lifebelt on, and her running shoes, and out to play. I was busy dressing, and I heard this funny sound. It sounded like one of the kids calling. So there I went, one shoe on, one shoe off, and here stood Mona, halfway out on the stiff leg, and said 'Come and get me, Mimi fell in.'

"When I got to her, only her little tiny face was above the water, and this lifebelt was pushing her little chin up, and the tide was pulling, really pulling, and she was within about three feet of a boom of logs there. I managed to grab her and set her up," said Elvera, "And she took off like a flash! 'I've got to go tell Bertha I fell in!'" Elvera shook her head in amazement. "She wasn't scared a bit!"

On another occasion, while the camp was being moved across the inlet to a little bay in Tahsis Narrows, a sudden storm came up, threatening to destroy the whole float. "We were towing the A-frame, and Gunnar Anderson's house was on there too," said Eric, "It was a glass calm day. Beautiful day. And we were putt-putting along there just fine, and all of a sudden this stupid wind hit. Just like a sledgehammer blow; sideways, you know. It wasn't two minutes and it was raining and blowing, picking up the water so I couldn't see," he said.

"We were probably making three miles, going ahead. But when the wind hit, then it started to blow over the other way, going four or five miles backwards." The float broke away from the towline and ended up on the flats at the head of the Tahsis Inlet.

"It was high tide," Eric said, "And we didn't think we'd get if off again. But the tide was higher the next day, so we managed to float it off."

The Gibson Brothers

When the McBride Bay sawmill closed down at the end of 1938, the small logging outfits were left without a local market. Eric said that Olson had only been logging for six months: he had just bought all his equipment and built sleds for the machines. "And no sooner did they get really going when, 'Shut her down. We're not taking any more logs.' All of a sudden, like a bang from the blue sky, you see," said Eric, "It was a heck of a letdown."

"I don't think it was financially stable anyway, because it *[the mill]* was in the wrong place. It was in a very bad place, nothing but rocks in there," he said, "The

Men booming logs into a raft.   Photo by Laura Anderson.

mill barely had room where it was located. And the lumberyard actually was about, I believe it was ten scows, there were great big huge scows that they piled lumber on. When the mill shut down, these scows ended up way up on the tide flats in Tahsis."

Olson shut down for a couple of seasons, leaving his camp tied to the side of the inlet. O'Malley went broke, said Laura Anderson, and Gunnar acquired part of his camp - the donkey engine, one or two bunkhouses, and a tugboat - which he used to set up his own outfit called Anderson's Logging. Eric Ericson went to work for Gunnar while Olson's camp was closed down. He said Gunnar sold his logs to a Victoria company, Lemon-Gonnason. It was during this period of instability that Gordon Gibson began to amass his holdings in the region in a process of consolidation that led almost inevitably to the construction, in 1945, of an export sawmill at the head of Tahsis Inlet.

By 1939, Gibson had several camps in the region. In addition to his Muchalat and Zeballos operations, he had purchased O'Malley's timber tracts and camps at Sandpoint and Chamiss Bay. In his autobiography, *Bull of the Woods*, Gordon writes that "one of our best purchases was the O'Malley camp at Chamiss Bay. The complete camp was offered for sale at an auction in Nanaimo for $5,000. For that amount our company acquired a large floating camp, cookhouse, bunkhouses, gasoline tug, blankets and supplies, four steam donkeys and a complete set of cables. But the finest part of the deal was the timber: half a million feet cold-decked (that is, felled and in piles of about a thousand logs, ready to be pulled into the water), two million feet fallen and bucked, and five million feet standing. It was a big step forward; now it was possible to build a really substantial camp."[8]

At about the same time, Gibson also took over a fairly substantial tract of timber at Sandpoint, on Tahsis Inlet. Purchasing one of the old North Vancouver ferries, the "No. 2," he converted it into a "floating bunkhouse" and towed it to Tahsis Inlet. "It was probably one of the most comfortable portable camps on the coast," he says.[9] It had a machine shop, filing room, electric light plant, dining room, individual staterooms, washrooms, and "well-appointed reading rooms to relax in."

On February 8, 1939, two weeks after arriving at its new site, the converted ferry was destroyed by a fire which burned down to the water line.[10] "Nothing was saved," said Gibson, "All the saws, axes, bales and even kitchen utensils were burned." But the setback didn't last long. According to Gibson's story, he and the foreman went out that night and towed in a nearby camp which had closed up for the season. "We were ready for work first thing Monday," he says.[11]

Gordon Gibson and his three brothers - Clarke, Jack, and Earson - were the driving force behind Gibson Brothers Industries Ltd. They started out working with their father, William, in the Gibson Mill and Shingle Company based in Alberni. They later moved to Ahousat where they established a sawmill and logging camp as well as ran the local store and post office. As "pioneer entrepreneurs" of the west coast, the Gibsons were involved in a variety of enterprises including fish packing, towing, logging and sawmilling, road-building, and even a short excursion into the fish processing and whaling business. During the war, Gordon Gibson's reputation for running tight camps won him contracts with the federal Department of Defense to clear land and build roads for the construction of airport landing facilities at Tofino, Cassidy Airport near Ladysmith, Prince Rupert, and Sandspit on the Queen Charlotte Islands.

Meanwhile, as the Gibsons continued to build up their business on the coast, smaller logging outfits were struggling to break even financially. Both Olson and Anderson were running small camps of about 20 to 25 men each. Their biggest difficulty was in getting their logs to market safely. With the McBride Bay sawmill closed, the nearest mills were in Port Alberni and Victoria some 100 miles away down the outside of the island. At that time, logs were made into Davis rafts and towed down the coast. But the Davis raft wasn't sturdy enough. "They had all kinds of trouble with those rafts because they towed them outside and the big wind came and they'd break up," said Eric, "And there were many of them lost, completely lost. I don't know where they went. Japan maybe."

Eric recalls working on one Davis raft, "a beautiful one," with over a million feet of prime logs in it. "They hooked onto it to tow it down to market, Port Alberni or somewhere around there, and it broke up. They towed it in somewheres and tried to fix it. Then they went out and it broke up again. By the time it reached Port Alberni, it must have been months went by, it was nothing but woodlogs, full of toredos. It was worthless. Today, that would be a small fortune, that same raft. And payrolls depend on the payments, you know."

In 1936, Gibson contracted with O'Malley, and later Olson and Anderson, to tow their logs from Nootka Sound to markets in the south. He used an old sailing ship, the *Malahat*, which had been converted into a self-loading barge in an effort to combat the loss of logs at sea using the Davis rafts. The *Malahat* was a 245-foot schooner built in Victoria by Canadian Westcoast Navigation Co., in 1917. The Gibson brothers purchased the ship for $2500., gutted it, and equipped it with two donkey engines to haul the logs on deck.[12] The *Malahat* broke down in 1937 and was converted to an ordinary log-carrying barge. In March, 1944, it was lost at sea in Barkley Sound.

"The *Malahat* had been the only self-powered, self-loading and -unloading barge, until MacMillan Bloedel built the *Haida Brave* in 1978 at a cost of $15 million. It cost six thousand times as much as the *Malahat* and carries only four times as much cargo at twice the speed," writes Gibson.[13]

During this same period, Gibson worked on developing a raft that would be able to withstand the beating taken on the open straits and down the outside coast. Launched in the early 1940s, the new raft proved successful:

"After three years of service under the most severe conditions to be encountered off the West Coast of Vancouver Island, the Gibson raft, designed by J.G. Gibson... is pronounced by its inventor 100 per cent satisfactory," reported the *British Columbia Lumberman.*

"Developed by Mr. Gibson for deep sea towing after the manner of the familiar Davis raft, the new Gibson raft is, he reports, much less expensive and simpler to build and to break down... So far...they have been so successful in towing through all weathers and all seasons that not a single loss has been incurred. On one occasion a Gibson raft broke away in a storm off Cape Scott and was five days adrift in heavy seas before being picked up intact...."[14]

But the Gibson raft came too late to help the small logging outfits struggling to survive in the remote wilds of Nootka Sound. Depressed lumber markets and a scarcity of labor caused by World War II and complicated by inaccessible markets, proved to be insurmountable. Anderson went bankrupt in 1941 and returned to Vancouver with nothing to show for his years on the coast. He abandoned his camp at the side of an inlet, his last shipment of logs hopelessly lost on the way to the mill in Victoria.

Olson, who had started up again after a two year layoff, operated in 1941 and 1942 before he, too, was forced to close. He had re-opened with the financial backing of a Vancouver-based firm, the Lamb Lumber Company. But Lamb decided to pull out and concentrate on its Sechelt operation. "It became quite a big deal to keep two outfits going financially, you see," said Eric, "So, it was up to Mr. Lamb to decide what he was going to do. And he decided Sechelt was within touching distance almost, whereas this was so remote, and he hardly got up to see it. And it was rather difficult in many ways to get rid of the logs, through rafting, and one thing and another. So he decided to drop the Tahsis part of his financing and concentrate on Sechelt."

Modern A-frames, operated by small independent contractors, are still in operation along the coast. Pictured above, A-frame at one of the inlets in Nootka Sound, June 1960. George Allen Aerial Photos. Tahsis Archives.

In November, 1943, the Gibson brothers bought all the assets in Olson's Logging Company. They gave Erik Olson $7,000. cash and paid off his outstanding debts. In return, Olson transferred his interest in the company to the Gibsons. Olson returned to the east coast of Vancouver Island, taking up where he'd left off in 1938. Erik Edward Olson, born March 18, 1887, in Sweden, died in 1970 at his home near Seattle, Washington. He was 83 years old.

"After Gibson Brothers bought the outfit, they got a lot more timber," said Eric, "And then, they had a lot more capital to work with, I imagine, and they had a lot more timber *[than Olson]*, so they could plan for years ahead. They could build roads and go in for miles where we couldn't reach it. Then of course they built the mill, which was a big deal in itself. They could mill it, then they could get the ships in to get the lumber right in there on the world market, you see."

"They had some far-reaching ideas," he said, "And the Gibsons were well-connected all over the world practically. To talk to people that really had the money to do things. Whereas Olson probably wasn't."

Although Gibson may have been considering the potential of building a sawmill in Tahsis at the time he bought Olson's Logging, it wasn't his most immediate concern. In late 1942, Gibson had contracted with the federal government to log spruce for the manufacture of Mosquito air fighter planes used during World War II. "We were given authority to take spruce from any location on the westcoast of Vancouver Island no matter who owned the rights to the timber."[15]

Spruce was a tightly-grained wood which was very buoyant and light-weight, ideally suited to the construction of the Mosquito bomber, a Canadian-built plane known for its speed. The federal government subsidized loggers by supplying the capital investment required to outfit a logging camp and by providing a guaranteed profit margin.[16] Many small logging outfits took advantage of the "Spruce Account" as a means of supporting what could only be described as a marginal existence. Gibson was one of the first and most aggressive. He started production at Ucluelet, Bowden Bay, Trout River, Zeballos, and Tahsis, logging "only the best straight-grained trees," he said.[17]

Spruce grew in the damp bottomlands of river valleys, and the Zeballos and Tahsis Rivers were prime spruce areas. But, unlike A-frame logging where the timber was easily accessible from the water, spruce had to be taken out by land. Gibson built a network of roads up the valleys, using tractors and lumber arches to pull the logs out of the woods and down to the booming grounds at the water's edge. Subsidized by the federal government, he was able to purchase the expensive equipment and machinery needed to undertake road-building and tractor logging. "They started building roads and using trucks, you see," said Eric, "There wasn't much A-frame logging left. So they made roads, and that took off, and those were more economical. Then the barges came in - self-loading barges and whatnot, and they can load timber much, much cheaper. And quicker."

The introduction of truck logging brought about the end of an era in Nootka Sound. The small-scale independent logger, with his floatcamp and A-frame, couldn't compete with the capital investment required for land-based logging. According to Gibson, one of the reasons he succeeded where others failed is that he had already-established markets for his product and was familiar with the local conditions.[18] That may have been part of his success. The other aspect had to do with his financial stability. Gibson Brothers Ltd. controlled the transportation links and was involved in several types of businesses; they could afford the risk of expanding into new areas.

As for the Ericsons, they have good feelings about their time on the west coast. "It's all interesting work, you know," said Eric, "I'd get up and have breakfast. Elvera made good hotcakes, fed me good, so I was happy going away to work. Sometimes it'd be raining and cold and whatnot, and you're always looking forward to a good supper.

"It was our life, you know. We knew when we were working we were making a dollar, and we had ideas what to do if we ever got enough, you see. Sooner or later we would maybe make a change. But while we were there, far as I was concerned, I was happy."

Eric and Elvera didn't miss city life. When they went to Vancouver - for a holiday, or to go to the doctor - they looked forward to returning to their home on the coast.

"I remember one time, we came back on the *Maquinna,* and that night - I had a good little skiff, a rowboat that I'd made - and that night, I rowed out right in the middle of the inlet, and I just sat there, drinking in the fresh air, and the feeling of being in clean air again," he said, "Sat there for a couple of hours...Glad to be back you see."

When Olson sold out, Eric went to work for Gibson, running a machine at the Gibson Brothers Jeune Landing camp near Port Alice on Quatsino Sound. Later, he and Elvera returned to the east coast of the island, settling in Sointula where Eric became a commercial fisherman until he retired, in 1980.

"It was beautiful. Even today it's a beautiful inlet," said Eric, recalling his days on the Tahsis Inlet. "Beautiful place to be. I've always had a feeling of wanting to go back there. We finally made it there a couple of years ago. We drove in, of all things, which when we were there it was an absolutely unheard of thing, to be able to drive into Tahsis. It was a beautiful full moon night when we went there. Great big full moon, and still. The water was still and everything.

"It reminded me of one winter evening, and the swans came in when we were logging in there. There was about eight swans, big white swans. And they were honking and talking across the bay there. And again I took my skiff and I rowed out, right among them, and I drifted in, right in the flock of swans. They were just talking away. They didn't worry about me at all, as long as I didn't chase them, you see. It was nice, really."

Notes

[1] Interview, Eric and Elvera Ericson (Sointula: February 15, 1988).

[2] Gordon Gibson, *Bull of the Woods* (Vancouver: 1980), p. 45. According to the *B.C. Gazette*, Sutton Lumber Co. was incorporated June 14, 1893 by William Sutton, William John Sutton, and James Edward Sutton.

[3] See Brian P. White, *The Settlement of Nootka Sound: Its Distributional Morphology 1900-1970*, unpubl. M.A. thesis, Simon Fraser University (Burnaby: 1972).

[4] Interview, Laura Anderson (Vancouver: September 5, 1987).

[5] Canadian Fishing Company, Journal entry for July 3, 1928, *Espinoza Reduction Plant - Records: 1928-1937*, Special Collections, University of B.C. Main Library, Vancouver.

[6] Interview, Budge and Alice Young (Victoria: July 22, 1989).

[7] Interview, Jack Gibson (Vancouver: July, 1987).

[8] Gordon Gibson, p. 132.

[9] Ibid., p. 134.

[10] George Nicholson, *Vancouver Island's West Coast* (Victoria: 1962), p. 24.

[11] Gordon Gibson, p. 135.

[12] Ibid., pp. 87-88.

[13] Ibid., p. 120.

[14] *Britsh Columbia Lumberman*, July 1948.

[15] Gordon Gibson, p. 147.

[16] White, p. 70.

[17] Gordon Gibson, p. 147.

[18] Ibid., p. 132.

CHAPTER 7   TAHSIS AND THE EVOLUTION OF TAHSIS CO. LTD.

The present-day community of Tahsis has been built near the site of what was once the winter home of Maquinna, a great chief of the Mowachaht tribe during the time of European contact. Each fall, Maquinna and his people would dismantle their summer village at Yuquot and travel up the inside passage to the head of Tahsis Inlet. Here, they spent the winter months sheltered from the harsh storms which battered the open coastline. And here, in 1792, Maquinna entertained European emissaries sent to negotiate the Nootka Convention. Britain's Captain George Vancouver and Spain's Bodega y Quadra were treated to lavish feasts and ceremonies during a three-day visit in October of that year. Archibald Menzies, a scientist on the Vancouver expedition, provides a vivid account of the celebrations in his journal of Vancouver's voyage.

The name 'Tahsis' is derived from an old Indian word, 'tashees,' meaning doorway or passage through.[1] It refers to a trail which led up the Tahsis River Valley overland to Woss Lake - one of two important trading routes which connected the northern Nuu-chah-nulth people with the Nimpkish on the east coast of Vancouver Island. Once across the divide, dugout canoes were used to travel down Woss Lake and the Nimpkish River to Nimpkish Lake, stopping in at Nimpkish fishing sites and villages along the way. The trail was an important trade and social link between the two groups. Another trail led through Tahsish Inlet in Kyuquot Sound and is discussed in more detail in the chapter on Kyuquot. A third route came down through Vernon Lake to Muchalat Lake and met up with a trail coming across the island from the Comox Valley. This trail was used by hunting parties from the Nimpkish and Muchalat people, and as a trade link with the Comox Indians.

Over the years, the Tahsis-Woss Lake trail was used more and more infrequently, although it remained passable until the 1930s and 40s. As the development of Vancouver Island grew, maritime trading routes on the east and west coasts took on a greater importance, both economically and socially. With the development of Friendly Cove as a maritime trading centre and later, the establishment of a store and steamship landing at Nootka Cannery, the Mowachaht gradually ceased their cycle of summer and winter homes to take up year-round occupation at Friendly Cove. The site at Tahsis, which started out as a local group site and was later Maquinna's winter home, became a seasonal fishing site for salmon. Today, several families maintain homes on the site, and continue to use it for picking berries, gathering grasses for basket-making, and fishing.

In the 1880s, the Tahsis trail was surveyed by the Dominion government. In the Surveyor's Report for 1887, Mr. Fry describes his route up the Nimpkish River to Woss Lake, "a magnificent sheet of water lying nearly north and south." He says there is some land suitable for agricultural purposes at the north end of the lake, but that "three miles up the lake the mountains close in and the shores are steep and rocky... Travelling 1 1/2 miles south from Woss Lake the summit of the divide is reached," he writes, "From this point the water flows to the West Coast. The divide is in a very narrow rocky gorge, between two snow-capped mountains, and in the lowest place about 970 feet above sea level.

"Continuing south for one mile we come to the head-waters of the Tahsis River, at this point a mountain torrent, falling about 300 feet for the first mile, then more gradually to the sea, a distance of 10 miles from its source....The valley is narrow but contains about 10,000 acres of good bottom land, easily cleared, with magnificent spruce and cedar, but a scarcity of fir timber. At the mouth of the river there is a large grass flat."[2]

Fry was part of a survey team sent to assess possible routes for the northern extension of the Esquimalt and Nanaimo Railway. Industrialists and developers were putting pressure on the government to open up the north end of Vancouver Island and reliable transportation was seen as the key. Tahsis was only one of several alternative routes being considered, one which Fry concluded would be virtually impossible: "The exploration through the Woss Lake country to the North Arm of Nootka Sound cannot be considered successful in view of railway construction, for although a road might possibly be built, very heavy grade would have to be made on a steep rock side-hill, or 2 miles of rock tunnel built to pass the divide between Woss Lake and the head-waters of Tahsis River."[3]

In the 1900s, the trail was used primarily by prospectors and trappers. Ernie Heevis had a trapline up the Tahsis River Valley in the early 1930s, selling his furs to the commercial buyer who came up the coast once a month on the steamship

Looking north up the Tahsis River valley with Rugged Mountain in the back. The first houses for mill workers and their families are shown in the foreground, circa 1947. Photo by John Perry. Provincial Archives of B.C.

Princess Maquinna. During the winters, Ernie used to hike deep into the valley to check his line for mink and fox. He built a small, one-room shack a few miles up the river where he stayed for five or six weeks at a time. He said other trappers used the old trail too, some of them occasionally crossing over to the east coast of Vancouver Island.[4]

George Harlow, a prospector with North American Mines, in 1934, said he used the trail while prospecting for gold up the Tahsis River Valley. "Right where the mill is, I used to have a little cabin there," he said, "And, a mile and a half up the river I had two big cabins on the sidehill there. Also, about four miles up, right at the branch of the rivers, I had a big cabin up there. When I say a big one, it was twenty-four by eighteen *[feet]*, something like that."[5]

During the war, Harlow was a member of the Westcoast Rangers, a volunteer group that was established to protect the west coast in the event of Japanese invasion from the Pacific. Harlow was in charge of evacuations, and he said the trail to Woss Lake was to be used to move people out in an emergency. When the Japanese shelled Estevan Lighthouse in 1943, the Rangers were put on standby alert. The shelling turned out to be a puzzling but false alarm, and the trail was never used for an evacuation.

In recent years, the idea of an overland route to Woss Lake has been resurrected as a partial solution to what the Village Council sees as a problem of isolation. As early as 1974, local politicians began lobbying the provincial government for a road

The sawmill at Tahsis is built on the flat delta at the head of Tahsis Inlet. George Allen Aerial Photos Ltd., 1960. Tahsis Archives.

to Woss which would link Tahsis with the North Island. They believe that being on a throughway rather than a dead end will improve their chances of attracting tourists and small industry to the area. But building a road through to Woss seems to have as much chance for success today as it did in 1887. According to the provincial government, steep grades and high costs make it impracticable.

Sawmill Town

There is no question that Tahsis is a sawmill town. Whether you arrive by air, sea, or boat, what dominates the landscape is the mill with its piles of sawdust and stacks of freshly cut lumber. Built on pilings, the plant sprawls at the head of the inlet, its docks jutting out over the water. Out in the harbour, log booms line the shores and the distinctive red and white Seaspan barges are piled high with chips, bound for the pulp mill in Gold River. Huge ocean-going freighters coming up the inlet to load are dwarfed by the steep mountains which rise straight up from the water. Up close, the ships stretch the length of the dock, looming large against the town which overlooks the harbor.

Tahsis is at the end of a logging road which cuts through the heart of prime forest land. The road winds and twists its way through some of the most rugged terrain on the coast. In one section, the grade is steeper than any other public access road on Vancouver Island. Although the road is deemed open to the public, it is also an active logging road where mammoth logging trucks command full attention.

Near Tahsis, the road comes out on the east side of the inlet, opposite the townsite. The final stretch into town follows the rocky shoreline around the head of the inlet, past the site of a cedar mill, closed down in 1986 and dismantled a year later; past a motel and the locally-famed 'Spar Tree' pub; across the bridge over the Tahsis River to the mill gate. Twenty years ago, the only way to get from one end of town to the other was through the millyard. The road has since been re-routed to skirt around the plant and now follows the west side of the inlet down to the hotel and shopping center about a mile and a half south of the mill.

In Tahsis, life revolves intimately around the sawmill. Social activities are planned according to shift schedules, and people know where they'll be on any given

Shift change at the mill, circa 1959. Photo by Anthony Carter.   Tahsis Archives.

day of the week by the shift they're working: days, "afters" (afternoons), or graveyards. Public meetings are usually scheduled twice in order to accommodate millworkers: once in the afternoon, and again in the evening. And then there is the shift change itself, marked by the sound of the horn blowing. Men coming off one shift swarm out of the main gate, grimy with sawdust, sweat streaked across their foreheads, hardhats pushed back or removed altogether, clothes grubby from long hard hours spent pulling lumber, sorting boards, working the boom. Some pedal off on bicycles, steel-toed workboots and all, lunchboxes slung over their shoulders. Others are picked up by wives or girlfriends waiting in cars at the side of the road. Still others set off on foot, singly or in pairs, home to a hot shower and meal, or maybe to the bar for a few drinks and a game of pool. The oncoming shift passes by with a hand raised in greeting, a shout to a friend or neighbor: clean clothes and full lunchboxes.

The mill runs 24 hours a day, five days a week, shutting down on weekends for maintenance. The sound of the buzz saws and noise of the machinery is a steady hum in the background. Shortly after I'd arrived, my first summer there, I remember waking with a start just after midnight one Friday night. Silence lay over the town. I listened to the sound of frogs in the creek across the road, the occasional distant bark of a dog down in the valley, the creaking of a screen door being opened in a trailer three or four sites away. What, I wondered, had woken me up? And then I realized that there was no sound from the mill. It had shut down at midnight and wouldn't start up again until midnight on Sunday. The stillness was noticeable in that it is the kind that comes only in the country where traffic and industrial activities are minimal. On weekends, the steady throbbing of tugboats can be heard miles away.

Building the Sawmill

According to Gordon Gibson, the idea for building a sawmill at the head of Tahsis Inlet came to him one day while he was sitting by the Tahsis River, sharing

Gordon Gibson, 1985.   Laurie Jones photo.

First shipment of lumber being loaded onto the Tipperary Park *in September 1945. Floatcamp and bunkhouses at lower right. Photo courtesy of Gordon Gibson.*   Tahsis Archives.

a bottle of whiskey with Bruce Haggart, a freight manager for the CPR. "Bruce," he said, "You won't believe it, but within a year I'm going to talk my brothers into building a sawmill here. We'll build a town where ships from all over the world will come to take away lumber." The way the story goes is that Bruce told Gordon to take another drink because "I've never heard you this drunk before," said Bruce.[6]

At the time, the Gibson brothers were considering buying the old Robert Dollars mill at Dollarton - what is now Port Moody - and shipping their logs from Nootka Sound down to the mainland. But there were still extreme difficulties in transporting logs south, despite the Gibsons' innovative use of converted sailing ships as barges, and improvements to rafting technology. "Even using the Gibson raft, we had been losing one out of twenty tows, and when we sent a raft of 1200 logs to Vancouver it would invariably arrive 50 to 60 logs short," he says in his book, *Bull of the Woods*.[7] Economically, it made more sense to build a mill in the heart of the resource rather than to continue shipping logs down the treacherous coast.

Construction on the sawmill started in February, 1945. Nine months later, the first load of lumber was shipped out, bound for Europe. "We had started with a dream and $100,000," writes Gibson. A dream which was financed in part by East Asiatic Company, a Danish shipping firm with international markets. Under the terms of an agreement signed on February 21, 1945, EAC advanced $75,000. to Gibson Mills Ltd. in exchange for an option on 50 per cent of the mill's total lumber production.[8] The Gibsons needed the capital in order to build the sawmill, and EAC wanted the lumber for their international export markets.

"The mill was built contrary to all rules of good construction," says Gibson. A

The freighter Barranduna *in the Tahsis harbor, circa 1948. John and Rhoda Campbell Collection.*   Tahsis Archives.

construction designer by the name of Charlie Broadbent was hired to plan the mill, but Gordon was in a hurry. The first ship was due in October and the mill had to be built and operating by then. He started driving in the piles immediately, and by the time Broadbent arrived with the plans and a civil engineer to lay out the millsite, the main building was nearly completed.[9]

"Broadbent's plans called for square timbers set on top of concrete pilings underneath the main deck of the mill," writes Gibson, "I had used hemlock and fir piles figuring that although these timbers would rot out in five years, we would either be able to replace them by that time or have gone broke. I had to use what materials were at hand because we were short of time and money. Broadbent had designed a Cadillac where we needed a secondhand Ford."[10]

The civil engineer, fresh from Vancouver, set up a transit and discovered that the floor of the mill ran downhill with about a six-inch difference from one end to the other. "I told him we had built it that way intentionally so as to have gravity favoring the roll of lumber as it left the mill," says Gordon, "Charlie Broadbent just shook his head, and we finished the mill without referring to his plans."[11]

The Gibsons didn't believe in paying for new when secondhand could do the trick. They purchased the equipment from the old Dollarton mill, dismantled it, and towed it up to Tahsis to be used in their new sawmill. The boilers came from the sawmill at McBride Bay. "They were haywire as heck, you know," said George Harlow, who worked for Gordon at Zeballos and Tahsis, "We used to get old mine wire and things like this, you know. Made do with what you could."

Jack Christensen, former president of Tahsis Company, agrees. "Haywire was a way of life on the westcoast," he said, "Everything was haywire. There was no money. They bought everything secondhand. If one thing worked, they made do with that. Sure it was haywire. But it worked." Jack says that the Gibsons, like many others of their generation and of that period in history, had a "Depression-era attitude" toward money. They didn't have any, so they couldn't spend any. Gordon didn't understand the concept of buying new, of investing in modern equipment, Jack says.[12]

Gordon, himself, called the mill a haywire operation, saying that the first superintendent they hired couldn't cope with that. He was used to building mills near urban areas, Gordon writes. "He didn't know that the impossible, with the right superintendent, only takes a little longer to accomplish."[13]

And what may have seemed impossible - finishing the mill in time to cut the first order of lumber by October - was made possible in large part by Gordon Gibson's drive and determination. The first log went through the sawmill on August 1, 1945. By September, the first order - two million board feet of lumber - was being cut. "Two weeks before the arrival of the first ship, we had only half the cargo cut and our wharf was still unfinished," says Gordon, "It seemed an unreasonable task to cut a million more feet of wood with an absolutely green crew and a mill that was not yet running efficiently."[14]

When the *Tipperary Park* arrived, the first ship to load lumber from the mill, they were still 300,000 feet short of a complete load: the last pieces of lumber were pulled off the saw two hours before the ship left port. "To load the first ship, we had to bring Indians in from Ceepeecee," said Neil McLeod, who came up to Tahsis in 1945, "We brought the loggers in, and that didn't go over very good, because we were loading clear lumber by hand, and they had caulk boots on."[15]

It took four days running round-the-clock shifts to load the first ship. At that time, lumber was loaded by hand, stowed piece by piece in the hold. It was only in 1970 that packaged lumber was developed, cutting down on the time - and labor - required to load a ship.

Three years after the first load of lumber was cut, the newly-built mill and community narrowly escaped destruction from a forest fire which raged down the Tahsis Valley, in June, 1948. The fire was started from the spark of a donkey engine about four or five miles out in the valley. "They had fishing boats from Ceepeecee and Esperanza and everything all ready to evacuate all the women and children," said Neil McLeod, "And, just through an act of God, I guess, and the efforts of the mill crew and the loggers, they saved the town and everything." The fire passed within fifty feet of the townsite, circled up the hill behind the houses and burned out a mile or two south.

"Two weeks later, the mill caught fire," said Neil, "Two-thirty in the morning. And it went like that. Just like that."

July 5, 1948. A welder was working on one of the saws when a spark landed in a pile of sawdust near the conveyor belt. "That mill went so fast," said Neil, "I was working near the edger. Dick Pilling was the fireman on watch, in the boiler house. And they were just practically across from each other. From the time Dick found out there was a fire in the mill and he got back and blew the steam whistle for fire, he couldn't get out of that boilerhouse. He had to go out the back. Just went like that."

The first mill was destroyed by fire July 5, 1948. John and Rhoda Campbell Collection.   Tahsis Archives.

There was no sprinkler system and no fire equipment. The crew had to go out to the woods and bring in the fire pumps from a logging site about two miles up the valley. But nothing could stop the fire. "Within five minutes the mill was like the inside of a red hot furnace with flames consuming the roof and machinery," writes Gordon Gibson.[16]

Things must have looked pretty bleak the next morning when the harsh light of day showed the still-smoldering and blackened ruins of the mill. But Gibson refused to allow the setback to destroy all his plans. That afternoon the pile drivers began pounding in new pilings in preparation for rebuilding the mill. "We had forty families dependent on us, and we knew that our orders must be filled immediately or we would go broke," he writes.[17]

"I guess the ashes weren't cold when we started clearing the area," says Neil McLeod, who remembers that Gibson was the first one on the bulldozer, clearing the rubble away.

"It was a great morale booster," said Jack Munro, chief accountant for Gibsons. "And we needed it, for the bottom had fallen out of our lives that day."[18] As it was, more than a hundred men decided they would leave on the *Princess Maquinna* the next day. The shaky future of the mill was obviously too much for them.

Rebuilding the Mill

Plans to rebuild began immediately, although initially, it seemed to be an impossible task. Gibson Mills didn't have the capital nor the borrowing power required to undertake such a major project. Meanwhile, they had purchased the Tidewater Mill in Port Alberni from Mrs. Grumbach in order to fulfill their contracts while the Tahsis mill was down.[19]

Work on rebuilding the mill began almost immediately. John and Rhoda Campbell Collection.

Tahsis Archives.

At the same time, East Asiatic was apparently considering building its own mill in the area, after hearing that the Tahsis plant had been destroyed. EAC had acquired considerable timber holdings in the Nootka Sound region and, as an international shipping firm, had certain lumber commitments that had to be met. Realizing that two large mills in the same area couldn't compete, EAC and Gibson Brothers agreed to form a partnership.

"East Asiatic proposed that we build a much bigger and better mill on a partnership basis," says Gibson, "They were so powerful and had control of so much timber in the area, that unless we went in as partners, they would build their own mill in competition with us. East Asiatic's proposition was fair and gentlemanly since they could have gone on without us."[20]

Mill and lumberyard before the fire, circa 1947. Houses have been moved off the floats and put on wood foundations.
Photo by John Perry.   Provincial Archives of B.C.

J.V. Christensen tells a slightly different version. He says that initially, the Gibsons wanted to cut their losses and leave the region. But EAC persuaded them to stay. The company saw the value of having an export mill on the west coast where it was accessible to international markets as well as being in the heart of the timber supply. And Tahsis was an ideal location with its level plateau at the head of the inlet, its natural deep-sea port, its protected waterway.

East Asiatic could come up with the capital investment that the Gibsons needed to build a new mill. What the Gibsons had that EAC lacked, says Christensen, was the experience in the day to day operation of a sawmill, and the drive to rebuild.

In January, 1949, Gibson Mills and East Asiatic formed a new company called Tahsis Company Ltd. Under the terms of the agreement, EAC advanced the money to build a new mill. They had a 51 per cent interest in the company as well as an exclusive contract designating them as selling agent for the lumber. The Gibsons, who had a 49 per cent interest in the company, signed their timber licenses over to Tahsis Company, but retained control of management and operations for a ten-year period.

Money was still tight, despite the financial backing of East Asiatic. Although the new mill was professionally designed and somewhat more substantial than the original plant, the habit of looking for a good bargain was hard to break. According to Frank Grobb, they used secondhand equipment and machinery wherever possible. Frank was in charge of locating and purchasing equipment for the mill, and he says he was "buying things on the cheap and dirty."[21]

On April 1, 1949, the Tahsis sawmill went back into production. It took a few months to work out the kinks of a brand-new operation, but by the end of the year, things were operating smoothly.

Building the Town

The company's main efforts concentrated on building the mill and getting it running properly. The town was secondary. As Christensen says, it grew like "topsy turvey." Houses were moved off floats and put on land "wherever the bulldozer found a space." There was no thought or planning put into laying out a community; that would come later.

In the beginning, when the first mill was being built, the crew lived in bunkhouses on the floatcamp which had originally belonged to Erik Olson. When Neil McLeod arrived in October, 1945, he said that the only signs of habitation were a floatcamp and a dock which "waved with the breeze." They were tied to shore near where the present-day mill office and loading dock are located.

By the time of the mill fire in 1948, the crew had grown and the town had begun to take on a shape of sorts. As more and more housing was needed, Gibson would buy up old abandoned floating camps from around the region and tow them into Tahsis. Three new bunkhouses were built which Neil calls the "California bunkhouses." They were two storeys high, built on open-deck fish scows, and provided accommodation for sixty men, altogether. In the spring of 1946, new bunkhouses were built on shore. "They were made out of wet hemlock," said Neil, "We used to take our blankets off the bed in the morning and put them around the stove to dry them out. I had a pencil and I used to mark the waterline on the walls where it was drying from the top down, you know."

Although a few families had moved up to Tahsis in the first year, there was a shortage of housing for married people. Neil said that those who were married, including himself, formed a committee and started "agitating," as he called it, for more houses. "One Sunday, we went out where the trailer court is today, just past the cookhouses, and that was all swamp. So then we went along the Valley road, and in those days they were logging out where the municipal yard is now. Taking

Looking north up the Tahsis River and first homes in "The Valley", circa 1948. Community hall at lower right. John and Rhoda Campbell Collection. From a postcard photo probably taken by John Perry.
Tahsis Archives.

spruce and fir out of there. And we decided that we could find a place to build our houses there.

"The original thoughts were that the Company would put the foundations down, which is hemlock blocks with a couple of ten by ten timbers on them, and we'd build the houses from there. They were just going to build the half shell, and we had to build the rest," said Neil.

According to Gibson, building housing for married couples was "one of the best innovations in our camps. With a crew of six carpenters we built houses about twenty feet apart along the bank of the river, the easiest place to clear... Our crew turned out a house every four days: just a crude affair with a floor covered in heavy tarpaper, a shingled roof, and a privy at the back."[22] The houses or "shacks" as they were commonly referred to by the people who lived in them, consisted of two bedrooms, a living room, and a kitchen. They were made of lumber rejects - wood not suitable for shipping out. Most if not all of those houses have since been torn down and were replaced, in the late 1960s, by modern two-storey homes built by Tahsis Company.

Up until the 1950s, living conditions in the milltown were relatively primitive. There was no electricity or running water, and women coming out to join their hus-

Neil McLeod's "shack" was the first house built in "The Valley" on what is now Rugged Mountain Road. It was completed on May 16, 1946. Photo courtesy of Neil McLeod.

First company-built houses on Rugged Mountain Road overlooking the Tahsis River, circa 1948. Photo courtesy of Neil McLeod.

bands found themselves cooking on woodstoves and using kerosene or gas lamps for lighting. Most came from Vancouver where they were used to paved streets, department stores, and all the modern conveniences of the twentieth century industrial world. Neil says the women deserve greater recognition for their contribution to the town:

"You're transported a hundred and sixty-five miles, north and west, back into the pioneering days, amongst the trees and the wind and the rain. Totally adverse conditions," says Neil, "Because when the old *Maquinna* would come in, and the women would come down the gangplank - and nine times out of ten, it was raining - they would go to a shack in the bush, which their husbands were trying to make into a home, under very trying conditions. And, no electricity, no running water, no electrical appliances, nor grocery store or supermarket. They really had it tough. I think some of those women should have been awarded a medal. But it was always the men that got the credit."

Conditions didn't seem to have improved much by the time Tom McCrae arrived in 1966: "We were living in what they called a duplex. Now, these had no resemblence to what people would normally term a duplex," said Tom. "None, whatsoever. They were two rooms and a bathroom. That's what a duplex was. Now, we were lucky. We got a bigger one, and it had an additional room. So, we had three rooms and a bathroom. So you had a kitchen, and a dining room, which was maybe twelve by fourteen. You had an oil stove and a stand-up old sink that you wouldn't believe how old that was. That was turn-of-the-century stuff. They probably imported that from some other old bunkhouse somewhere. And you had a stand-up shower because there was no room for a bathtub. And maybe you could put your fridge in the living room. And then you had the bedroom. Anyway, that's what they called a duplex."[23]

What services that were installed were done during spare time and on days off, and everybody pitched in, regardless of the job. "When you're building something, you only got so many tools to build with," said Neil, "As you expand, you got to use the same tools and spread them out." When the south townsite was being built, there was no one to do the blasting, so they called on Neil, even though he didn't have a blasting ticket. Then, he was asked to help put in the sewer and water lines and "I had to read up on that!" he said.

"We put our own water system in," said Neil, "There's a creek coming down just about where the school is now. And they used to call that McLeod Falls. So, we went around and scrounged all the pipe we could find around the sawmill and logging camp. And one Saturday and Sunday, we put in our own water system. And it worked great until summer came, and then the falls went dry. So then we put a pump in the river and we would take turns: I would start the pump in the morning, someone else would turn it off at night."

Tahsis, circa 1952. The new mill was completed April 1, 1949. New elementary–secondary school is seen on small hill overlooking the mill yard. The hill is locally known as School Hill and is now the site of teacherages belonging to the school district. Photo by John Perry. Provincial Archives of B.C.

Turnover

Despite efforts to build a town and to develop the community spirit necessary to drive it, Tahsis suffered from a problem which afflicted all small, isolated camps along the west coast at that time: turnover. "They used to say that when the *Maquinna* comes in bringing a new crew it's brought ten thousand and there's nine thousand and nine hundred ready to go," said Neil. One shift coming, one shift going, and one shift working was the slogan of the day, until as recently as the late 1970s when the turnover rate seemed to slow and stabilize.

"Some men even came up here, just took one look, never even came ashore," Neil said. "Because the living conditions were atrocious. And I guess in British Columbia they always have been. You know, somebody's got to go in, somebody had to start. And it's not like Vancouver when they were building Expo. You got everything there, nice highrises to live in. Up here, you had to suffer it out. And it doesn't rain vertically on the west coast in the winter," he said, "It rains horizontally."

The first resident manager to take over from Gordon Gibson, in 1950, was Frank Grobb. He blames the high turnover in part on the bunkhouses. "We didn't have very many families living there, and of course, your married people are the backbone of any community. So we had a large single community, and they were constantly turning over."

Frank started out with the Gibsons in 1947. He was in charge of their Vancouver employment office. At that time, logging outfits hired their crew through the Logger's Agency or had their own hiring offices, all of which were located around the Carroll and Hastings Street area in Vancouver. Loggers wanting a job out in the camps would go from one office to another, searching the notice boards for a suitable posting. Frank said that more than a hundred men a day went through his office, looking for work. There were always vacancies, he said, and when men hired on

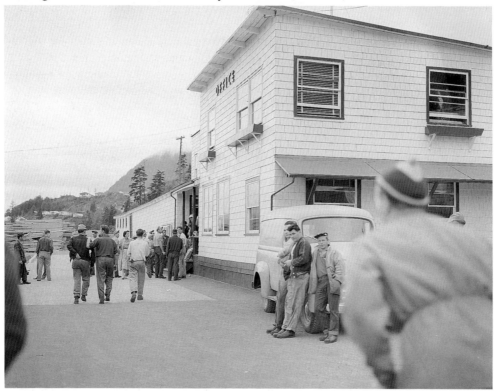

Millworkers in front of the office. Photo by Anthony Carter.　　　　　Tahsis Archives.

they were given a contract, told to buy a good pair of caulk boots, and issued a transportation ticket on the *Maquinna*.

"Well, we soon found out that what a few of them would do would be to go and try to sell the transportation ticket and not bother showing up," said Frank, "So then it became a case of making sure they signed a contract and then meeting them down at the boat to make sure that they showed up and did go on."

Twenty years later, the problem of high turnover hadn't changed significantly. Gerry Hill, assistant personnel manager in Tahsis from 1964 to 1967, said that up to 2,000 people a month would go through the Vancouver office. He said the sawmill hired between one hundred and two hundred people a month. "Our turnover was very, very high," said Gerry, "People went up there, made enough money in a few months, and left. Or they sometimes only lasted a day. Some never even got off the boat.

"Our selection techniques weren't too advanced. We'd hire drunks. They'd be drunk when they got there and drunk when they left." It was an occupational hazard. Sometimes it was the poor living conditions or the isolation. Sometimes it was alcohol. "The old demon alcohol," said Gerry, "You'd have your finest sawyer ruined with booze. And they were just geniuses in their trade. Just tremendous people. And then they'd get into the sauce, and they were nothing. And you couldn't rely on them, so off they had to go."[24]

At the end of each week, Gerry would put in a call to the Vancouver office to order more men to replace the ones that had left or didn't work out. "About the middle of the week I'd check with the head bull cook and see how many empty rooms we had and figure we'd have a few more drop by the wayside by the end of the week, and a few people quit over the weekend, so that's how we'd determine how many people to order each week," he said, "By the number of beds we had, and how many we'd extrapolated we'd have by the end of the week, and fill them all up. And that always seemed to work."

"Mondays were awful. Because that's when all the new guys came staggering out from the cookhouse and their bunkhouses, having arrived the night before." Mondays were "new people day," the bane of the foremen who had to train a new batch of people again, juggling crew and jobs to fill the gap while the rookies got oriented. Bob Kilmartin, a former resident manager, was a mill supervisor in 1967. He said he used to average ten new people a day. "I didn't know them because they turned over so quickly. I'd look at their shoes, and if he had a brand new pair of safety shoes on, I knew he was brand new today."[25]

Loading lumber by hand. Photo courtesy of Neil McLeod.

Consolidation and Expansion

In 1952, the Gibson brothers sold out to East Asiatic Company. EAC was interested in expanding its timber holdings, and was considering building a pulp mill in the region. In September 1951, the company applied for a forest management license to cover 132,000 acres in the Gold River watershed. In addition to their existing timber licenses, the company was requesting another 35,000 acres. Prince Axel of Denmark, the chairman of the board of directors of EAC, visited Vancouver Island in the fall of 1951 to discuss the application with the provincial Cabinet. According to a

Until the development of packaged lumber in the 1970s, all lumber was loaded by hand onto freighters.   Provincial Archives of B.C.

report in the *Victoria Daily Colonist,* "Dr. C.D. Orchard, deputy minister of forests, declares that the company wants the forest management license in addition to privately-owned timber, to provide a sustained yield operation sufficient to warrant the building of a pulp mill and sawmill and possibly a plywood plant.."[26]

The application was fiercely opposed by the communities of Campbell River and Courtenay, and two large forest companies already working in the region, including Bloedel, Stewart and Welch, predecessors of MacMillan Bloedel Ltd. They argued that the timber supply should support existing communities and mills rather than build up new communities by taking away from the old.[27]

EAC's application was turned down on the basis that it didn't have a concrete plan for developing its project.[28] But the debate over the granting of forest management licenses had only just begun, and in fact, was the major point of contention which eventually drove a wedge between Gibson Brothers and EAC.

Gibson was a strong and vocal opponent of the government's new forest policies. He argued that under the system of forest management licenses, the small independent logging companies, such as his, would be wiped out or become "just hewers of wood subject to the whims of the larger companies which held the Forest Management Licenses."

"Our days were numbered: we had five or six years at best before an independent logging company such as ours would be forced out of business because it could not secure sufficient cutting rights to maintain its camps and make a profit."[29]

For moral and political reasons, Gibson refused to accept EAC's ambitious plans. "Our family considered it wrong to accept a policy that was so detrimental to the province. Between East Asiatic and our company, we had twenty-five years of timber, which was all we felt necessary to amortize our capital. But East Asiatic felt differently. They liked the idea of having forestry rights in perpetuity."[30]

So, in July 1952, in what one newspaper called a "surprise move," East Asiatic acquired the Gibsons' interests in Tahsis Company. At that time, the Company employed approximately 650 workers in sawmills at Tahsis and Port Alberni, and loggers in camps at Chamiss Bay, Zeballos, and Muchalat.[31] The sale made each of the four Gibson brothers millionaires in their own right. It was the first time, according to Gordon, that he ever had more than a few dollars to spend. The Gibsons continued to operate their other businesses, including their interests in shipping and whaling ventures.

Government Policies and Tree Farm Licenses

According to the provincial government, forest management licenses were part of a plan to put the responsibility of forest management in the hands of the private sector. The policy was developed from a report by Chief Justice Gordon Sloan who conducted the first Royal Commission on the forests. His report, released in 1945, recommended greater management and control of the forests, including

Tahsis sawmill looking south down Tahsis Inlet, 1962. Bunkhouses for single men in the foreground. George Allen Aerial Photos Ltd.
                                                                      Tahsis Archives.

establishing large blocks of timber to be allocated to companies on a long-term basis. In exchange for cutting rights, companies would be accountable for replanting logged-off areas, and for protecting forests from disease and fire.

The new policies favored an integrated approach to forest utilization, and supported the consolidation of operations. At that time, the concept of integration was just beginning to take hold. Paul Cooper, chairman of the executive committee for the Western Division of the Canadian Pulp and Paper Association, described the integrated approach as "multiple unit operations comprising sawmills, shingle mills, plywood plants, pulp mills, hardboard plants, plus various directly related secondary operations consuming leftover wood."[32]

Gibson was not alone in his opposition to the new policies. By the 1950s, the question of who controlled the forest resources had emerged as a subject of great public controversy. Small independent logging firms were opposed to turning over large blocks of timber to a single company. While the industry talked in positive terms of "close utilization" and "integrated operations," the small contractors faced economic extinction. Like the small A-frame logger of the 1930s, the contractor of the 1950s had neither the capital nor the resources required to construct mills and develop reforestation techniques on the scale required to compete with the larger companies. Many expressed concern that capital would leave British Columbia and end up in eastern Canada and the United States.

An editorial in the *Victoria Daily Colonist* criticized the government's forest management licenses. "The emergence of big logging groups and little logging groups with sharply opposed interests is not a furtherance of the scheme. It has never been the intention to turn the woods over to a handful of powerful operating mergers to the exclusion of the rest of the field. Nor should that ever be done. On the contrary, if forest management is good for the "big" interests, it must be made equally good for the "little" interests, else we shall have a fresh and entirely unwanted monopoly on our hands before the end of the present century."[33]

As of March, 1952, twelve Tree Farm Licenses had been issued since the introduction of the legislation in 1948, and another nine applications were pending approval. H.J. Welch, then MLA for Comox, warned that great timber dynasties were being created at the expense of the small loggers. "I am just as sold on forest management as the minister is," he said in one news report, "It's the license I deplore."[34]

Certain changes to the policy, in late 1952, held companies more accountable to the public for the management of their Tree Farm Licenses. Under the new legislation, companies were required to contract a certain percentage of their timber to small, independent operators; to provide public access on logging roads during weekends and off-hours; and to establish permanent settlements in remote areas.

In Nootka Sound, the new policies had some immediate and long term consequences. The Muchalat logging camp was moved off floats and relocated on land at Jacklah River. Later, a road between Campbell River and Gold River was opened to the public. And eventually, a brand new town was built at the mouth of the Gold River (see Chapter 8 on *Gold River: Modern Expansions*).

The conflict over forest policies came to a head in late 1954, when concern arose over the American takeover of Canadian forest companies. "There is a growing tendency under the forest management license system for our vital timber resources to fall into a few hands. The trend is toward American control... What seems to be happening is that some of these companies, securing licenses giving control over vast acreages of timber lands, are turning around and selling them at large profits to other interests... It is not a bad thing in itself that American capital should help develop our resources, since that development creates jobs and invest-ment. But foreign control of our forests is another thing. It is a perpetual control and since our forests are so vital to our economy it can become dangerous whenever it suits the American owners to manipulate things to suit their interests in the U.S."[35]

Of particular concern were four giant forest license areas, granted originally to Canadian companies, but recently purchased at that time by U.S. companies. In December, 1954, Chief Justice Sloan bowed to public pressure and agreed to head a second inquiry into B.C.'s forests. The inquiry opened in February, 1955. A full report was handed down in 1957.

In the meantime, East Asiatic had re-submitted its application for a forest management license. And in July, 1954, EAC was awarded the 19th Tree Farm License in the province (TFL #19), covering some 398,000 acres (162,000 hectares) in the Nootka Sound region, of which about 192,000 acres (78,000 hectares) was estimated to be productive forest land. The company now had the long-term tenure it had said was required in order to fully develop the region's resources. But the issue of TFL's and who controls the forests, continues today.

Town Development and Stabilization

With EAC's takeover, and the establishment of TFL #19, the community of Tahsis began to take on a more permanent shape. Town services were upgraded, new houses were built, and the mill was gradually modernized. "E.A.C. had more money," said Christensen, "They worked at getting rid of the haywireness."

One of the major improvements was the provision of electricity. The mill's steam plant and its five huge boilers generated enough power to drive the sawmill as well as the town. The electricity was free, as long as residents stayed within the limit of 300 kilowatts a month. If they used more than that, they were charged for it. But it didn't seem to be a problem staying within the limit, said one resident. Aksel Ostergaard moved to Tahsis with his wife, Edith, in 1955. "Tahsis had electricity all the time," he said, "But of course it was a struggle, because whenever anything went wrong in the mill, if one of the generators was down, then things were tough. They would shut off the lights to town and keep the mill going. So we would sit in the dark here and look down and see everything lit up down there at the mill."[36]

The water system was another eccentricity of life in Tahsis. "It was a pretty haywire water system," said Jack Munro, "A lot of things were haywire. But this water system - I think it was a half-inch line, maybe an inch line. Well, there wasn't any pressure. Every time they were using a lot of water down in the mill, we never got any up at the Point."[37]

Jack, who had worked for Nootka Packing Co. at Nootka and at Port Albion near Tofino, moved to Tahsis in 1949 with his wife, Jean. One day, Jean invited a newly-arrived neighbor over for tea. As it happened, there was no running water to the townsite that day: Jean had her bathtub taps open waiting for the first drops to come through. After enjoying her tea, the neighbor turned to Jean and asked where she got the water from. "Jean, she had a hot water bag, and she went and poured this into the kettle and cooked it," said Jack, "So that was the first cup of tea that Mrs. Dyer had, and she never forgot that!"

During the first years of the town's development, residents worked together to build the kind of community they wanted. "If there was something to be done, everybody went in and helped," said Neil, "It was real close working conditions." The water system was one such co-operative project. Another was the decision to re-route the main road through town. "Originally, the road went from about the office, right through the mill yard," said Neil, "Now, part of the mill yard was all

The main road used to run through the mill yard. Pictured above are the mill office with the Co-op store in the low building to the side. George Allen Aerial Photos Ltd.

mud in those days. And it was just stumps, up where the new planer mill is now. So, one Saturday, we just took all the machinery - one and a half cats we had here - and we built the road on the outside. Did it all on our own."

The United Church, the Catholic Church, the fire hall: all were built in a similar fashion. "I'm Protestant," said Neil, "But there was a lot of us worked building the St. Joseph's Church, the Catholic Church here. Then, in nineteen-fifty-eight, fifty-nine, when we built the Tahsis United Church there was fourteen of us working: and there was twelve Catholics and two Protestants. We all worked together."

The Catholic Church was built in 1955-56, and the United Church opened in 1960. Before that, congregations would hold their services in the community hall, the Shantymen's church, and various school gymnasiums, scheduling times to accommodate each group. At that time, Tahsis was served by the United Church Marine Mission. The pastor, Reverend Bill Howie, travelled up the west coast from Bamfield in the mission boat *Melvin Swartout,* visiting the isolated logging camps, lighthouses, Indian villages, and other communities along the way. Every six weeks or so he stopped in at Tahsis, holding his services in the community hall where he "competed with the jukebox," says Charlotte Tasker.

Charlotte came to Tahsis in 1956, joining her husband, Ken, who had come up a few months earlier to take a job as a lumber inspector with the Pacific Lumber Inspection

Bureau. Both she and Ken became active in the community and were instrumental in helping to build the United Church. "It became evident that if we wanted to have a church we would have to build it," she said, "The Company said yes, they would do it, but they would have to be assured that the town was back of it."[38]

Charlotte helped circulate a petition through the community: it came back with forty signatures, more than enough to convince the Company to donate the lumber and the land for the building. And it was truly "'a house builded upon the rock,'" said Ken, quoting a passage from the Bible. The church was built on the side of the mountain overlooking the mill yard: solid rock that had to be blasted in order to make room for the A-frame structure.

"When we had a 'first dig' ceremony, the president of the Company came in from Vancouver," said Charlotte, "He was a real card: Kenneth Frederickson. He took the spade that we'd borrowed from the Company store. He goes in and it goes clang! And he couldn't get it any further. And he goes somewhere else and it goes clang! He looked up at Doug Abernethy *[resident manager at the time]*, and says 'Don't you think we can build this someplace where I can dig?' He didn't dig very far because of the rock!"

School

Another focal point for community activities was the school. The first school was established shortly after families began to arrive. It was a one-room schoolhouse

The school played an important role in community life, from the first two-room schoolhouse to today's modern elementary– secondary school. George Allen Aerial Photos Ltd., 1960. Tahsis Archives.

near the river, a converted bunkhouse operated and paid for by the Gibsons. In 1948, the school was taken over by the provincial government, and Andy Anderson, who had been teaching at Ceepeecee and Esperanza, was hired as the new teacher. "We had such good support for the school," said Andy, "When we had Christmas and Easter programs, it wasn't just the school - the whole town would turn out to see it."

The community hall would be packed, standing room only, and all the mothers would pitch in, making fancy cakes and serving tea and coffee, and even, said Andy, bringing in tablecloths to make the place look festive. As Lorna, Andy's wife, said, "In those days, anything you had, the whole town turned out. Because it was the only recreation, the only change that you had. Unless you flew to Vancouver."[39]

A Parent Teachers' Association was formed to support the school and organize activities. And according to many old-time residents, the school and the association became a kind of common meeting ground in a town which was split by union and management tensions. Lorna said that personal differences were set aside to make sure community events succeeded. "I think the school really was a focal point for the whole community," said Andy.

The Andersons arrived shortly after the mill fire, and everything was "just a shambles," said Andy, "Just a shambles." During his first year, he taught all grades in

One of the first classes in the Tahsis High School.
Photo courtesy of Neil McLeod.

one room. By the second or third year, another room had been added and a second teacher was hired to take the primary grades, while Andy taught grades five to seven. When East Asiatic took over, in the early '50s, a larger school was built on top of what is now called School Hill. It had four rooms and a teacherage nearby.

"Schools were the most expensive part of running a town," said Jack Christensen, who was instrumental in building the new school, "But I consider them the most important." Shortly after the new school was built, it was nearly destroyed by fire. But Neil McLeod, then fire chief, managed to save it by pumping water from the river up to the top of the hill. "I wasn't too popular with the kids after that," he said, "For saving the school, you know."

Lorna says she thinks part of the feeling of pulling together as a community, in those days, came from a strong sense of sharing common experiences. "One spring, everybody's pipes froze," she said, "A bad cold spell. Well, when everybody is using melted ice water and melted snow for washing - you took spit baths and everything else - you share all those things together. And the kids learn to cope."

In 1958, a high school was built on the site of what is now the hospital. When a new and completely modern secondary school was built several years later, in 1972, the old high school was converted into teacherages. In 1976, an elementary school wing was added and the new complex was renamed the Captain Meares Elementary-Secondary School.

Company Ownership and Control

Until the town's incorporation in 1970, Tahsis Company owned and controlled everything: the land, housing, roads, recreational facilities, waterfront. The company was employer, landlord, and town boss all rolled into one. And being a resident manager in Tahsis was very different from being the manager of a mill in Vancouver or Victoria.

"You were faced with being a referee in all sorts of domestic problems which you would not normally come in contact with," said Frank Grobb. "You became involved with people who, although you were renting the houses there at a very nominal rate, always wanted something added, something fixed, or something new. The company, at that time, ran the general store and we were always being criticized because the food prices were too high. So, as well as manager of the mill per se, you had to act as unofficial mayor, referee, and politician."

Shiploaders did double duty as the town's clean-up crew. Between ships, they would help repair houses, deliver sawdust for furnaces, and do general maintenance work around the community. In 1967, a Royal visit from the Princess of Denmark sparked a flurry of clean-up activity. "They nicely painted all the fronts of the houses here," said Aksel Ostergaard, "In a hurry, so she could go around and see all these beautiful houses. But only the fronts were painted." Not the sides, not the backs— just the fronts.

Prince Axel's visit, in the 1960s, caused a similar response. "I think the last forty-eight hours before he came, they were spray-painting all over the blooming place. Everything swept, everything absolutely spotless. For him to come here and stay for oh, maybe four or five hours," Aksel said.

It wasn't just Danish Royalty who received the special treatment. Bob Kilmartin says the town was kept in such good shape mainly due to "orders from the top."

"The sawmill was spotless. They painted it every year. I had two Dutchmen from Victoria that had a contract. They would go into the townsite and just, paint the houses. Like, if you had a rosebush in the way they just painted over it. And what we used to do, we used to hire a guy from General Paints, and he would tell us what colors to paint the houses. Like a code. He had a chart. Like, this house was purple, this house was blue, this house was white.

"The reason we did it was because our president, when he would come into Tahsis - naturally he flew. And he'd circle Tahsis, you see, and observe what it looked like. And the color code was excellent."

Christensen admits he had high standards for the community. He says he was very conscious about maintaining a good relationship with the people who lived in Tahsis, and that meant making sure living conditions were good. Jack, who made regular and frequent visits to Tahsis, said he made a point of walking around the mill and townsite, talking to people and asking them about their work and families. He said he always checked the washrooms in the mill to make sure they were clean enough that he would use them. "If not, there was hell to pay!" he said.

Jack's approach to running a single industry town was somewhat different than the Gibson brothers before him and CIP after. "You were together with the community. You were not responsible for the community," he said, "The com-

A bowling alley, community theatre and coffee shop were the center of Tahsis' social life. Note the small cars parked in front, circa 1965.
Tahsis Archives.

munity cannot live without the mill, and the mill cannot do without the other." It was a sentiment strongly echoed by other top management of Tahsis Company at that time.

When EAC first took over from the Gibsons, the town was desperately in need of more family housing. And families were an important element to a town because they added stability and, more importantly, a sense of long-term permanency. The first housing construction undertaken by EAC was in the south townsite, on the hill overlooking the inlet. A few years later, new houses were built in the Valley or north townsite, replacing the shacks built by Gibson in the late 1940s.

The community was loosely divided into three social groups, according to where you lived and what your job in the mill was. Supervisors, management, and skilled tradespeople generally lived in the south townsite or what was popularly referred to as "Snob Hill." Hourly-paid workers and their families lived in "the Valley." The two sections were separated by the Tahsis River which often flooded in winter, cutting off people in the Valley from the rest of the town.

"This town was built, in some respects, like a small town in Denmark," said Tom McCrae. "The boss lived on the highest point in the community and everybody lived subsequently in layers below him. There were two distinct areas of the community. One was this particular area that this building is in now *[Village Office]*,

Aerial view of Tahsis, 1960. Centre foreground, Capt. Meares Junior/Senior Secondary School with playing field and "Snob Hill". Air landing strip and housing in the "Valley" at back. George Allen Aerial Photos Ltd.   Tahsis Archives.

and the other was down in the Valley. And you knew how you were progressing in the company as you moved closer to this end of the community. Because, of course, the store and the hotel and everything was down at this end of the town. As you got a little bit more up in the strata of things, and were considered to be on better terms with your supervisors, and one thing and another, you progressed from the Valley slowly up towards "Hamburger Heights" as we called it in those days."

The single men living in bunkhouses were a group unto themselves, and most residents didn't consider them to be part of the community. Many were married men who had wives and families on "the outside," but were forced to live in the bunkhouses because of a lack of housing. For others, married and unmarried, bunkhouse living was a way of life, an opportunity to make a stake and, eventually, leave.

Gerry Hill remembers that Slippo Malecki, head flunky in the cookhouse for many years, tried to leave town several times, but never quite made it. "He'd save up enough money to go down to Reno for his vacation. But he'd get conned into going to the Poker Shack, and lose it all, so he would never leave," said Gerry, "It happened over and over again." Slippo was in Tahsis when Gerry arrived and was still there when Gerry left, three years later.

There seems to be several explanations for the hierarchical arrangement of housing based on class structure. One had to do with the quality of the houses and

New houses going up in the townsite subdivision, 1960. Preference was given to married men with families in management or key skill areas. George Allen Aerial Photos Ltd.

facilities themselves. Initially, houses in the south townsite were more modern than those in the Valley. According to Gerry Hill, they were built in compliance with National Housing Administration standards. Electrical wiring and plumbing was up to code, they were generally larger and, perched on top of the hill, they commanded a breathtaking view down the inlet. Houses on the hill also had the advantage of being closer to town services. The co-op store and post office, the high school, the churches, and the public wharf where the *Maquinna* docked, were all within walking distance. Later, the hotel and shopping plaza were also built at that end of town.

Houses in the Valley, on the other hand, were a mish-mash of old floathomes pulled up on land and the "shacks" built by Gibson and his crew. If you lived in the Valley, it was a "long trudge" to the center of activity, said Gerry.

In Tahsis, as in all of the isolated logging camps and mill towns which dotted the west coast, accommodation was a critical factor in attracting and keeping workers. The availability of housing was used by management as both weapon and carrot. Because housing was owned by the company, management decided who got a house, what kind of house they got, and where it was located. Gerry says the decisions were made at monthly townsite meetings by the mill manager and his assistant, the personnel manager, the production superintendent, the townsite manager, and the maintenance superintendent.

Aerial view of housing in the "Valley", 1960. George Allen Aerial Photos Ltd.   Tahsis Archives.

"We'd all come in with lists of people that had requested houses," he said, "The personnel office used to have a book and people would come in and sign up for a house. Sometimes they were in a little two-room shack and had two babies now and needed something bigger. Sometimes they were in the bunkhouse and wanted to move into their first house."

The list was prioritized according to whether the person applying for a house was needed in the mill, was a good worker, and whether he already had a house or not. It was a "very subjective" process, admitted Gerry. And the meetings could get fairly stormy. For example, a sawmill isn't much good without a sawyer, so they carried a fair amount of weight in the allocation of houses. Management staff, skilled workers, and people in key jobs were almost certain to get a house. "Sawyers and filers and your tradespeople are the backbone of the sawmill. Without all of them, you haven't got a sawmill," Gerry said.

For Ken and Freda Sturdy who moved to Tahsis from Port Alice in the 1960s, having a house to go to determined whether or not they accepted the job in Tahsis. "The accommodation was very, very limited," said Ken, "Because it only depended on who left for the next person to get a house. They weren't building any homes, and they had to reserve a lot of accommodation for their supervisors and salaried staff. Otherwise they wouldn't have got them, you know. There was no way we could have gone down there if we hadn't got suitable accommodation."[40]

Vehicle Restrictions

As private property, the town was subject to company rules and policies, including one which restricted the size of cars to ten feet eleven-and-a-half inches long. It was one of the first things to hit you when you arrived, said Ken Sturdy, particularly in the 1960s, when cars were fairly large. "Let's put it this way. The Volkswagon bug was too big. This was one of Doug Abernethy's little pet deals. He and I had a lot of arguments over this. But he was the boss, so that's what we had to do. He had a little car, and he really didn't want to have other cars there. He wanted to keep the town very much, you know, a small town."[41]

The company issued its own license plates - miniature in size to fit the small three-wheeled Isetas and British-made Morris Minors and Austin Minis which crowded the roads. One of the explanations for the size restriction was that the company was afraid of accidents, and according to Gerry Hill, it was a good rationale. "There were few roads. They were winding and narrow. No way to get in and out. Very, very narrow roads in some spots. If one car was coming the other car would have to stop and let it through."

One of Gerry's responsibilities was enforcing the vehicle restrictions. Any time a new car came in on the boat, he said, he was there with his measuring tape. And there were some dicey situations. "There was a school teacher that decided to heck with it, and she brought in a VW bug. And one of our mechanics, he said to heck with it, and he brought in a bigger car." It was the beginning of the end. Usually a warning letter from the manager was sufficient notice to offenders. "But these two individuals challenged it, and won. They just held on. For one thing, you couldn't fire a teacher. And mechanics you needed. So, they just toughed it out."

When the town was incorporated, in 1970, the roads became public property, subject to provincial legislation, not private rule. The company no longer had any authority to restrict car size. Then, when the road to Gold River opened three years later, it became more feasible - and practical - to bring in larger cars.

"The strange thing is that there were no accidents, absolutely no accidents, whatsoever, when the standard-type cars came in, that could be attributed to the fact that they were bigger cars," said Ken.

The 'Booze' Boat

Marine transportation was a vital link between people on the west coast and larger centers in the south. In Tahsis, one of those links was supplied by Slim Beale and the *Chamiss Queen*. Slim operated the liquor boat. He made the run from Zeballos to Tahsis two or three times a week, taking orders on one trip, then returning to Zeballos to fill them for delivery on the next trip. "Legal bootlegging," Aksel Ostergaard calls it. But it wasn't really bootlegging. As there was no liquor store in Tahsis, and the nearest one was in Zeballos, Slim was authorized by the provincial government to bring liquor in at cost: he only charged freight.

"All the fellows used to line up down at the dock and there was lots of kibbitzing," says Mrs. Beale, of the times she would accompany her husband on his run. "They used to call him 'doc' and I wondered why, and Slim said 'Well, that's because I'm the one that brings the medicine.'"[42]

In the twenty-one years he operated, Mrs. Beale only recalls him missing two trips. "They relied on him in Tahsis, and he never let them down," she said. They may have relied on him too much, say some workers. There seems to be little doubt that the 'booze boat' was important, maybe too important. "The drinking got so bad here that, one time, Gordon Gibson told Slim he wasn't to bring in any more liquor for a certain period of time," said Neil McLeod. Slim used to bring groceries in too, so one Saturday, he was in and Gordon went down, wanting to buy a bottle off Slim. "Slim says 'Gordon, you said there was no liquor to be brought in here, and that goes for you too.'"

Before the *Chamiss Queen* there was the *Mary Meade,* and before Slim there was Chuck and Ethel Harvey. They brought the *Mary Meade* up to Tahsis from Maple Bay in 1946 or '47, operating it first as a water taxi and then as a liquor boat between Tahsis and Zeballos. The Harveys left the area in 1949. A year or two later, Slim bought the *Mary Meade* and took up where the Harveys had left off. "And it's been a satisfying life," he said after close to 25 years on the water, "Look at it this way: there are people, tourists, who pay thousands of dollars to cruise the way I do every day, and I'm doing it making a living."[43]

The *Chamiss Queen* made its last run in May, 1974, attracting reporters from all of the major newspapers in British Columbia. Slim retired to the Comox Valley to listen to "the cows mooing the chickens clucking and the stuff growing."[44] There was no longer any economic rationale for a liquor boat. Delta Hotels had opened the Tahsis Chalet in 1965, and its beer parlor was one of the main attractions. Later, after the town was incorporated, the provincial government made plans to put in a liquor store. The outlet opened in 1974, shortly after Slim made his final run.

Municipal Incorporation

The Company's priority was to make a profit, "To try and make as much lumber as you could as economically as possible on order - because we had orders in there from all over the world - and try to get it out on time and get paid for it so you could meet next month's payroll," Frank Grobb said.

"And we all knew that if we didn't make the mill profitable, and we didn't cut the orders on time, and we didn't ship them on time, and we didn't ship them according to grade and everything, that the company wouldn't get paid," he said, "And therefore we wouldn't have any money to pay the mill."

But while the primary business was to run a sawmill, it was difficult if not impossible to separate the town from the mill.

"You say without the mill there wouldn't be any town," said Frank, "But without the town there wouldn't be any mill. It's a very close relationship."

Initially, the company owned the town out of necessity to attract and sustain its workforce. People came to Tahsis for one reason only: to work at the mill. But there were disadvantages, from the company's perspective, to owning the town. In terms of a profit-motivated business, being a landlord wasn't cost-effective. Statistics showed that it cost more to cut lumber in Tahsis than in a similar-sized operation elsewhere. "The lumber production per man-day was lower than other mills," said Aksel Ostergaard.

The company challenged the figures, saying it was an unfair comparison because the Tahsis operation included the bunkhouse-cookhouse facility, townsite services, town maintenance, and so on.

"All the cookhouse people are included in the man-day production even though they're serving food, not cutting lumber," said Aksel, "All the people that are looking after the houses, the carpenters, the townsite foreman, and all the plumbers - they're included in that, not to mention the amount of money going out of the company's pocket. Why not sell the whole damn thing and let people pay for these services? Which is correct. And now our man-day is coming up."

"The manager of a mill," says Ken Sturdy, "His prime reason is to produce the mill's product and make money doing it. So the management of the town is a

George Allen Aerial Photos Ltd.

TAHSIS COMPANY LTD.

Townsite housing, upper left, with the mill manager's house on top of a small knoll overlooking the whole community. George Allen Photos Ltd., 1960.

Tahsis Archives.

secondary interest. I guess now, nobody would think twice about it. It's an open town. And there aren't very many company towns left any more."

The move to incorporate was a company decision, based on what management considered "sound business sense." The residents had little choice in the matter. It was purely a question of the company shedding its obligations as landlord. The provincial government took over some of the responsibility, the new municipality shouldered the remainder.

Discussions regarding the incorporation of Tahsis began as early as 1964, at about the same time as plans were announced to build a pulp mill at Gold River, and along with it, an "instant" town. During this same period, revisions to the Municipal Act made it easier for a company town to become incorporated. Under the new legislation, only five landholders were required to petition the government for municipal status, as opposed to the previous laws which required five hundred petitioners.

In July, 1969, the Company announced its plans to incorporate Tahsis at a public meeting in the town hall.[45] Jack Christensen, president of Tahsis Company, outlined the company's plans which included more and better housing, a mobile home park development, improved water and sewage systems, new recreation facilities, and a new school. At the same time, Christensen announced a deal between Tahsis Company and B.C. Hydro that would bring both hydroelectricity and a road into the remote community. In fact, road-building was already underway. Existing logging roads were being connected to complete the link between the communities of Tahsis and Gold River.

According to Christensen, the incorporation of the town as a municipality was essential. It meant "local responsibility for the community and, as always, the inevitable taxes for everyone," he said, "Community development is underway and the Tahsis Company shares completely the view that the future lies in achieving 'open' town status."[46]

The move to incorporate was a problematic one, fraught with tension and anxiety. Most residents were angry with the company for reneging on its responsibility to the community's well-being. The town was and continues to be dominated by a single-industry - forestry - and a single company - Canadian Pacific Forest Products. The mill is the town's largest employer: other small businesses are in the service sector. The sawmill's payroll carries the town and keeps small businesses afloat.

But, even as the company spoke of independence and self-government, it retained its control of the land. With very few exceptions, the whole foreshore - prime land for future development - is owned by the company. The municipality has very little land of its own.

Not much has changed since Gordon Gibson's era when he first conceived of the sawmill. The town may have grown larger and become more stable, but it has remained economically tied to the sawmill. When the company relinquished ownership, it was merely shifting the burden of responsibility for hydro, water, sewer, and schooling onto the residents.

Difficult Transition

The transition period from a "closed" company-owned town to an "open" municipality was a difficult period. The residents were resentful and bitter, their fear of the future only slightly allayed by the promise of a road to the outside. "They were a little bit reluctant, a little bit scared," said Edith Ostergaard, "Because we were so protected. If we wanted to build anything, we could get wallpaper and paint for the houses. You moved into the house, everything was given to you. We were really, in a way, pampered. And a little bit scared: now we all of a sudden had to start to pay for things!"[47]

It also meant shouldering the huge task of looking after the roads, the water and sewer systems, garbage collection, and all the large and small things that come with administering a town. "All our water lines were then becoming about twenty-five years old," said Ostergaard, "They were just about ready to pop." Aksel was appointed to the town's first council, and, shortly after, was elected to a term as mayor. One of his first concerns was upgrading the water system. According to the municipal legislation, the town was required to have a sewage treatment plant and a proper water system. "You are now incorporated. You are now a legal entity. You must abide by the law. Privately, before, the company could do anything that pleased them. And we had outbreaks after outbreaks of hepatitis in town," he said, "Because our water supply was not proper."

Another big concern, at the time, centered around housing. The company was planning to sell its houses to residents who, after years of low rents, were concerned about having to purchase a home in a town where housing values rose and fell according to the economic well-being of the mill. Many were not interested in making the long-term commitment to the region that buying a house signified. They were happy with renting: it gave them a feeling of being able to leave at any time. And the company itself was concerned that by turning over all the houses they would lose their ability to attract workers to the area. Houses were often used as bait to lure skilled tradespeople to work in the mill.

They dragged their heels on the housing issue for several years after the town was officially incorporated. Houses were finally put up for sale in 1974, four years after incorporation. One of the reasons had to do with surveying the lots and roads. "And we went through quite a bit of hassle trying to figure out how to subdivide," said Sturdy, "We had to use what they call a non-conforming system. The town had been built without any attention to legal lots and layout of roads, etcetera."

The decision to incorporate was a difficult one for both parties, and the complexities of the issue continue to be discussed in the town today. "The president of the company, Mr. Christensen - I knew Jack for a lot of years and had a lot of dealings with him," said Tom McCrae. "I'm sure he really felt in his heart that that was the best thing for the company to do, both financially but also from a humanistic point of view, because I found that Jack always did have a bent towards the people. I'm sure the people thought, initially, that that was the right thing to happen...

"But, looking back and trying to armchair quarterback anything - you know, second guess what was going on when you weren't really there, involved in it - is pretty damn difficult. It's pretty hard to say that 'This was right and that was wrong.' I think, personally, it was wrong, without more of the homework being done, and without more of the assurances to the people that the systems would go in place, that our infrastructure needs would be properly looked after. I think that part was wrong. For the rest of it, I think you could flip a coin and you would find that you'd come up heads more times than tails, so far as the advantages to the community on a long term."

In theory, Tahsis has been an "open" town since 1970. But in practice, it took a few years before it could really be called a self-governing community. Initially, members of the new council were appointed by the government at the company's recommendation. The first elections were held in 1974, the first time the town could finally say it had representatives who spoke on their behalf.

Before turning the town over to the village council, the company upgraded the water system, built new housing in the Valley, put in a mobile home park, and contributed toward the building of a new sewage treatment plant. All of this helped bring the town up to government standard: something that didn't need to be considered when it was privately owned.

At the same time, a new cedar mill was built on the other side of the inlet from the existing sawmill. Nootka Cedar Products, opened in 1971, was a joint venture between Tahsis Company and Paul Shew. Initially, the mill employed 100 men working two shifts. But poor lumber markets in the early 1980s eventually resulted in the mill's closure in 1986. The mill has since been dismantled and the site is now used as a lumberyard.

Upgrading the town's facilities, the new sawmill, and the access road were all part of the company's overall strategy of investment in the region. A strategy which included building a pulp mill and townsite at Gold River, moving the logging camp at Fair Harbor into the town of Zeballos, and building a road link between Zeballos and the North Island. It was a strategy that was ultimately tied to Tahsis Company's application for an extension to its tree farm license. In 1964, the company applied for and was subsequently awarded an extension to TFL #19. Under the terms of government forest policy, the company was required to invest in the long-term development of the region and its communities.

The physical and economic changes to the town also had their social and emotional implications: "Nine times out of ten, you could get to know the president of the company by his first name," said Tom. "He would ask you about your family, and one thing and another, on his visits up here. There's a total isolation from that, of course, a total impersonal approach to everything, now. And that is being felt throughout the whole community. It's becoming sterile in the effect of human communications. And that's very sad."

What seems to have had the most significant impact on Tahsis was the opening of the road to Gold River. The company agreed to clear and log the hydro line right-of-way in exchange for B.C. Hydro's commitment to string power lines in from the Gold River substation. A network of logging roads already in existence were connected to form the final link between the two communities.

When the road first opened up in 1972, "It would take us anywhere from three to four hours to get to Gold River because the road was in such terrible shape," Aksel said, "It was meant for four-wheel drive only, to service the hydro line."

The road was so bad that then-mayor of Tahsis, Bill Lore, initiated a walkathon to focus public attention on the rugged terrain and difficult road conditions between Tahsis and Gold River. In the first Great Walk, groups set out from Tahsis and Gold River and met halfway. Today, the Great Walk has become an annual event. Starting in Gold River before sunrise, walkers, hikers, and even joggers, young and old alike, set off early in the morning in order to cover the 40-mile stretch to Tahsis by sundown.

The road has gradually been improved over the years, but it will be many years before it becomes anything more or less than it is: a gravel logging road, meant for heavy-duty trucks and machinery. Some of the steepest grades on Vancouver Island are found in the area between Gold River and Tahsis, and sharp corners, narrow passes, and dangerous drop-off's make the road an interesting one to travel on. Today, instead of four hours in a four-wheel drive vehicle, the 40-mile stretch takes just over an hour-and-a-half to drive. On a "good day," locals shave off another fifteen minutes.

Today, the mill continues to exert a powerful influence on the residents of this tiny community, not only by its sheer physical presence, but also by its economic importance to the town's survival. The town lives and dies according to labor relations, technological changes, and the market for wood products. Uppermost in people's minds these days is the fate of their community. They are concerned about the loss of jobs, and the company's application for an extension to its Tree Farm License. If approved, the extension would further strengthen the company's hold on what is already a single industry town, and on a region they already control.

Notes

[1] Philip Drucker, *The Northern and Central Nootkan Tribes* (Washington D.C.: 1951), p. 228.

[2] Legislative Assembly, *Sessional Papers* (Victoria: 1888), p. 173.

[3] Ibid., p. 174.

[4] Interview, Ernie Heevis (Ceepeecee: July, 1985).

[5] Interview, George Harlow (Ladysmith: July 9, 1985).

[6] Gordon Gibson, *Bull of the Woods* (Vancouver: 1980), p. 177.

[7] Ibid., p. 173.

8   Ibid., p. 174.

9   Ibid., p. 175.

10   Ibid., p. 175.

11   Ibid., p. 175.

12   Interview, Jack Christensen (Vancouver: September 8, 1987).

13   Gordon Gibson, p. 176.

14   Ibid., p. 178.

15   Interview, Neil MacLeod (Tahsis: June 26, 1985).

16   Gordon Gibson, p. 186.

17   Ibid., p. 187.

18   *Nootka Sound*, March, 1974.

19   *Nootka Sound*, March, 1974, says 'Grumbach.' Gibson, in *Bull of the Woods*, p. 187, says 'Strumbach'. The actual name, according to the Port Alberni Museum and Archives is 'Grumbach.'

20   Gordon Gibson, p. 188.

21   Interview, Frank Grobb (North Vancouver: June 2, 1987).

22   Gordon Gibson, p. 177.

23   Interview, Tom McCrae (Tahsis: April 9, 1988).

24   Interview, Gerry Hill (North Vancouver: May 21, 1987).

25   Interview, Bob Kilmartin (Tahsis: April 28, 1988).

26   *Victoria Daily Colonist*, (September 16, 1951).

27   Ibid.

28   *Victoria Daily Times*, (November 29, 1951).

29   Gordon Gibson, pp. 160-161.

30   Ibid., p. 199.

31   *Vancouver Sun*, (July 15, 1952).

32   *Daily Province*, (December 7, 1951).

33   *Victoria Daily Colonist*, (December 20, 1951).

34   *The Province*, (March 19, 1952).

35   *Vancouver Sun*, Editorial, (November 15, 1954).

36   Interview, Aksel and Edith Ostergaard (Tahsis: June 24, 1985).

37   Interview, Jack and Jean Munro (West Vancouver: July 13, 1985).

38   Interview, Ken and Charlotte Tasker (Tahsis: July 30, 1985).

39   Interview, Andy and Lorna Anderson (Surrey: September 7, 1987).

40   Interview, Ken and Freda Sturdy (Courtenay: July 9, 1985).

41   Doug Abernethy was long-time resident manager of Tahsis. He and his wife also seem to have developed a close relationship with the community and many of its residents.

42   *The Province*, (May 13, 1974).

43   Ibid.

[44] Ibid.

[45] *Nootka Sound*, (August, 1969).

[46] Ibid.

[47] Interview, Aksel and Edith Ostergaard (Tahsis: June 24, 1985).

CHAPTER 8   GOLD RIVER: MODERN EXPANSIONS

As the community of Gold River began making plans for its 25th birthday celebration in 1990, the company which gave birth to the town was readying itself for yet another expansion, one which promised economic growth to the region. Gold River got its start in 1965 as an "instant town." Carved out of the rainforest to support Tahsis Company's $60 million pulp mill then under construction at the mouth of the Gold River, the town was incorporated as a district municipality before residents had even moved into their new homes. The pulp mill marked the beginning of a bright new future. Twenty-five years later, the construction of a modern newsprint mill and expansion of the existing mill brought similar expectations.

Building the Pulp Mill

In 1960, the decision to build a pulp mill on the west coast of Vancouver Island made good business sense to Tahsis Company. They had been actively logging in the region since the late 1940s and in 1954 had acquired the timber rights to some 398,000 acres (162,000 hectares) under Tree Farm License #19, an area which encompassed virtually all of the undeveloped land in the Nootka and Kyuquot Sounds. According to then-president Jack Christensen, the company had more timber than it could handle. Most went to the sawmill in Tahsis to be cut into lumber, but chips from the mill and pulp logs - logs that couldn't be used in the sawmill - were exported to overseas markets or sold to pulp mills. "If other companies were benefiting from our surplus," said Jack, "why shouldn't we?"[1]

What the company needed to fully utilize its timber resources was a pulp mill. A research team from Stanford University in California spent close to two years studying the feasibility of the project, and recommended that the company build a mill which would produce kraft pulp rather than sulphite. The markets for sulphite pulp were dwindling, said Jack, even though B.C.'s pulp and paper industry at the time was producing mainly sulphite pulp. By 1963, the company had decided to take the plunge. Lacking experience in the pulp and paper industry, Tahsis Company approached Canadian International Paper for expert advice and consultation. The Montreal-based firm was a subsidiary of International Paper Ltd. in New York and had several large pulp and paper plants in Ontario and Quebec.

"At that time, one of the responsibilities that CIP had was to arrange for the financing of the pulp mill," said Henry Funk. "I'm sure this was no trade secret, but what they arranged was a loan for fifty-five million dollars with a number of banks and insurance companies involved, and trust companies. The lead bank was the Chase Manhatten Bank in New York. They were the lead bank and we arranged this fifty-five million dollar loan which was raised for the purpose of building the pulp mill. That was CIP's responsibility." Henry Funk was the secretary and treasurer for Tahsis Company in 1965.[2]

"The other responsibility that CIP had," he continued, "Was to provide the technical know-how for the construction and the operation of the pulp mill. And the reason East Asiatic and Tahsis were looking for a partner like this is that East Asiatic Company had been in the lumber-timber industry for many, many years...East Asiatic had virtually a world-wide network in the marketing of timber, which was logs, and lumber. So they had the know-how in the sawmilling end of it. Whereas, IP-CIP had a number of pulp mills as well as newsprint and other mills, and they had a subsidiary in New York called International Pulp Sales that had a network of offices around the world for the selling of pulp. This is why East Asiatic was looking for a partner that had that expertise...So this made a good marriage."[2]

In October, 1964, Tahsis Company announced its intentions to build a new 750-ton-a-day bleached kraft pulp mill at the mouth of the Gold River. At the time, Jack felt that it would be cheaper to bring industry to the heart of the resource rather than ship the resource out to the industry. The provincial government of the day agreed: "The Social Credit party was keen on developing the backwoods - with our money," he said. Site studies indicated that the flat delta land at the mouth of the river, the ease of access to ocean-going freighters, and a good source of water made Gold River an ideal choice. There had been some discussion about locating the new mill next to the company's sawmill at Tahsis, but the lack of a steady water source made it impossible.

Gold River logging camp at the mouth of the Gold River on Muchalat Inlet, 1960. George Allen Aerial Photos Ltd.

The Tahsis Co. pulp mill was built on the former site of the logging camp at the head of Muchalat Inlet. The photo above was taken as construction neared completion, circa 1967. Chuck Diven photo. Tahsis Archives.

"The concept of Tahsis was good, and the concept of Gold River was good," said Jack, "and if they had been together it would have been better. There just wasn't enough suitable waterfront around that could handle both plants."

Survey work and site clearing began in February 1965. A few weeks later, on April 1st, Canadian International Paper officially joined East Asiatic as an equal partner in Tahsis Company. CIP immediately appointed several of its experts to oversee construction of the new mill:

"I was part of the package deal from CIP," said Henry Funk. "One of the arrangements in the EAC-CIP agreements was that the president would come from the East Asiatic side of the family, and the financial officer was to come from the CIP side of the family, and I was the financial officer of the company. That was part of the arrangement." At the same time, Jack Christensen resigned as president of East Asiatic and took over as president of Tahsis Company.

By the time Henry Funk became involved, the two companies were down to "pretty serious negotiation," he said. "They were doing financial studies, both from an operational standpoint and from a marketing standpoint. They had to look into it because at that time I think they had decided where the mill was going to be and they had decided it was going to be a pulp mill rather than a newsprint mill. So I came in at that point."

The site chosen for the new town was a 300 acre section of land on a plateau overlooking the juncture of the Gold and the Heber Rivers. Chuck Diven photo, 1966.

There were five people that did the legwork on the studies, including two engineers, an economist, a cost-accountant, and Henry, who got involved in the overall financial aspect of the project. "We worked on these things and we pulled together oh, many many different 'what if' situations: what happens if this was to occur in the market? What happens if this was to occur?"

The Need for a Town

Tahsis Company's plans included building a brand new town to serve the needs of the pulp mill. "It was a necessity," said Jack. When finished, the Gold River facility was expected to employ some 400 people in its pulp division and another 200 in its logging division. Those workers, and their families, needed a place to live. Jack envisioned a modern, well-planned community which would be completely separate and independent from the company. "I did not want to have a company-owned town," he said, "There are too many problems with them." For one, companies are in the business to make a profit, not to be landlords. For another, he believed that the residents would be more committed to the town if it was their own. Recent amendments to the Municipal Act whereby five landowners in a community could apply for incorporation, made it easier for single-industry towns to become self-governing. Gold River, company-built but not company-owned, was incorporated as a district municipality on August 26, 1965 - the first town in B.C. to have its charter while still under construction.

The site chosen for the new town was a 300-acre section of land on a plateau overlooking the juncture of the Gold and the Heber Rivers. Located about nine miles up the Gold River Valley, it was the only site available that was suitable for development. Here, the steep narrow walls of the river canyon opened out into a large, bowl-shaped area, ringed by mountains. The location turned out to have an added bonus: the town was far enough away from the mill to escape the worst of the noxious pulp fumes and remain somewhat independent of the plant's day-to-day operations.

In summer, the plateau was a natural heat collector: it was sheltered from the open waters of the inlet and had a southwest exposure. "This little spot was like a desert in the summertime, it was so hot," said Jim Fiddick. Jim is a forester who worked for Tahsis Company in Gold River in 1959 and the early 1960s. "We'd be coming in from work on the early shift, and we'd drive across this piece right here. And when you put your hand out, it would be just like putting it in an oven. Then you'd get down to the straight stretch, where you'd get the breeze off the ocean, and it would be nice and cool."[3]

Work clearing the townsite began in February, 1965. By mid-October, families began to move into their new homes. Above, Bill Hawkins, engineer who later became the first superintendent of Public Works for the new town.   Village of Gold River.

The town's first residents were loggers and their families who had been living in Tahsis Company's logging camp at the mouth of the Gold River. The camp had to be relocated to make way for the new mill, and that meant moving some 35 families up to the townsite almost immediately. Bulldozers began clearing the land in February of 1965 and by mid-October, families had begun to move into their new homes. Among them were Des Stewart and his wife, Mae, who had lived at the Beach Camp since 1962.

"Just to show you how fast things happen," said Des, "We moved up here in October, on Hallowe'en. I'd left some paint down there in the attic and thought, 'Gee, it would be nice to have that up here.' I went down the next morning to get it, and my house was gone. It had been loaded onto a barge for Tahsis. That's how fast it was."[4]

The new subdivision in Area A of the town plan, was known as Loggers' Row. Later named Dogwood Drive, the crescent-shaped street was perched on a small knoll at the edge of town. For the first year or so, the families from the logging camp had the townsite to themselves. They watched as houses went up all around them. Construction crews worked feverishly to finish on time. The pulp mill was scheduled to go into production by the summer of 1967, and the new employees needed a place to live.

Doug and Betty Wilson, former Beach Camp residents, said the houses had been built so fast that the wood was still wet when they moved in. "Everything was damp. We were in them three months, they said, before we should have been. That's

Another view of the townsite under construction. Dogwood Loop or "Loggers Road" is seen in the upper right. Road to Campbell River comes in from the lower right.
Village of Gold River.

why everybody had such high hydro bills in the beginning, because the houses had to dry out," said Betty.[5]

The finishing touches were still being put on as people moved in. Doug said that a representative from the company would come around two or three times a week to make a list of things that still needed doing, and then send a carpenter around to fix them. Little things, said Doug, like doors out of line or putting wood molding around the floors. And in the beginning, the power and water service was sporadic.

"When we first moved in, we never had power and water together for the first two months. You either had power and no water, or water and no power. They never got the two together. We cooked on gas stoves. A nice, brand-new home, and gas stoves in your fireplace!"

The day the Stewarts moved in, their kitchen wasn't finished yet, and the cement sidewalk had just been poured. "We had to put planks over it so that we could get the furniture in," laughed Des. It was an adventure: "I'd always dreamt of pioneering," said Mae, "And here it was, handed to me on a silver platter.

A Planned Community

The new town of Gold River was - and still is - in sharp contrast to most other forest industry communities on the west coast. Billed as a "Model Community" and "Canada's first all-electric town," it boasted underground wiring, modern schools, and all the amenities of urban living. We had to have a town, and we had to offer the "best of everything" in order to attract people here, said project coordinator Mike Norris. "Because the fact is that no matter how you slice it we are still out in the

SHOPPING CENTRE AT GOLD RIVER FOR MacKENZIE MANAGEMENT LTD

Artist's conception of the shopping centre which forms the commercial core of the fully planned community.

Village of Gold River.

171

bush, not at the corner of Georgia and Granville. With the pulp mill expansion in B.C. skilled personnel are highly prized. But unlike loggers, they won't live in bunkhouse camps."[6]

The town was professionally designed by a team of architects, town planners, and landscapers. The residential area is built around a centrally-located commercial core which is within comfortable walking distance from anywhere in town. Wide curving streets and tree-lined boulevards sweep gracefully through neighborhoods where houses are set well back from the road, screened from their neighbors by strategically-placed carports and greenery. Instead of building row upon straight row of tract houses, architects provided prospective homeowners with several different housing styles to choose from, laid out on irregularly shaped lots. And throughout the small community, attention to detail is evident in the ornamental plum and cherry trees which line the boulevards, and in the numerous footpaths and trails that connect one area with another, or wind through the parks and along the river banks.

A market research study determined Gold River's immediate and long-range needs, taking into consideration the town's isolation from larger centers. Among the services proposed in the initial plans were a supermarket, drugstore, and 50-room hotel. Land was designated for the future development of a recreational complex, four churches, a town hall, and several parks and ballfields.

"Why settle for a logging camp in the virgin forest?" asks one Tahsis Company ad, "Gold River will be just about as unlike a logging camp as you can get...It will be a place where families can settle and enjoy the good life to the full."[7]

There is little doubt that the new town of Gold River offered all the modern conveniences and amenities a logging camp lacked. But what it didn't have in those formative years was a soul. You can build the physical structures of a town, but you can't create community spirit. That can only develop over time, and through established relationships. "We were hesitant about the move in one sense, we really were," said Mae. "Because we really didn't want to be uprooted. But we had no choice."

The Beach Camp

The community's earliest and longest-term residents are Bunty and Carole Sinclair. They had lived at the Beach Camp since it's establishment in 1955, and before that, had been at Tahsis Company's Muchalat Camp across the inlet at Jacklah River. Like the Stewarts, they had some initial misgivings about leaving the tiny community and moving to a larger one.

"We were like one big happy family down there," said Carole, "You knew that once it became a town, it would get bigger and bigger." They liked the intimacy of the logging camp, and felt they would lose that in a larger town where people seemed to keep to themselves more. "We were closer-knitted I think in a place like that," said Bunty, "Right now, I've got to think who my neighbors are and I've probably lived alongside of them for ten or fifteen years."[8]

What people seem to remember most about living at the Beach Camp is the strong sense of community that drew everyone together. "Everybody knew everybody," said Carole, "If you needed something, or ran out of something, you could always go to a neighbor." People visited more, and they seemed to have more time to relax and enjoy life. When Mae first moved into the camp, she said it didn't take her long to get to know people.

"Two days after I'd moved in, I looked out my kitchen window, and here's a man walking into my yard with the largest fish I've ever seen in my life. Threw it

George Allen Aerial Photos Ltd.

Tahsis Company's logging camp at the mouth of the Gold River, 1960. Bunkhouses for the single men at front of the camp, over-looking the water's edge. Schoolhouse and community centre at far right of the playing field. Housing for married men and their framilies at back of camp. George Allen Aerial Photos Ltd., 1960. Tahsis Archives.

on my lawn and said 'Would you like to can this?' You know, that's the kind of thing that went on. Took me two days to can it. What was it, sixty-four pounds? Never met him before in my life," she said, "But you see, that's the way things were down there."

There were about 35 families who lived in camp all year round, and the company did it's best to make them happy. "They made it a very, very nice living camp," said Mae, "A lot of thought was given to the people that lived there. Our gardens were all beautiful. Just snap your fingers and you'd get a load of soil if you needed it." Bunkhouses for the single men were at the front of the camp, just up from the dock. The married quarters were towards the back, separated from the bunkhouses by a huge playing field with a schoolhouse in one corner and a paved tennis court in another. Next to the tennis court was a community hall, housing a small store, the post office, and a cafe.

Housing was provided at a nominal rent which ranged from $15. a month for trailer sites to $31.50 for the largest house in camp - a four-bedroom, two-storey building in the middle of the settlement. "As far as cheap living, you couldn't beat the price," said Bunty, "We had a four-bedroom home there, twenty-five dollars a

There was a waiting list for housing at the Beach Camp. Initially, there were about 25 permanent houses for married men and their families. Later, more houses were built and trailers brought in to meet the increased demand. George Allen Aerial Photos, 1960.
Tahsis Archives.

month for rent, and the company supplied everything. If any repairs were needed, they sent someone around to do them." The rent included garbage pick-up as well as electricity supplied by the camp's generator plant.

Housing was limited. Initially there were about twenty-five permanent houses for married men and their families. By 1962, the company had built another seven homes and land had been cleared at the back of the camp for about fifteen trailers. There was a waiting list for houses, but not everyone was eligible.

"You see, in the logging camp they used to offer houses according to your ability of logging, and how badly they needed you," said Bunty. "You couldn't just come and say 'Hey, can I have a house?' and get one."

Key employees, people skilled in a particularly specialized job, were given priority for a house. Foremen, loader operators, cat drivers, riggers, and head loaders were among the positions the company considered critical to their logging operations. Without them, they couldn't log. Houses became a way of attracting qualified personnel and ensuring a reliable workforce. Doug Wilson was a grapple yarder, and the offer of a house came at the right time. "We were going to buy in Courtenay, but we were sort of undecided," said Betty. "Then he came up here and they offered him a house, so we moved up."

Usually a house came open every few months. Somebody either quit, was fired, or was transferred. When Des first came up to Gold River in 1960 to drive a logging truck, he had to stay in the bunkhouses, commuting home to Cumberland, on the east coast of Vancouver Island, on the weekends to visit his wife and three children. He was promoted to truck foreman after about a year, and only then was he put on the waiting list for a house. "I just had to wait my turn, which wasn't very long," he said. "I was quite lucky because a house came up in short order."

As a community, the Beach Camp learned to become self-sufficient. People depended on each other for companionship, support, and entertainment. They had to: there was no one else. They were isolated from other settlements, and didn't have the basic services that are taken for granted in today's more urban settings, such as doctors and dentists, libraries and department stores.

Until 1958, the only transportation was by floatplane or boat. Pacific Western Airlines operated regularly-scheduled passenger and mail flights to Vancouver. Groceries and heavier freight came in every ten days on the *Tahsis Prince*, a Northland Navigation boat out of Vancouver, or the *Uchuck II* which at the time was based in Port Alberni and served the logging camps and communities in Nootka Sound. Later, when the road was pushed through from the east coast of the island, groceries were ordered from Campbell River and shipped in by bus or freight truck.

The Uchuck III *at dock at the Beach Camp, 1960. Until the road to Campbell River was opened to the public in 1964, the* Uchuck *provided the camp with transportation and freight. Today, the* Uchuck III *continues to ply the waters of Nootka Sound. George Allen Aerial Photos.*
Tahsis Archives.

"I have to laugh,"said Carole, "Because now when people get eggs and that, it's right into the fridge with them. Well, back then, when I ordered groceries I used to order a case of eggs at a time, which was fifteen dozen. I never once put them in the fridge. Just kept them in the cupboard and they always kept."

Fresh produce, fresh meat, fresh anything was difficult to get in on a regular basis. People either did without or learned to make do. The Sinclairs, for example, raised their kids on canned milk cut with water. "We went down to Bunty's sister's one time for Christmas," said Carole, "And at Christmas dinner, the kids said 'Ugh! That milk tastes horrible!' Of course, Helen says 'What do you mean? Is it sour?' I taste it, and 'Oh,' I said, 'Forget it. My kids are used to canned milk.' I mean, that's all they ever had after they got older. And then to have fresh milk, naturally it tasted funny."

Carole's parents had opened a small store next to the community hall in 1955 when they first moved into camp. Carole said that it carried a few things, but not many. It was primarily for the men in the bunkhouse, and carried work clothes, work boots, cigarettes, and pop. It was later taken over by Dudley Moore who ran it as a co-op for years. He would get fresh meat and produce in every weekend but "you had to be quick," said Bunty. The co-op carried more than the little store, but it was expensive, and didn't have everything. Most people ordered their groceries from Vancouver or went out to Campbell River to stock up, using the co-op as a corner store if they ran out of anything.

Road Access

The road between Gold River and Campbell River was finally completed in the summer of 1958 in order to bring in fire-fighting equipment. A major forest fire had broken out in the Upana Valley, said Bunty, and tankers had to be brought in to help put it out. As it was, the region was criss-crossed by a network of logging roads. Elk River Timber was logging in an area northeast of Tahsis Company, and had already built a road along the north side of Upper Campbell Lake to an area just west of the Elk River. By the late 1950s, Tahsis Company had started logging up the Ucona River Valley, and had pushed a road part way along the Heber River. It didn't take much to connect the two.

"From Elk River's Camp Ten out here, which is about four or five miles out, it was just a goat trail," said Des, "It was just a kind of cat road that joined up our road here. And the buses would bang and jangle over them."

When it was first opened, the road was restricted to logging trucks and buses. Vancouver Island Coachlines had the franchise to operate a bus service between Gold River and Campbell River. Buses ran once a day, carrying people, mail, groceries, and freight. On Friday and Sunday nights, two extra buses were put on to accommodate men in the bunkhouses who would go out for the weekends. And, from time to time, the bus doubled as moving van when someone moved in (or out) of camp: the seats were removed and furniture was loaded in their place.

Travelling conditions were terrible. The roads were gravel, designed for heavy-duty logging trucks and off-highway driving, not for ordinary vehicles. During fire season, smoking wasn't permitted on the bus and passengers weren't allowed to open the windows for fear a casually-tossed cigarette butt would start a major forest fire.

"You got onto the bus, and away you went without a stop except to unlock gates until you got to Campbell River," said Anne Fiddick, "It was about two hours on a logging road, and you signed your life away at the Strathcona Dam trestle. The

View of the Beach Camp at Gold River, looking east up the Gold River Valley. Bunkhouses for single men at front of camp, playing field, school and community centre/co-op store immediately behind them. At back, housing for families. George Allen Aerial Photos.
Village of Gold River.

Pinkerton guards came aboard the bus and said 'Sign here' when you came in, and 'Check out' when you checked out."[9]

The road belonged to Elk River Timber and was, strictly speaking, a private access road. A gate manned by security guards blocked the Campbell River end and all vehicles were required to have a pass in order to use the road. Anyone not employed by the company and travelling on company business, travelled at their own risk. Bus passengers signed a waiver absolving ERT of any and all responsibility for injuries or damage to personal property in the event they were in an accident while on company property. At the Gold River end, Tahsis Company had a similar gate at the top of the road coming into the Beach Camp. Although unmanned, it too was locked at night.

In early 1964, the road was opened to private vehicle traffic after working hours. Residents were permitted to use the road from 6 o'clock at night to 6 o'clock the following morning. Drivers were still required to sign in and out, and ERT continued to issue permits at the Strathcona Dam trestle.

As road conditions improved, however, people were able to get out more often. Some drove to Campbell River every two weeks or so to do their shopping. "We used to go out just about every payday, and stock up," said Betty, "And at the Beach Camp, if I knew you were going to town, and I couldn't go, I would give you my list, and vice versa. In a small place like that, everybody does for everybody else."

Not everyone went out to Campbell River. Mae said she would send her grocery list in with the bus driver one day, and her order would be filled and on the next bus the following day. "I wasn't that interested in going out," she said, "Lots of other women went out, maybe every weekend. But I liked the camp life, I was happy. And I'm not a shopper, so I was saved that way."

"There's never been any question in my mind that a paved road between here and Campbell River is the single most dramatic factor that has changed the community," says Anne Fiddick, now mayor of Gold River. "Open access, a paved highway... The minute you have reasonable access you have a change take place in the community. People have choices. You allow them choices between this and the next biggest community... I can't honestly say there is a disadvantage to the road, apart from the fact that it's a rather dangerous piece of highway ... But, disadvantages? It's opened up the west coast of the island, if that's a disadvantage."

A Sense of Community

Isolation has sometimes been referred to as a state of mind. Certainly there were the objective factors of geographical remoteness, difficult access, and minimal

The cookhouse had an excellent reputation for its pastries and baked goods, as well as for its steak nights; some men would load their plates with two or three steaks at a time. George Allen Aerial Photos. Tahsis Archives.

services. But to suggest that these were hardships or deprivations is to impose another, more subjective, perspective. Most of the former Beach Camp residents I talked with did not feel disadvantaged. At least, they don't recall suffering or feeling deprived and isolated. Instead, they remember the close community ties that bound them to their neighbors and fellow workers. Ties that were important to morale and the very social fiber of life. And it is in that deeper more intimate sense that social activities were extremely important. Not because of the isolation, but because that is what makes a community. As Mae said, "the community is what you bring to it, what you make it."

"I liked it down there," said Gail Shillito who first moved to the Beach Camp in February, 1963. "I like being out in the wilderness. We had neighbors, but there weren't too many people. We got to know everybody. I never felt isolated. A lot of people do, even up here. I just enjoyed that type of life. Such an easy-going, relaxed period."[10]

The Stewarts never had the sense of being isolated. "It was a very, very happy life, and we hated to leave. Our children especially," said Mae. "It was real primitive in those days," said Des, "But an awful nice camp. Peaceful. Laid out perfect. And we had our own little entertainment. And I liked driving logging truck. I really enjoyed it, I really did."

"As far as I was concerned, Gold River was a great place to be," said Jim, "Because I like the solitude. I don't like crowds, I don't like traffic. I could just go

School was held in a two-room school house in the middle of the camp. George Allen Aerial Photos, 1960.   Tahsis Archives.

out there and be by myself, do my own thing, go hunting, fishing, hiking. I did a lot of hiking. I climbed all the mountains around here."

"We used to have shows brought in twice a month, and everybody would go to a show. And usually once a month there was a dance. You know, you made your own fun," said Gail, "For recreation, you made your own recreation. Which is too bad that we've lost that. Because everybody had fun."

There was no television, and radio reception was poor - "You could pick up CKWX down there," said Gail, except at night when so many radio stations from as far away as Alaska and sometimes Montana crowded the frequency bands so that all you could hear was a muted babble fading in and out until the early morning. And, as in any other small community, there were parties for the kids, a visit from Santa Claus at Christmas, and New Year's Eve for the adults.

Limited resources forced residents to draw upon their own initiatives and talents to create the kind of community they wanted. They relied on themselves and each other to provide entertainment and recreation activities. Dances at the community hall, movies once a week - popcorn and "everything you wanted" from the small cafe next door - softball in the huge field outdoors, badminton and basketball inside during the long winter nights. Evenings were spent visiting or playing cards, and weekends were usually reserved for pot-luck dinners and Saturday night socials.

Schoolhouse at the Gold River camp was later moved to Tahsis Company's logging camp at Fair Harbour on Kyuquot Sound and then to Zeballos. George Allen Aerial Photos, 1960. Tahsis Archives.

"It was and it wasn't" a dry camp. Liquor was served at the dances, and every second Friday was a beer night or "smoker" where you could buy beer at the community hall. At that time, the only liquor store in the region was at Zeballos, and once or twice a week, Slim Beale, who ran the water taxi from Zeballos, would come into camp and take orders for liquor. The 'no liquor' rule was primarily for the bunkhouses. In the married quarters, the restrictions were looser and less easy to enforce.

"Every Saturday night was a smoker," said Jim Fiddick. "You could buy beer - the camp was a dry camp, but in the community hall you could buy beer. So all the single guys went over to the community hall. They had tables set up, and you'd sit around and b.s. and have a few beers. They were called 'smokers.' Once a month there was a party, where the wives were invited. Other than that, the wives generally didn't go to the smokers."

Social activities were a focal point and involved the whole camp. No one was left out, not even the single men in the bunkhouses. Residents formed a community club which organized events and activities year-round. They usually had monthly meetings and planned a month in advance for entertainment.

Dances were "more like a big house party held in a community hall," said Mae. Women got together to cook the food, and everyone met at the hall for an evening of music, dancing, and a generally good time. "It was just like a big happy family, because you knew everybody there," said Betty. "There was no such thing as a wallflower."

"And then for New Year's, it practically cost you nothing to go out for New Year's Eve," said Bunty, "We'd dance to the tune tapes, and everybody brought food and your own liquor, and had a heck of a good time at the dance. And then the next day, everybody brought the heels of their bottles and went down, cleaned the hall up."

And then there was Bill Forde's punch bowl. Bill was the camp superintendent: "He used to be really proud of his punch," said Doug, "Six bottles of gin and a little bit of lemon squeezed in it. You only needed one drink and you could water it all night."

The men were at the logging camp because it was their job, their work, their livelihood. The women came because they wanted to be with their husbands. Some couldn't handle life in a logging camp on the remote west coast. They soon left. Those who stayed preferred it to city living. They enjoyed the peacefulness, the solitude, the slower pace, the close ties and atmosphere of a small community. They all agree that it was an excellent place to raise kids: they too learned to "make their own fun," enjoying the outdoors and relying on each other for company.

Nearly all the families at the Beach Camp were young couples in their early twenties just starting out. They all had families, young kids and pre-schoolers. The oldest was in grade eight, and there was usually someone with a baby in diapers around.

"You spent a lot more time with your kids than you do today," said Betty, "Raising kids all day, they kept you busy."

"Kids learned to make do without having that boob toob there, or somebody to entertain them," said Jim, "They entertained themselves. It was great for the kids; it was the best time they ever had."

School was held in a two-room schoolhouse near the community hall. In the beginning, there was only one teacher. Later on there were two. "Our second son, Clifford, he was always first and last in his grade because he was the only boy of that age in that grade," said Mae. "That was the type of school it was."

The Gold River Valley was known for its prime timber. Above, logging was the driving force behind the area's economic growth. George Allen Aerial Photos, 1960.　　　Tahsis Archives.

Early Operations

"You might call me a tramp logger," said Bunty. "That's what we were known as. Whichever way the wind blew and there was a job in that direction, that's the way I'd go. Just go up and down the coast and there was always plenty of jobs. I just happened to end up here at one point," he said. "And when I seen this country - I didn't expect to stay very long because I was still not finished seeing everything - I said to a guy that was with me, 'Boy,' I said, 'When I get to retire, I'm gonna come back to this camp. To this country.' I just liked the country. I never thought I'd be here thirty some odd years later!"

The west coast of Vancouver Island has long been recognized for its natural resources, and the Muchalat Inlet area is no exception. Interest in its rich timber

Logging operations, Gold River division. Grapple yarder swings logs onto truck. George Allen Aerial Photos, 1960.

potential began as early as 1884 when William Parsons Sayward, pioneer lumberman from Victoria, purchased 726 acres at Jacklah River on Muchalat Arm, and along the Gold River, a few miles up from the site of the present-day pulp mill. In 1893, the Sayward Mill and Timber Company leased another 9,974 acres up the Gold River and Heber Creek valleys at ten cents an acre. There is little evidence to indicate that Sayward did any extensive logging in these areas at that time. According to the Nootka Land Registry, Sayward's original purchases were transferred to a man by the name of John Ash, and the Gold River and Heber Creek leases were taken over by the Pacific Coast Lumber Company. As Brian White has suggested elsewhere, these early timber leases were primarily speculative in nature, and were taken out in anticipation of the proposed northern extension of the Esquimalt and Nanaimo Railway and the region's future development as a port.[11]

Active logging in the Gold River area began in the mid-1930s when small, independent contractors roved up and down the inlets with float camps and A-frame operations. Laura Anderson says that in 1935 and 1936, Eric O'Malley was logging in Muchalat Inlet before he moved up to Tahsis and then to Chamiss Bay. And in January 1938, Gordon Gibson got his start in Nootka Sound. He made a deal with a Seattle Company to purchase the rights to several blocks of timber along the shores of Muchalat Inlet. At the time, Gibson had been logging at Malksope in Kyuquot

Log dump at the mouth of the Gold River, near the Beach Camp. George Allen Aerial Photos, 1960.

Sound, and had run out of timber. He towed his A-frame and floatcamp down to Muchalat where, he said "we were to spend the next two years making our greatest start in the lumber business."[12]

By mid-1940 Gibson was operating four profitable logging camps in the Nootka Sound area, including his main camp at Muchalat, and had just taken over another large timber tract at Sandpoint. Eighteen months later he had pulled all his operations out of the region.

"I was in our Muchalat camp on 7 December 1941 when word came to us that the Japanese had bombed Pearl Harbor," Gordon says in his autobiography. Because the Pacific coast was considered vulnerable to a possible attack from the Japanese, the Canadian government acted immediately to construct an airport and defense post at Tofino on the west coast of Vancouver Island. Gordon Gibson was contracted to assist in road-building and in clearing the ground for the airport.

"During a spell of cold, clear weather in January 1942 I towed all the floating logging camps and equipment that we had in the Nootka Sound area behind the old *Joan G* through forty miles of outside waters into Clayoquot Sound and up to the Tofino airport site," writes Gibson. "But the floating houses took such a beating rounding Estevan Point that they disintegrated, and though we saved our machinery, our bunkhouses were a total write-off."[13]

Truck in for repairs at the logging division, Gold River. George Allen Aerial Photos, 1960.

Tahsis Archives.

Gibson returned to the Nootka Sound area in 1942 but concentrated most of his logging activities in the northern reaches of the sound, along the Tahsis and Zeballos Inlets. One or two small-scale logging outfits continued to work the southern end of the sound, but their operations were marginal. A significant impact on the overall utilization of timber resources didn't occur until East Asiatic and Gibson Brothers joined forces in the 1950s.

East Asiatic's initial involvement in Nootka Sound began during World War II, independent of its association with Gibson Brothers and the Tahsis sawmill. In 1943, one of EAC's ships, the *M.S. Europa,* was bombed in the North Atlantic while under the Canadian flag. Because of monetary restrictions during the war, the $2 million insurance money had to remain in Canada. East Asiatic deposited the money in its Vancouver account and used part of it to purchase large blocks of timber along Muchalat Inlet and up the Gold River Valley. A few years later, the company acquired additional timber leases at the northern end of Nootka Island and at the mouth of the Gold River. In 1948, East Asiatic joined Gibson Brothers to form Tahsis Company Ltd. eventually becoming sole owners of the firm.

House parties, Saturday night socials, and other informal gatherings brought people together for fun and entertainment in the logging camps. Above, Muchalat Camp at Jacklah River, circa 1954.

Village of Gold River.

Jacklah River

Tahsis Company intensified its logging activities in the Gold River area in the 1950s. The lumber market was good and increasingly more raw logs were needed to supply the Tahsis sawmill. Several small independent contractors - George Green, Vic O'Hara, and Taylor Way Logging - were already working for Tahsis Company and operated logging camps in Muchalat Inlet. Deciding to expand its operations in order to more fully take advantage of the area's rich timber supply, the company established a main camp at Jacklah Bay. "Just a typical logging camp is all it was," according to Bunty.

But unlike most of the other camps at that time, Tahsis Company's Muchalat operation was beached on land and had housing for some of the married loggers and their families. About fifteen families lived at Muchalat, said Carole. She moved there in November, 1952 a few weeks before her sixteenth birthday. A one-room schoolhouse and playing field, a small post office, and a community hall set it apart from the small floatcamps in the area. The school went up to grade eight - "there must have been sixteen, eighteen kids in camp," - and the older kids, such as Carole, took correspondence courses.

Mail came in by plane three times a week "if the plane flew," said Bunty, and parcels arrived every ten days by freight boat. Northland Navigation took over the route once served by CPR's *SS Princess Maquinna,* running first the *Nootka Prince* and later the *Tahsis Prince* out of Vancouver and Port Alberni.

Carole's father was president of the community club, and he helped organize picture shows once a week and dances on the weekends. "They used to turn the generator off at 11 o'clock at night," said Carole, "So one night we decided we'd have a dance and we'd get the superintendent's wife to go, figuring he wouldn't shut off the power if his wife was there. We figured that if she was having such a good time, he'd leave the power on. But no such luck. Off it would go at at 11 o'clock."

Carole's mother opened a cafe in the community hall towards the end of 1953, serving hamburgers, soda pop, chocolate bars and "stuff like that," said Carole. It became a popular hangout, especially for the single men in the bunkhouses. "It was something for them to do rather than sit in camp," said Bunty. "Where, if you're married there, you've got a family to go to."

The one-room schoolhouse at the Muchalat Camp at Jacklah River went up to grade 8.

Photo courtesy of Del and Inez Birtch.

Relocating the Townsite

Tahsis Company's application for Tree Farm License #19 was approved by the provincial government in 1954.[14] In January, 1955, the Muchalat camp was moved across the inlet to the mouth of the Gold River. The company had run out of timber in the Muchalat Inlet area and was anxious to start logging up the Gold River Valley. "Gold River was the big thing," said Bunty. "There was a lifetime of timber up there."

But there was also a major stumbling block in the way, one that eventually cost Tahsis Company millions of dollars to remove. In order to gain access to the timber supply in the interior, a road had to be pushed through from the inlet. And in order to build the road, they had to cut through several miles of narrow, rock-walled canyon in the spectacularly beautiful but almost impenetrable Gold River Valley. "There was no way through it," said Des Stewart. "They had to blast all that rock and make that road to get to the timber in the valley here. And it took them a couple of years to get through it."

The road was in place by the time the Muchalat camp had been moved across from Jacklah River to the flat open land just up from the water's edge. The houses were towed across on floats and jacked up onto logs at their new sites. Except for a new location, life in the logging camp remained pretty much the same. Carole's

Building the road through the Gold River Valley required blasting through several miles of the narrow rock-walled canyon.   Village of Gold River.

mother re-opened her cafe in the community hall, and started a general store. Social activities continued to play an important role in the community and they were still, as Carole says, "like one big happy family."

Today, two water towers at the edge of the pulp mill are the last reminders of the Beach Camp. When the camp was closed to make way for the pulp mill, the buildings were put on skids and towed to other areas along the coast. A few of the houses went to Tahsis while others, including the original Muchalat camp schoolhouse, were sent to what was to become Tahsis Company's main logging camp at Fair Harbor. The general office was moved up to the new townsite and turned into a clubhouse which was shared by several groups, including the Golf and Country Club, the Lions, and so on. The community hall and general store complex was

The Muchalat logging camp was moved from Jacklah River to Gold River in 1955. Above, houses are towed across the inlet and

dismantled and moved up to a site just below Dogwood Drive where it was used for several years as - what else? - a community hall and local movie house.

The move from the logging camp to the new townsite was somewhat more complicated than the move from Jacklah River to the mouth of the Gold River. When the camp was first moved, residents kept their original homes, whereas moving from the Beach Camp into the town meant not only moving into a new house, but having to purchase that house as well. Tahsis Company attempted to ease the financial burden, somewhat, by arranging low downpayments and interest-free second mortgages, and agreeing to repurchase the house at any time during the first five years. "I think it was quite a deal when we moved up here," said Bunty. "We only paid five hundred *[dollars]* down on this place, and they paid the full mortgage for the first year, half of the mortgage for the second year, and gave us the property after staying here five years."

Accustomed to company housing and low monthly rents, the decision to buy a house was a major one for most Beach Camp residents. For the Sinclairs, it meant going from twenty-five dollars a month in rent to one hundred and nineteen dollars in monthly mortgage payments: "Thinking it over," said Bunty. "I thought, 'Well, now even at that there's no place I can get a four-bedroom home, anywhere, for my family for anything close to that.' So when I came into this place, I didn't care whether I made money on it or lost it, it was just cheap rent. As it turned out, it increased its value."

"When we moved up here," said Gail. "My husband said 'Don't go putting any nails in the walls because we might not stay.' This instant town he wasn't sure of. And going into a big house, he just didn't know whether we could afford it either."

After the project was first announced, company officials and the project designers held a series of general meetings at the community hall. "We were all very well informed," says Doug. The Beach Camp families were given first choice of lots in the Dogwood Drive area, and could choose from three basic house designs, ranging in size from two- to four-bedrooms. Everything was done by paper: lots and houses were selected from architects' drawings, and residents took home pamphlets of paint samples and tile colors. And sometimes, what you saw wasn't quite what you got:

put on skids.

Photos courtesy of Del and Inez Birtch.

"This house actually is backwards on the lot," said Betty. "Our back door is really supposed to be our front door."

What might have looked good on paper had to be modified in practice. Given the rocky terrain and limited amount of space suitable for construction, plans for service alleys running behind the houses - a decidedly urban characteristic - were scratched in order to give residents larger backyards. Many of the houses in the Dogwood area were, inexplicably, placed on the lots backwards, so that the lofty and elegant cathedral entrance faced away from the street and onto the back. The plain and ordinary back doors became front doors, opening into the kitchen instead of the living room. But these stories are told with smiles as residents freely admit to preferring the casualness of the kitchen entry to the more formal cathedral entrance. They've grown to accept what was, at first, a disappointment.

'Instant' Municipality

Under the 'instant town' legislation, Gold River was governed by an interim council of one Reeve and five councillors, all of whom were appointed by the government. The official papers were issued August 26, 1965. Swearing-in ceremonies were held in the old community hall on September 2, 1965 and were presided over by the distinguished magistrate, Roderick Haig-Brown, from Campbell River. Taking the oath were the newly appointed Reeve, Bruce Chisholm, a mill engineer working out of Tahsis Company's Vancouver office, and councillors Frank Grobb, manager of operations, sawmill and services division; Donald Kilpatrick, assistant to the president of Tahsis Company; William Tymchuk, woods foreman; William Forde, logging superintendent; and Mae Stewart, housewife and wife of the assistant woods foreman. Of the six, two were non-residents and a third, Mr. Chisholm, moved to Gold River once housing construction had been completed in Area B of the townsite.

The town's official dedication came a few days later on September 8th, when Dan Campbell, then Minister of Municipal Affairs, formally presented the town charter to the first council. On that same day, the Minister of Lands and Forests, Ray Williston, ceremoniously began construction of the pulp facility by pouring the first yard of concrete in the mill's foundation.

Gold River was originally incorporated as a district municipality in order to take advantage of anticipated growth and expansion to a population of 5,000. The town later re-incorporated January 1, 1972 as a village municipality to reflect smaller population size.

The first council for the new town of Gold River was sworn in on September 2, 1965. Shown in the photo above are Bruce Chisholm, Donald Kilpatrick, Mae Stewart, Bill Forde and William Tymchuck. The Honorable Dan Campbell, Minister of Municipal Affairs, is second from right. George Allen Aerial Photos. Village of Gold River.

Roderick Haig-Brown (left), distinguished magistrate from Campbell River, congratulates Bruce Chisholm, Gold River's first Reeve. George Allen Aerial Photos, 1965. Village of Gold River.

As with any change, the transition was at times difficult, although in the beginning, the Beach Camp community managed to maintain a certain amount of cohesiveness. "It might have been 'instant,' but it was still basically all the same people from down at the Beach," said Gail. The old community hall was moved up to a site just below Dogwood Drive, and while the shopping center was under construction, it held the co-op store and post office, a branch of the Port Alberni Credit Union, and a small library. Along with the building came many of the same traditions which kept the Beach Camp together: movies, Saturday night socials, and recreational activities. Anne Fiddick remembers the Christmas concert as being one event in particular which, year after year, manages to bring the whole community together: "It was the same in the Beach Camp," she said. "It moved from the Beach Camp up here, and still maintains that community spirit. Because everybody, including the single men who lived in the bunkhouses, came to the Christmas concert. The community hall was just busting at the seams."

But that sense of community closeness only lasted for a couple of years, said Mae. Then it started to drift away as more and more people moved in. A massive influx of pulp mill workers in late 1966 and 1967 had a significant impact on the town, both materially and socially. The population nearly tripled, jumping from a relatively stable core of about 600 to close to 1800, almost overnight. Turnover was

The 'instant' town of Gold River was billed as a "Model Community." Professionally designed by a team of architects, planners and landscapers, it features wide curving streets and tree-lined boulevards.
Village of Gold River.

high - nearly 40 percent, according to one report - and the newcomers had to adjust not only to a strange town, but to neighbors who were themselves newcomers, and to loggers who had already established themselves as the area's first residents.

"Your kids were going to school one year in a one-room little trailer, and the next year they were in a school with all these kids they'd never seen before," said Betty. "It was a shock to everybody. A different way of life. We'd lived in our own little cocoon, and everybody helped everybody, and everybody spoke to everybody. Then all of a sudden, there's all these new people and we don't know any of them."

Initially, there was some tension between the loggers and the pulp mill workers, the "oldtimers" and the "newcomers." Differences in occupation were aggravated by the sudden increase in population and the fact that the loggers and their families lived in their own neighborhood: Dogwood Drive, popularly called "Logger's Row," was located on a small hill at the northeastern edge of town.

"The logging division was their own bunch, and the pulp mill were their own bunch," said Des. "And it took many, many years to break that down. They're a different breed, I'll have to admit. They're a different breed."

"The mill-workers were 'cake-eaters' to us," said Betty. "At one time this whole neighborhood was loggers. And for a cake-eater to move into the logging area was unheard of."

"We figure they got pretty jammy jobs, that's why they're called cake-eaters," said Doug. "So a logger goes into the pub and he'll say 'Any "cake-eaters" in the pub?' It's said mostly in good fun. But every now and again, a couple of guys feeling fairly frisky, looking for a battle, say 'Any "cake-eaters"?' So sometimes it gets a little iffy."

Gradually over the years, as the town stabilized, loggers and millworkers learned to live together. They met over various community issues, joined the same organizations, participated in the same sports. "We used to play hockey and we'd get intermixed with the 'cake-eaters'," said Doug. "They'd be playing on our team, and we actually realized that 'Hey, these are not bad people; we can live with them.'"

There was also some friction within the community over the issue of an appointed council. Four of the six appointees were company executives, and two of those four lived in Vancouver. Concerns were raised over whether or not the council was merely a puppet of the company. "They thought the company had appointed us and that we were working strictly for the company," said Mae. According to one former mayor, it seemed to be a question of attitude. "They accepted things the Tahsis Company proposed without too much argument," said Les Cartwright a few years later. "I don't think the present council would do that."[15]

Gold River was not a company-owned town. But as a single-industry town, it continued to be company-dominated. At the time, Tahsis Company paid $825,000 of the $1 million in taxes the town received annually, and controlled all of the land: the municipality had very little it could call its own, and none for expansion. As one report put it: The company has perhaps played the part of the company father who wants the most for his children, wrote Pete Louden in the *Victoria Daily Times*. "But as most parents come to realize, one day children want to make their own decisions."[16]

Muchalat Arm, 1896. Little is known of the cannery which operated for a few years near the head of Muchalat Inlet. It was most likely built to take advantage of the rich sockeye streams nearby. Edgar Fleming Photo. Royal B.C. Museum, Ethnology Division.

The growing tensions between town and company and between loggers and millworkers came to a head in September, 1968, when the pulp mill went out on strike for ten days. The main issues were town policies and company control. "In the second year, the pulp mill union started rumbling about the way we were carrying on, and what we were doing and such like," said Mae. "So we went back to the government and asked them if we could hold an election. So they opened the letters patent and allowed us to have an election."

The town's first open election was held December 7, 1968, almost a year before the appointed council's four year term was up. There was a 71-per-cent turnout at the polls, "one of the highest" in the province-wide municipal elections that year.[17] All five aldermanic seats were hotly contested, as was the mayoralty race. Three of the original appointees stood for election, and all three were returned: Bruce Chisholm was elected mayor, and incumbents Mae Stewart and Bill Forde were returned to finish out their one-year terms as aldermen. But the top vote-getters were newcomers Gar H. Westlake, and A.T. Lampard, and T.G. Ellwood and Les D. Cartwright: all four were elected to aldermanic seats.

Politics and conflicts were all part of the process during the early years of building the community. The company had built the structures; it was left to the council to fill in the blanks. The town needed health and social services, a police force and a fire department. Budgets, taxes and administrative structures had to be established and by-laws enacted. Decisions had to be made on the installation of water and sewer systems, hydroelectric power, telephones. A Municipal Hall had to be built and streets had to be named. In short, the town had to plunge immediately into the business of operating a municipality.

"Three of us named the streets," said Mae. "The municipal clerk and Bill Tymchuk and myself. We just sat down one night over a cup of coffee and did it."

Looking up Muchalat Arm, 1912.   Provincial Archives of B.C.

Streets were named according to three themes: in the westerly section of town it was trees; in the easterly section, Native Indians, and in the center, birds. "We were all at Bill Tymchuk's house and we couldn't come up with one final name of a bird. We had a terrible time, and of course, you get silly after awhile," said Mae. "Bill's wife was out in the kitchen, making coffee and dessert for us, and she started singing that song, 'Hummingbird Lane.' So she was the one who named that street!"

As the town grew, so too did the need for more and more recreational activities and facilities. Groups and organizations proliferated, from exercise classes to church auxiliaries to basketball leagues. Almost overnight, the number of groups mushroomed to a high of more than twenty-five in the late 1960s. And they flourished. Memberships were large and interest was keen during those early, formative years.

The organizations fulfilled vital needs in the community. The Take-A-Break Club, for example, was a women's group which organized crafts, guest speakers, films, and discussions. It met once a week and provided free babysitting, giving women a break from their daily routine and an opportunity to meet other people. With the opening of the road to Campbell River and increased employment opportunities for women, interest began to wane until the group eventually disbanded. In 1987, a version of the Take-A-Break Club was revived under the auspices of the Rainbow Society, again with a mandate to provide a variety of services to women.

Close-up of the Tahsis Company Ltd. pulp mill at Gold River, 1967.

Village of Gold River.

Another long-lasting group which got its start in 1968 and continues to play a key role in the community today, is the Rod and Gun Club. Once formed, the group immediately undertook the construction of a hand-built, log-style clubhouse which opened in early 1971. Bert Donovan, writing in the *Gold River Record* in 1973, describes the lodge as a rustic building with great charm: "The Gold River rushes through the backyard and trees tower skyward all around, like dark sentinels. There is none of the slickness of factory manufactured objects which we find in modern buildings. Everything is hand-made out of raw materials. Labor and skills were volunteered and the only reward for the immense toil was the love of construction and creation." Upon entering, continued Bert, there is an "unashamedly ugly wood-burning heater, a black monster of welded steel plates with an insatiable appetite for wood."[18]

Those words were to have fateful significance. Fifteen years later, the log cabin was destroyed by fire: a fire that was caused by smoldering coals in the woodstove.

For most residents, the lack of recreational facilities was seen as a serious problem. When first designing the town, architects had included several parks, ballfields, and tennis courts in the community plan. Provision had also been made for a recreation center located on a site adjacent to the shopping plaza. But the town had difficulty coming up with the money needed to build the center: the council was already in debt for construction of the public safety building, housing the municipal hall and the fire and police departments, and was restricted from borrowing any more money until its first loan was paid off. In 1967, the Gold River Golf and Country Club was formed for the immediate purpose of building a curling and ice skating arena. It's long-range plans included a swimming pool, tennis courts, and a 9-hole golf course.

Finally, in the summer of 1969, after several dismal attempts to raise the money locally, Tahsis Company stepped in with an offer to build the arena-curling rink complex, on condition the municipality agreed to take over operations and maintenance of the facility once it was built. It was a deal. The 21,000 square foot arena included facilities for ice skating and hockey, and five sheets of curling ice. As a bonus, the company threw in a $20,000 grant to cover capital and operating costs for the first year.

The arena opened to great fanfare on November 20, 1970, and was to be the nucleus of a much larger recreational facility which now boasts a meeting hall, activity rooms, a lounge, an outdoor swimming pool and, most recently, an indoor pool. In 1987, land was cleared for a 9-hole golf course, the final step in the realization of the Gold River Golf and Country Club's long-range plans.

The process of building the community began in 1965 and continues today. Piece by piece, through local organizations, fund-raising drives, and dedicated volunteers, the town has filled in the blanks. A Legion Hall was built in 1970. An emergency health clinic in 1973, and North Island College established a Gold River center later that same year. Today, a new shopping mall and plans for a multi-use cultural center are signs of the town's continued development.

The community has also enjoyed the benefits of its own, locally-produced newspaper. Established in February, 1968 the first paper, *Between the Gold and the Heber,* was the brainchild of the Reverend Dave McKay, head of the Recreation Commission, his wife Joan, and a small but dedicated group of volunteers. The paper was taken over in 1970 by husband and wife team Bert and Joan Donovan who are credited with successfully establishing the newspaper as a permanent fixture in the community. Re-named *The Gold River Record,* the paper was published twice a month, at first by hand on a secondhand A.B. Dick machine, then later shipped out to Campbell River to be printed as a tabloid. Through the years, other newspapers came and went: *The Gold River Nugget, The Beacon,* and most notably, Tahsis Company's own *The Nootka Sound,* a monthly, tabloid-style newspaper which was published out of the company's Vancouver office from 1968 to 1976. The Donovans retired from the newspaper business in 1986, selling *The Record* to Dave and Miriam Trevis who ran it for a few short months under the name *Nootka News.* In 1987, Gerry and Lesley Hunter took over from the Trevis', renamed the paper *The Record,* and have been running it ever since from the basement of their home in Gold River.

Coming of Age

Gold River "came of age" in 1990 when it celebrated its first twenty-five years as an official municipality. And in coming of age, the town still faces some of the problems it had to deal with when it was newly carved out of the wilderness. Among them is the growing need for land in order to expand and diversify into rural acreages and subdivisions; the constraints of economic dependency on a single industry; the double-edged problem of remoteness and lack of services.

And yet, even as some things remain the same, others change. In 1987, the pulp mill workers and their families marked twenty years in Gold River. Like the loggers who lived at the Beach Camp before the townsite was built, veteran mill workers are bound together by shared experiences of coming to work in a brand-new pulp mill and to live in a brand-new town. Second generation sons (and daughters) have followed their fathers to work in the woods or the mill, and third and fourth generation children attend Gold River schools.

"I think we have a history, but the people in the community don't think they have roots or history," says Mayor Anne Fiddick. "I think we've got the history, I don't think we have the roots. That can only happen over time, and when this community is forty or fifty years old, it will have roots. But the history of the area is important to making people feel that sense of permanency, that sense of circular time. Like, 'I'm here for awhile but it will carry on.' In a young community there's always the sense 'Well, it could be just another ghost town, you know,' in another 'X' number of years. Which makes people reluctant to invest, either commercially or in homes. It makes people unsure about the future of it."

Anne says people need to know that Gold River really does have a history, one that is something to be proud of. "I think people need that pride in community as well. They're proud because it's clean and tidy and is a very nice community to live in, as far as that's concerned," she said. "But you also have to have pride in what came before. There is a history to the community and it's unusual, it's unique, and they can take some pride in it."

As the town comes into its own, another industrial expansion is playing a major role in the community's growth, an expansion which, like the one in 1965, could put Gold River on the map as the hub of Vancouver Island's northwest coast. In September, 1987, Canadian Pacific Forest Products announced construction of a $320 million newsprint mill adjacent to the pulp mill. Also included in the expansion plans was the addition of a new type of pulp-making machine. According to CPFP officials, the new paper mill, with a scheduled start-up of October, 1989, would create 120 permanent jobs and boost Gold River's population by another 600 people.

"Today you don't know hardly anybody any more," said Gail. "It's like any other town. You only know the people around you and who you associate with.

There are so many new faces in town now, you just wonder 'Do they live here or are they from Tahsis?' "

"A population of twenty-five hundred is a good figure to aim for," said Mayor Anne Fiddick. One day soon, Gold River may finally fulfill its planners' expectations of a thriving urban center of 10,000 people.

Notes

1   Interview, Jack Christensen (Vancouver: September 8, 1987).

2   Interview, Henry Funk (West Vancouver: September 4, 1987).

3   Interview, Jim and Anne Fiddick (Gold River: May 12, 1988).

4   Interview, Des and Mae Stewart (Gold River: July 2, 1987).

5   Interview, Doug and Betty Wilson (July 2, 1987).

6   *Vancouver Sun*, July/August 1965.

7   *Vancouver Sun*, (May 25, 1965), p.15.

8   Interview, Bunty and Carole Sinclair (Gold River: July 9, 1987).

9   Interview, Jim and Anne Fiddick (Gold River: May 12, 1988).

10   Interview, Gail Shillito (Gold River: May 4, 1988).

11   Brian White, *The Settlement of Nootka Sound,* (Burnaby: 1972), p. 25.

12   Gordon Gibson, *Bull of the Woods* (Vancouver: 1980), pp. 129-130.

13   Ibid., p. 143.

14   In 1965, Tahsis company was awarded an extension of its Tree Farm License to include an additional 60,000 acres of land, bringing its total coverage to about 458,000 acres, or 185,000 hectares. In 1987, Canadian International Paper, predecessor of Canadian Pacific Forest Products Ltd., reported 200,000 hectares in TFL #19.

15   *Vancouver Sun*, by Neale Adams, (July 7, 1970).

16   *Victoria Daily Times*, (August 22, 1967).

17   *The Nootka Sound,* (December 1968).

18   *The Record*, (June 13, 1973).

North of Nootka Sound lies Kyuquot Sound. Remote, rugged, and sparsely populated, Kyuquot is noted for its natural wilderness. Historically, the impact of logging on Kyuquot Sound has been minimal, the area's remoteness helping to preserve the pristine beaches, waterways, and forests. In recent years, however, as logging companies go farther afield for their trees, Kyuquot Sound has been under siege by the increasing demand for logs and a growing concern on the part of residents about the destruction of their wilderness environment.

Bounded on the north by Brooks Peninsula,[1] a rocky, tree-covered promontory jutting out into the Pacific Ocean, the region encompasses Kyuquot Sound and Checleset Bay, the steep bluffs of the peninsula forming the upper corner of what Captain Cook called Hope Bay, in 1778. Point Breakers, near the entrance to Nootka Sound, formed the southern end of the so-called bay. Solander Island, just off Cape Cook, was a landmark for early European traders who gave the unusually shaped island the name "Split Rock."[2]

Early Contact

By a combination of geography and happenstance, Nootka Sound and not Kyuquot became the center of the European fur trade and subsequent developments. The entrance to Kyuquot Sound is riddled with rocky shoals and reefs. Numerous small islands scattered throughout present an imposing threat to ships seeking sheltered anchorages. Cook, searching for just such a safe harbor, rejected the northern entrance in favor of Nootka, in the south. Rough seas and stormy weather prevented him from sailing north. "As I could not fetch up the first I bore up for the latter," he noted in his journal.[3]

James Strange, aboard one of the first trading ships on the coast, offers this description of the coastline near "Woody Point," as Cook named the forbidding peninsula. "The aspect of the Coast as we approached it, was by no means flattering; its appearance was both bleak and Rugged. We frequently sounded during the day, but found no Bottom with a line of 180 Fathoms...."[4]

During Strange's stay in Nootka Sound, he sent an exploring party northwards towards Woody Point to determine the extent of the trade in sea otter pelts. Alexander Walker was a member of the expedition which travelled up the coast on July 13, 1786. "We weathered a ridge of Rocks, and entered a large opening, of which the ridge forms the South East boundary. Upon entering, we discovered, that we had gotten into a considerable Sound, which afforded good Anchorage, and secure cover...."[5]

He offered a word of caution to other sailing vessels, who "must be careful to keep close in with the East Point, as several Rocks lie on the opposite shore; but these are easily avoided, as they appear above-Water... On the East side are several Bays, forming commodious and safe Harbours: On the west side are many small Islands."[6]

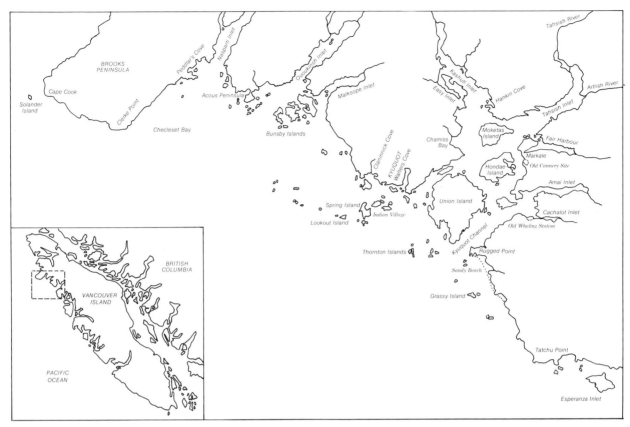

Kyuquot and Checleset Bay.

From Margaret Sharcott: *Place of Many Winds* (1960), pg. 1.

Once past the reefs, Walker was so impressed with the Sound that he called it "Safe-anchorage Sound," a short-lived and little known name. However: "Between Safe-anchorage and Nootka Sounds there are many Reefs of Rocks, that run a considerable way into the Sea, and there are multitudes of sunken Rocks, which render the Navigation dangerous even for Boats."

Thus, during the initial period of contact, Nootka Sound, and not Kyuquot, became an important center of the maritime fur trade on the North Pacific coast. Maquinna controlled the trade by acting as the agent or middle man between the fur traders and Indian hunters. Written accounts and journals from this period note that Maquinna would prevent other Native groups from dealing directly with the European and American traders. Walker notes that by the middle of July during their time in port, the Nootka Sound Natives, having exhausted their stock of furs, made several trips to the south and the north, returning with a fresh supply of the rich pelts. "Strangers were never entirely excluded from trading with us, but this was only done with the permission of the Inhabitants of Friendly Village. The treatment these gave, to their Northern and Southern Neighbours, was exceedingly different. The former were not allowed to trade with us directly, but had to use some inhabitant of Nootka as an agent. Those who came from the south, on the other hand, could sell their own goods directly to the traders."[7]

It's likely that the Indian groups living in Kyuquot Sound and Checleset Bay supplied their furs to the Nootka Sound groups, at least initially. Walker says that on his exploratory trip northward they encountered a party of Nootka Sound Natives returning south. "We told them whither we were going, and they advised us not to proceed farther; as they had just come from the same pursuit, and had been able to procure nothing, but a few small pieces of Fur, north."[8]

Walker says the meeting was "proof of a communal intercourse existing of considerable extent." Esteban José Martínez, the Spanish commandant of the fort at Friendly Cove, notes that the Nootkas traded with the Caiyuquat *(Kyuquot)* and Chiachsult *(Checleset)* groups to the north,[9] as does Jewitt who refers to the Cay-u-quets *(Kyuquots)*.[10]

Later, arriving in Kyuquot Sound, Walker describes the people as being poorer than their neighbors to the south. "They had disposed of all their Skins to the People of Friendly Harbour," he writes, "but attended us all Day endeavoring to dispose of their fish, tho' they had neither the variety nor plenty of fish, to which we had been accustomed at Nootka." He adds that he seemed to recognize some of the people, possibly from their visits to Friendly Cove.[11]

Despite heavy marine traffic along the coast during the late 18th Century, records dealing with Kyuquot Sound are relatively scarce. Vessels generally made their way directly to Nootka, concerned less with exploration than with profit. The marine charts of the day show sketchy details of the coastline between Esperanza Inlet and Brooks Peninsula, indication that traders had little interest in the northern sound.[12]

Later, as tension over the Spanish occupation of Nootka Sound grew, American vessels began frequenting Checleset Bay. Martínez, sent from San Blas to take charge of the Spanish fort at Friendly Cove, in 1789, was given orders to treat Russian and British vessels with "tact and civility."[13] American traders, on the other hand, were not given the same courtesy: "you may use more powerful arguments with the subjects of the independent American colonies..." He is told to take "any steps that may seem practicable and convenient" to let them know that Spain had control of the coast.[14]

By the same token, the American traders were warned to steer clear of the Spanish. Captain John Kendrick of the ship *Columbia* was ordered to avoid Spanish occupations during his voyage to the Pacific Ocean, in 1787. "You are strictly enjoined not to touch at any part of the Spanish dominions on the western continent of America, unless driven there by some unavoidable accident...."[15]

The voyage of the *Columbia* and the *Washington,* in 1787, was the first trading expedition to the northwest coast launched by the Americans. They left Boston with Kendrick in command of the *Columbia* and Captain Robert Gray in charge of the *Washington.*

In the course of their travels along the coast, in May 1789, winds drove the *Columbia* into Hope Bay, "a place called by the Natives Checleset where there is every appearance of a good harbor."[16] The crew was told of an Indian village about two leagues to the east called Cauquot, which was likely the name of the local group site from which the name Kyuquot was eventually taken. The ship did not remain long enough on that first visit to do any exploring, leaving at daybreak the next day to continue on its journey north.

Two years later, the *Columbia* returned for a more extensive examination of the area. Journals kept by Robert Haswell, John Hoskins and John Boit, provide us with some of the first written accounts of Checleset Bay and Kyuquot Sound. On June 20, 1791, the *Columbia* anchored in a small cove off the entrance to Nasparti Inlet near what is now called Jakobsen Point. "Thus situated we are entirely landlocked in an excellent harbour on the west side of the Sound," wrote Hoskins, "This harbor was named Columbia's Cove; but we were afterwards informed by the Natives that they call it Naspahtee."[17]

What we now know as Nasparti Inlet, the Americans named Bulfinch's Sound, in honor of Dr. Thomas Bulfinch, a prominent Boston physician. "The land about the sound is high and mountainous; well-covered with trees to its summits..." writes Hoskins. "The only inhabited part of the Sound is the small village on the eastern side, called Opswis; which I suppose contains about twenty or thirty inhabitants: no doubt, various other parts of the sound are occasionally inhabited; as they appear to have no abiding place; but move about as fancy or inclination suggests. The head village is in the next sound, where the Chief resides, and is the one I visited; it is situated on an island...at the bottom of a small bay or cove; the village consists of about thirty houses; which contain between two and three hundred inhabitants. besides this, there are two or three other villages scattered about the sound; whether they are subject to the same Chief or not, I don't know."[18]

On the 22nd, sent to explore the immediate coast, Haswell discovered that the main village was located in the next inlet, but the rocky shoals and reefs in the bay prevented him from approaching it.[19] Instead, he returned up the inside coast, stopping to visit a small village called Opsowis on the eastern side of Nasparti Inlet.[20]

Two days later, Hoskins embarked on a visit to the head village, paying close attention to the sunken rocks and narrow passages noted by Haswell. "I was received at my landing by the old Chief, who conducted me, with Mr. Smith, to his house," wrote Hoskins, "He seated us by a good fire; offered us to eat and drink of the best the house afforded; which was dried fish of various sorts, roasted clams and mussels; water was our drink, handed in a wooden box, with a large sea clam shell to drink out of...

"After this entertainment, we were greeted with two songs... These were sung by a grate concourse of Natives, who came from all parts of the village to see us, for it is very probable we are the first white people that ever was at their village, and the first many of them ever saw."[21]

But at some point during what appears to have been a pleasant and friendly visit, Hoskins and his crew sensed a shift in the mood. Growing suspicious of their hosts' intentions, Hoskins quickly returned to the boat, admonishing his crew "not to show the least signs of fear."[22] Beating a hasty return to Columbia's Cove, the ship weighed anchor at dawn on the 26th.

Gray later planned to winter at Columbia's Cove but bad weather and strong winds forced him to turn back, and he spent the winter further south, in Gray's Harbor off Clayoquot Sound.

Relations between the American traders and the northern Indian groups were often uneasy and fraught with tension. On May 29th, 1792, fighting between the Indians and the crew of the *Columbia* left several Native Indians dead and others wounded. Hoskins reports that, according to Captain Gray, the ship was attacked by the Natives, forcing the crew to kill "a neat number of them."

The Indians have a very different account of the attack. According to the Spanish records, on June 3, 1792, several Indians from up the coast arrived at Friendly Cove seeking the assistance of Bodega y Quadra, then commandant at Nootka. They said the Americans had attacked their village, killing seven people and wounding others. The Indians said they had been unable to agree with Captain Gray on a price for their sea otter pelts. The Captain had then fired upon the village and taken the skins by force.[23]

Gray and the *Columbia* weren't the only ones to engage in battle with the Checleset and Kyuquot Sound Indians. Later that same summer, Joseph Ingraham on the *Hope* entered Kyuquot Sound on his way south from the Queen Charlotte Islands. "Never neglecting an opportunity to obtain a sea otter skin," says F.W. Howay, Ingraham made his way up the interior waterways of Kyuquot Sound, stopping to trade at one or two villages along the way.

Howay, who edited Ingraham's journal, goes on to say that "He seems to have been suspicious of the Natives, for his first step on entering was to seize two of them as hostages, an action which he does not appear to have taken in any other place."[24]

Whether this action or some other incident triggered the Indians' anger is not clear, for there are no written accounts of the Indians' version of the event: we have only one side of the story. According to Ingraham, fifteen large canoes filled with Indians in regular battle array bore down upon the *Hope*. Warning shots apparently went unheeded and Ingraham fired upon the canoes which then turned back across the bay. Abandoning all hope of trading, Ingraham set sail for Nootka.

The difficulty with interpreting the reports of violence and aggression is that we usually only get the European side of the story. We do not know what may or may not have been done to provoke the attacks and battles, nor do we know who initiated them. The Natives were quite likely defending themselves against the very real threat of the larger, better-armed trading vessels. Clearly, when it came to force, the British and the Americans were in a dominant position.

The *Columbia* and the *Adventure* returned to Nasparti two more times before leaving the westcoast in September, 1792, for their final voyage back to the east coast. They used Nasparti to make repairs to their boats and on both occasions found the Native people to be quite cheerful and amiable. Today, the fact that the first white ship in the area went to Ououkinsh (Checleset) is a well-accepted fact in Kyuquot, says Susan Kenyon in her study of the Kyuquot. "The Checleset people still claim details of these stories as their private property and celebrate them in potlatches and song," she notes in *The Kyuquot Way*.[25]

The Checlesets

Two groups of Indians inhabited the region north of Nootka Sound. From Cape Cook to the top end of Kyuquot Sound lived the Checleset group with villages and fishing sites in the Nasparti, Ououkinsh and Malksope Inlets. According to Phillip Drucker, the Checlesets were a single tribe with one winter village at Acous (ai'qo'as) near Battle Bay. By the late 1880s, their summer site at Opsowis (apsuwis) had become the group's permanent year-round village.

The Checlesets had several fishing stations on the major salmon spawning rivers, including the Ououkinsh and the Malksope. Kenyon says the sites were located at Hisnit (Power Lake), Mahope, Ououkinsh, Owas, and Malsope.[26] Several other temporary sites for halibut fishing, sealing, and fishing were located along the outer coast when necessary. Along with the Kyuquot, the Checlesets shared certain rights with the Nuchatlaht and Ehattesaht to fish for dentalia at Tachu Point near the entrance to Esperanza Inlet.[27] More recently, a detailed archaeological survey of the coastline between Esperanza Inlet and Brooks Peninsula shows hundreds of other sites used by the west coast tribes for fishing and food gathering.[28]

An overland trail across Brooks Peninsula connected the Checleset with their Kwa'kwa'la-speaking neighbors to the north. The Checlesets were once bilingual, says Kenyon, and they mixed regularly with the Klaskino, Quatsino, Koskimo, and Gopino groups on the other side of the peninsula. And, in 1888, the Reverend Lemmons reports attending a potlatch to which the Checlesets had invited their northern neighbors and spoke courteously to them in their own language.

Kenyon, who lived in Kyuquot for several months while researching her book, was told that the Checlesets were "all one big family in the old days. They had only one chief who was head over all and the others were just heads of where they came from." They were apparently well-respected by their neighbors and noted for their independence and aggressiveness, particularly in contrast to their peace-loving

Kyuquot neighbors: "Today it is still the Checleset people who are known for the best war stories in the area," writes Kenyon.[29]

The Checlesets began moving down to Kyuquot after the opening of the commercial fish camps there. At first, they only came down during the summer fishing season, returning to their homes at the beginning of fall. Later, in the mid-1930s, they started staying year-round so their children could attend school. By this time, there was no longer a school in the Checleset area. Most services, including the school, a store, and medical facilities were located in Kyuquot, the main center of economic activity.

The last of the Checlesets moved down to Kyuquot in the 1950s, temporarily abandoning their former home to the wilds of the rainforest. They were given house sites on Mission Island and the two bands formally amalgamated in 1963.[30]

"They pooled their finances and reserves and now share an elected band council," wrote Kenyon in 1982. "Both peoples, however, continue to have their own hereditary chiefs and traditional property rights and they continue to distinguish themselves in terms of their former, rather than contemporary, band affiliation whenever possible."[31]

Little evidence remains of the Checlesets' ancestral homes, although they

One of two human figures remaining at the old village site of Opsowis. Royal B.C. Museum, Ethnology Division.

still retain rights to their original fishing sites and villages. Margaret Sharcott, long-time Kyuquot resident and author of *Place of Many Winds,* describes the abandoned and overgrown villages she and her husband encountered on their many trips along the coast in the 1950s and '60s.

Of Malksope she writes: "We headed for the narrow channel between Malksope and Ououkinsh Inlet where the Kyuquot people had told us that we would find an Indian village and strong, well-made wooden floats." The tiny cove was protected on one side by the Bunsby Islands, on the other by the mountains of Vancouver Island. "At the head of the floats we saw the Indian village known as Hollywood *[probably the old village of Opsowis].* It consisted of three shacks, unoccupied then, used only in the winter months when their owners tended traplines in the surrounding bush."[32]

In the tiny village, they found once-lush gardens, now overgrown, as well as apple and plum tress in a neglected orchard. "At the top of the creek bank, a wooden flume swayed through the bush on rotting poles. Once the houses had had water piped from the upper creek to their doorsteps. Now the flume was broken and to all appearances no one had repaired it in years."

Hidden in the overgrown bushes were two old totem poles: "Small carved figures, standing only about five feet high, they were so ancient that huckleberry

Human figure at the old village site of Opsowis.
Royal B.C. Museum, Ethnology Division.

bushes sprouted from the head of one. They were unpainted except for traces of red pigment, grey with age and weatherbeaten. An old-timer at Kyuquot told us they had once depicted a male and a female figure. 'No need to guess as to which was which either,' he chuckled."

When Sharcott asked about the figures, she was told that they had once been corner posts in a lodge. "When the old cedar board communal dwellings were replaced with modern shacks, the totems were set outside," she says.[33]

The Sharcotts discovered other carved figures in their wanderings up the coast: at the long-deserted village of Opsowis they found one small totem pole still standing, and the carved figure of a bear, laying on the ground: "No one lives at this village now," writes Margaret Sharcott, "And according to old Indian custom it would take another feast to move the carvings to another village."[34]

Today, the Checleset people are still strong and their culture is still alive. Although few people live year-round in their traditional territory, they continue to maintain strong links to their ancestral homelands through seasonal fishing, hunting, and food gathering.

"The Checlesets like to be remembered as great songsters, people who made up the best songs on the Coast and traded them all over the place," writes Kenyon, "They remember their home up west as being the most beautiful of places with lots of daffodils in spring (unusual in this area) and wild lilies, sunflowers, thrift and other blooms in summer; with water so fresh that one drank it on the spot; with herring eggs or blackberries so abundant that they never lacked them; and where nobody was ever in need."[35]

The Kyuquot

The Kyuquot confederacy was probably the oldest and the most stable of confederacies along the coast, according to Kenyon. Earlier fieldwork suggests that the Kyuquot was a large grouping of four tribes composed of fourteen local groups, each named after the salmon stream it owned.[36] Their winter villages were at Markale (maxqet), Chamiss Bay (ca'wispa), (Cachalot) qwixqo, and Houpsitas, site of the present-day village. During the summer, the four tribes came together at Actis on Village Island.

"There were 27 houses on Actis remembered by informants," writes Kenyon, "Each of the houses of the winter villages was supposed to have been erected at the summer village, duplicating even the carvings of posts and beams. The houses at Actis were said to have been arranged in a single row along the beach, with but two in a second row behind the first."[37]

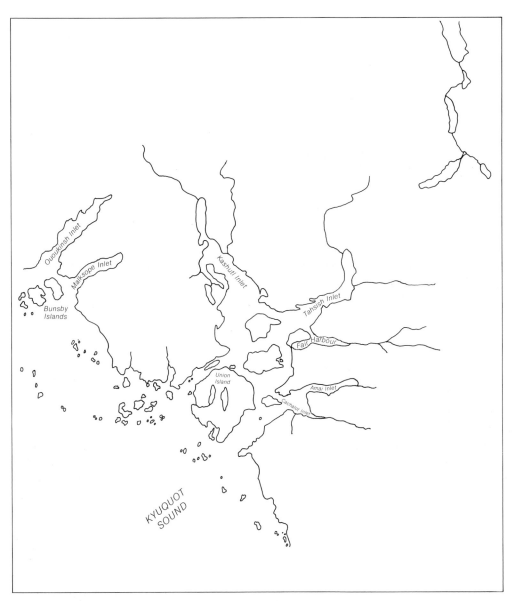

Traditional Kyuquot and Chelcleset area.

With the advent of the dogfish oil trade and the sealing industry, Actis, originally the summer home of the Kyuquot, became a year-round base. Trading ships and sealing schooners stopped off at the village on their way up the coast - the one to buy dogfish and shark oil, the other to take on seal hunters for the Bering Sea. By the end of the 19th century, most people were spending summer and winter at Actis, with each local group given land on which to build a house.

"Actis, a windswept island situated near the outer waters, is regarded as the more traditionally oriented point of the Indian community and is also the most isolated," notes Kenyon.[38]

When Kenyon first visited Kyuquot, in 1972, about twenty houses were still standing on the sheltered inner beach: "The buildings stretch along the shore in virtually a single line," she writes, "The houses all face the water and the mainland, and a well-trodden path, running just below the houses and at the top of the beach, connects them together. A second pathway runs behind some of the houses, ending at the school and church."[39]

In 1805, John Jewitt wrote that the Kyuquot were a "much more numerous tribe than that of Nootka,"[40] and he estimated their population to be about 2,000. Sixty years later, in 1865, Lieutenant Hankin from the survey ship *H.M.S. Hecate,* put the population at between seven and eight hundred, a figure which corresponds to Father Brabant's calculations a few years later. According to Brabant and Father Lemmons, the resident priest at Kyuquot, Kyuquot's population went from 800, in 1874, to 430 in 1897. By the early 1900s it had dropped even lower: to 257, in 1906, and to 124 in 1925.[41] Smallpox, measles, and venereal diseases had taken their disturbing toll.

"Older people in Kyuquot recall with nostalgia the Actis of their youth, around 1920," writes Kenyon, "Then, it is claimed, the Village was a large and lively place, with as many as 1,000 people staying there and more than 40 houses occupied."[42]

Houpsitas

Thirty minutes away from Actis, by small motor boat, is the present-day community of Houpsitas. Situated on the mainland of Vancouver Island, the brand-new

Village of Actis, circa 1910.   Royal B.C. Museum, Ethnology Division.

Sealing schooner anchored off Indian village at Kyuquot.   Provincial Archives of B.C.

village faces Walter's Cove, the predominantly white fishing community located on a tiny island at the entrance to Kyuquot Sound.

Houpsitas is the traditional winter village of the La'a'ath people of the Kyuquot confederacy, and has been continuously occupied by a handful of families since before the time of European contact. In the 1970s, the village was expanded as more families began moving to Houpsitas in order to be closer to the commercial center of Walter's Cove. In 1972, there were about ten homes at Houpsitas. By 1974, they had more than doubled in number. The Band had purchased fourteen new homes from the Navy, trucked them from Vancouver to Fair Harbor, and floated them down to Houpsitas.

"When more new homes were purchased for the band, the rest of the Houpsitas reserve land was cleared of forest and a band meeting held to determine the ownership and composition of sites," Kenyon writes, "I was told that this was done on a first-come, first-served basis. Priority was given to sites with a view of the sea and near the beach."[43]

The last of the people moved from Actis to Houpsitas in 1974. The school, which had operated since the mid-1950s, was closed down and the few children remaining at Actis were sent to attend school with the white children at Walter's Cove. That summer, many of the old houses and buildings on Actis were torn down. Abandoned and left to rot, the Band Council decided it was unsafe to leave them standing. Not everyone agreed. One man criticized the Council's decision: "Houses are like people, he felt, or like anything else in this world; they should be allowed to die in peace and dignity and not deliberately be disposed of."[44]

Today, Actis is still considered the main village of the Kyuquot. Although only a few houses remain on the flat, windswept shore, people talk of one day returning to live in their traditional homes. Many have already returned. Nonetheless, Houpsitas and Walter's Cove are now the modern hub of Kyuquot Sound.

Roman Catholic Mission

In 1880, a Roman Catholic Mission was established in Kyuquot. The Mission of St. Marc was located on Kamils Island, also known as Mission Island and Graveyard Island, just off the village of Actis on Village Island. Father Peter Joseph Nicolaye, 36 years old, took charge of the Mission in September of that year.

The first visit by missionaries was in April, 1874 when Father Brabant, along with Bishop Seghers, stopped in at Kyuquot as part of their survey of the west coast. While in Kyuquot, they baptized 177 children and erected a 24-foot cross on Kamils Island. The cross was constructed out of wood by the Swedish mate of Captain Spring's trading ship the *Favorite:*

"It was placed on three canoes and about 50 young men took charge," writes Father Brabant in his journal, "An immense number of Indians followed us in canoes to the foot of a small island opposite the shore, then unoccupied and seemingly abandoned. And there it now stands in sight of the tribe."[45]

During that same trip up the coast, Brabant and Seghers visited the Checleset at Acous where they baptized 46 children. Returning to Kyuquot later that year, Brabant notes that they made their headquarters in the "old and unoccupied store" belonging to Captain Spring. The store was most likely used seasonally during the dogfish and shark oil trade.

By 1878, Brabant was making plans to establish a permanent mission base at Kyuquot. On August 28, 1879, he went to Kyuquot for the express purpose of "feeling the pulse" of the people over the idea of stationing a priest in the area. "The Chief not only told me that he was anxious to have a resident priest but he promised

Village on Kamils Island, 1894. Freeman photo.   Provincial Archives of B.C., Newcombe Collection.

to grant all the land required for the use of the missionary, free of charge," writes Brabant, "Other important men also spoke and expressed their happiness at the idea of having a chance to have their children properly educated. My opinion of the Kyuquots is that it will be hard to manage the old people. As regards the boys and girls, of whom there are hundreds, I consider it to be the very finest Mission. Not only on the Island, but in the diocese."[46]

An inventory lists the Mission of St. Marc as consisting of a church and school, a three-room house for the priest, a hospital, and various outbuildings including a stable and a chicken house. Two orchards of fruit trees, five head of cattle, one goat, a cat, a dog, and a canary rounded out the Mission's tiny settlement.[47]

The first school opened August 6th, 1883, in a classroom at the back of the church building. Father Lemmons reported that the school had a regular attendance of about 40 children, although it must have been a tight fit: According to the inventory, although the school had "a full set of books and slates," it only had eight writing desks.

Father J.N. Lemmons took over as resident priest from Father Nicolaye on August 1, 1883. Nicolaye remained at the Mission, but he spent a great deal of his time in the field. Kyuquot Mission served a large region which included the Checleset, Nuchatlaht, and Ehattesaht territories. Nicolaye would often spend several weeks at a time visiting the various other centers. A resident priest was stationed in Kyuquot until 1911, after which it was served from the Christie Residential School at Kakawis on Meares Island near Hesquiat.

At some point during the 1880s, Father Nicolaye staked village lots on the land adjacent to the mission. Here, families with children attending school, could build houses on the island. "These were the new, small one-roomed homes," says Kenyon, "So much commended by Church and government officials, and intended to replace the traditional big house which was still in use at this period."[48] When the Church closed at the end of the nineteenth century, the population of Mission Island declined. Later, when the Checlesets moved down from the north, the Kyuquot gave them places to live on Mission Island.

At the beginning of the twentieth century, a new resident priest arrived in Kyuquot and another church was rebuilt on a new site in Actis, on Village Island. In the 1940s, a third church was built, although there is some confusion over the details. According to a report by the Christie Residential School, the church was erected, in 1941, by Father Sorenson in the name of St. James. Kenyon, however, says the church, which is still standing, was built in 1945 and was dedicated to St. Michael. A new schoolhouse was built next to the new church at around the same time and was opened, in 1949, by the Department of Indian Affairs under the guidance of Mrs. George Green whose husband operated a logging camp in the area.

The 1920s and '30s are remembered as one of the most difficult periods in Kyuquot's history, says Kenyon. There was a concerted effort to Christianize the Indians: to eliminate their old ways and force them to learn the new. Children were removed from their homes - sometimes forcibly - and sent to the Christie Indian Residential School, far from home, where they were forbidden to speak their own language or practice their culture.

"Today," says Kenyon, "Older people who grew up in this atmosphere are puzzled by the enthusiasm whites express for the traditional Indian culture. 'Now it's crazy,' said one man, 'They are trying to bring everything back, culture, language, after taking it all away from us.' "[49]

Dogfish Oil and Sealing

The advent of a brisk and lucrative dogfish oil trade and the rise of the fur sealing industry had direct economic and social impact on Kyuquot. It became a regular port of call for the various traders and small sailing schooners engaged in trading along the west coast. William Eddy Banfield and his partner, Peter Francis, were among the first to take advantage of the region's commercial potential during this period. Banfield and Francis were independent merchants and traders based in Clayoquot. They operated sailing schooners which traded along the west coast of Vancouver Island in the mid-1800s. In 1855, they opened a second trading post at Kyuquot where they purchased dogfish oil from the Indians.

"The oil procured from this colony is procured from the Native tribes inhabiting the west coast of Vancouver's Island, and is manufactured by them from the whale and dogfish," wrote Governor James Douglas in 1855. "It is of excellent quality, and has a high character in California where it brings from two to three dollars a gallon..."[50]

The Indians began spending their summers fishing for dogfish and harpooning mud sharks, processing the oil themselves for sale to the traders, who in turn sold it to the Hudson's Bay Company.

Banfield's trading post on Mission Island was short-lived. Their storekeeper, Peter Cornelius - nicknamed "Barney" - was killed, along with three Kyuquot men, in an attack by Clayoquots off Estevan Point. As there are few records of this period, it is difficult to determine whether or not Barney was ever replaced.

The fur sealing industry employed men from Kyuquot as hunters aboard sailing schooners in the Bering Sea.   Provincial Archives of B.C.

In the 1860s, Captain William Spring entered the west coast trade with the vessels *Alert, Surprise* and *Favorite*. Spring was well known on the coast as he provided the only reliable means of communication with the outside world. Spring became involved in the sealing industry in the late 1860s and was the first to successfully engage Native Indians as hunters. Schooners would stop at the Indian villages along the coast to take on Native hunters and their canoes. The hunters were often gone three to four months at a stretch while the sealing fleet went down to northern California to meet the northbound herds, follow them up the coast to the Bering Sea, and then down to the coast of Japan.[51] Schooners carried ten to fifteen canoes at a time, with crews of up to 30 Indians. Since two or three schooners could get a crew from each village, they often competed for the best spearman of the tribe.

An entry in Father Lemmons journal for January 15th, 1885, provides a glimpse into the nature of the sealing industry: "Mr. Spring proposed to give $2.50 for a large seal skin. The Natives come to the conclusion not to go out sealing at all. February - Busy times with herring spawn. Speeches are made at every *makmas* gathering not to seal for less than $5... April 3 - News arrives that seal skins are being raised to $4. Some start sealing... May 3 - Mr. Spring arrived per canoe, gave four boxes of biscuits to the Natives of Kyuquot, and left, satisfied that the Indians were willing to go out sealing on a schooner. May 8 - The schooner *Kate* dropped in. Captain Riley got a fresh crew in no time, and off he was on the waves of the ocean. She had about 250 skins."[52] When sealing was outlawed, in 1911, the schooner trade dropped off dramatically.

Cachalot Whaling Station

By the time the sealing industry came to a close, another marine industry, whaling, was already flourishing in Kyuquot Sound. In 1907, Pacific Whaling Co. began construction on the Cachalot Whaling Station at Narrowgut Inlet, since renamed Cachalot Inlet.

The Pacific Whaling Company was established by Sprott Balcom, a pioneer whaler based in Victoria. At the time, whaling licenses in B.C. were restricted and allocated according to specific criteria. According to Robert L. Webb's book on

The Cachalot Whaling Station, operated by The Pacific Whaling Co. from 1907 to 1925, was located in Narrowgut Inlet, since renamed Cachalot.

commercial whaling in the Pacific Northwest, Balcom submitted applications for four sites on the west coast of Vancouver Island, including one called "Rose Harbour" on the northeast side of Catala Island in Esperanza Inlet. His application was complicated by several other contenders vying for sites in Nootka Sound, including William J. Corbett, John O. Townsend, and G. F. Pearson.

In 1905, Balcom was granted a license for a site in Barkley Sound where he built Sechart, his first whaling station. Meanwhile, the government was prepared to accept John O. Townsend's application to build a whaling station at Plumber Harbor in Nootka Sound. Balcom protested, arguing that he had applied first. He immediately submitted plans and specifications for a factory to be built at Esperanza Inlet, and included an $800. cheque to cover the first year's fees.

Balcom was granted his second whaling license in January, 1906. The plant at Esperanza was never built. Instead, Balcom went to Kyuquot: "Just as Sechart was situated close to La Perouse Bank to the southwest and Swiftsure Bank to the southeast, so the Kyuquot site was immediate to even larger shallows, some barely fifteen fathoms deep," says Webb. "The upwelling of currents on these shallows brings nutrients up from the sea floor to the surface, and the invertebrate animals and small schooling fish that make up the food chain provide a vigorous supply of food for visiting filter-feeding baleen whales. The circumstances promised years of good whaling."[53]

Balcom contracted a Norwegian firm which specialized in supplying ships and men to the whaling industry. They built the *Orion,* the first steam "chaser" boat to be used on the coast, and sailed it across from Norway to the west coast of Canada. Many of the Norwegian crew remained in B.C. to work for Balcom and the Pacific Whaling Co.

Whaling at Kyuquot was immediately successful. The first shipment from the 1907 season included 639 barrels of oil and 815 bags of guano from Cachalot. By the end of the summer, in 1911, the Kyuquot harvest totaled 416 whales that season, including 293 humpbacks and 86 giant blues, among others.

J.E. Gilmore was station manager at Cachalot for ten years. In correspondence with the Provincial Archives, he says there were 80 men on the payroll, with Indians comprising about half the crew.[54] The majority of the Indians were from Kyuquot, "living with their families in small houses supplied by the company, they enjoyed their life there, and were good faithful workers."[55]

The few white men employed were managers, foremen, office staff, and skilled tradesmen. "The crews being composed of Indians, Japanese, and Chinese laborers," writes Mr. Gilmore, "The white men consisting of the heads of different departments and crews of whaling steamers (about 50 or 60 all told)." When the cannery was in full operation, the total payroll was over 200.

Gilmore notes that during the first few years of operation "whales were so plentiful that one steamer was able to keep two stations busy (Cachalot and Sechart). She would get enough whales in two or three days to keep one station busy for a week, and would then go to the other and repeat the process; but the practice of killing females with their young depleted the schools rapidly and this plentiful supply lasted for only a couple of years." The total take at Kyuquot was 4,765 whales.

The main products of whaling were oil and fertilizer. The oil was used, initially, as fuel and as an ingredient in lubricants and margarine. After World War I, all oil produced at Cachalot was shipped to Proctor and Gamble in Cincinatti, Ohio for soap products. Fertilizer in the form of guano was sold to California for use on their orange groves.

Meat shortages during World War I prompted an increased marketing campaign, in 1917, to entice the public to buy whale meat. A pamphlet entitled "Whale Meat as Food: Twenty Delicious Whale Meat Recipes, Tried and True" listed such delicacies as Curried Whale Meat on Toast, condensed whale milk, and pickled whale tail. Newspapers also encouraged readers to take advantage of "sea beef" and printed recipes for Whale Stew and Whale Meat Shepherd's Pie. Whale meat, however, was never popular in North America and the return of beef brought a quick end to attempts to market "sea beef" domestically.

A sulphur bottom or "blue" whale being prepared for processing. Length: 103 feet.   Provincial Archives of B.C.

In the meantime, whaling plants geared up to meet the anticipated demand. In Kyuquot, cold storage facilities were added and special equipment for canning whale meat was installed.[56] Records for that period show that Kyuquot canned 60,000 cases of whale meat for domestic consumption. Another 29,585 cases were prepared during armistice for shipment overseas.

In 1918, the Pacific Whaling Co. was incorporated under a new umbrella company, Consolidated Whaling. Three years later, poor markets and depleted whale stocks forced Kyuquot and the other whaling stations to close for a season. Although they reopened in 1922, production levels had dropped significantly. In the summer of 1925, Kyuquot reported 1280 barrels of whale oil and 181 barrels of sperm oil from "a meagre take of 82 animals."[57]

The Cachalot Whaling Station closed down after the 1925 season. Its wharves and buildings were transferred to Orion Fishing and Packing Co. Ltd. and its reduction machinery went to an Alaska plant. In 1926, writes Webb, Orion operated the Cachalot station as a pilchard reduction plant.

The highly profitable and successful whaling industry had a detrimental effect on the whales. Between 1908 and 1923, over 5,700 whales were killed and processed at Sechart and Kyuquot stations. "But only the industry could be favorably impressed with these figures," say Richard Inglis and Jim Haggarty, anthropologists with the Royal B.C. Museum. "The stark reality was the near annihilation of coastal whale populations. Analysis of daily kill records from both the Sechart and Kyuquot stations document the rapid demise of specific whaling populations."[58]

Pilchards

For a brief period during the late 1920s, a handful of fish canneries and reduction plants operated at various sites along the inside shores of Kyuquot Sound. The records are sketchy. Margaret Sharcott says a Japanese-owned saltery operated out of Chamiss Bay, providing salted salmon to the Chinese market. The saltery closed down in the 1930s due to the Sino-Japan war. B.C. Packers' records show that Gosse Packing Co. leased the Chamiss Bay site in 1927, apparently with the intention of building a cannery or reduction plant there.

At Cachalot, in 1926, Orion Fishing and Packing Co. Ltd. operated a pilchard fishery out of the old whaling station, and on Easy Creek at the head of Kashutl Arm, Dominion Packing Co. Ltd., fish canners, applied for a lease, in 1928, in order to build a reduction plant. In that same year, records show that the Anglo-B.C. Packing Co. operated a single line cannery in Kyuquot Sound,[59] possibly at Markale, a now abandoned cannery site at the entrance to Fair Harbor.

"Old-timers had told us how boards, wooden floor beams and windows had been taken from these old buildings to become parts of many of the earlier Kyuquot homes," Sharcott writes. "A red-brick chimney, once part of the cannery equipment, had been carried away, brick by brick, to make chimneys for the fishermen."[60]

Kyuquot Trollers' Co-op

Fishing is fundamental to Kyuquot's survival and is an important element in its history. With the closure of the Cachalot Whaling Station, many of the Norwegian and Scandinavian whalers remained in Kyuquot Sound, settling down in the area near the present-day community of Walter's Cove. They turned mainly to commercial fishing as a source of income.

"When the men are not actually fishing on the grounds they are talking about fishing," writes Margaret Sharcott, "Wherever they gather together, on the wooden floats, on the docks or in the galleys of their boats when the weather is fine, or in the kitchens and sitting-rooms of their homes in winter, fishermen discuss fishing, which

Floatcamp at Chamiss Bay, operated by Tahsis Co. Ltd. Logging is beginning to replace fishing as the primary industry in Kyuquot Sound. Photo by Commercial Illustrators. Tahsis Archives.

gear to use, where to fish and whether it is more profitable to work at all types of fishing, each in its own season, or stay with the principal one for our area - trolling."[61]

Kyuquot is best-known as a salmon trolling centre and on April 2, 1931, the Kyuquot Trollers' Co-op Association was established to represent the trollers fishing off the west coast of Vancouver Island. The Co-op was organized to collect and market members' fish, a task which had become increasingly difficult over the years, as the fishing industry became more centralized. The Co-op expanded and its headquarters were eventually moved to Victoria. In 1950, the Kyuquot Trollers' Co-op amalgamated with the Fishermen's Co-op Association and, four years later, consolidated with the Prince Rupert Fishermen's Co-op.

Nelson Brothers

The need for more permanent and consistent fish-buying opportunities prompted two Kyuquot fishermen to organize buying on the west coast. Richard and Norman Nelson, trollers themselves, bought a small packer to carry their fish to market. They soon began carrying fish for others and expanded their modest operations, purchasing larger packers and establishing permanent fishcamps along the coast.

In 1929, Richard and Norman Nelson, along with two other brothers, Ralph and John, incorporated as Nelson Brothers Fisheries Limited. A few years later, in 1934, they purchased Ceepeecee in Nootka Sound. Originally built as a reduction plant, in 1926, Nelson Brothers added a cannery to the operation shortly after they took it over. Later, Nelson Brothers built stores at Ceepeecee and Zeballos. The store in Zeballos was later sold to Seth Witton.

Nelson Brothers Fisheries grew to become one of the principal fish processors of B.C., their success attributed in part to the "outstanding loyalty" of fishermen and staff to what has always been a family-run organization. Nelson Brothers recently amalgamated with B.C. Packers making B.C. Packers and Canfisco the two largest fish companies in British Columbia.

Walter's Cove

Walter's Cove is predominantly a fishing community with a heavy Scandinavian influence. The Scandinavians came by way of Quatsino Sound and Winter Harbor, or had worked at the Cachalot Whaling Station before it closed down in 1911. About thirty full-time residents live year-round at Walter's Cove, a community spread out over several small islets in Nicolaye Passage, near the entrance to Kyuquot Sound.

With the establishment of the Trollers' Co-op and the fish-buying camps, Walter's Cove became the commercial centre of Kyuquot Sound. A boatways was built in the 1950s, and for several years, a small sawmill operated, cutting lumber for the local market.[62]

For many years, two stores operated out of Walter's Cove. One was the original trading post which serviced the dogfish oil and sealing industries. When the fish-buying camp and co-op were established at Walter's Cove, the store moved from Actis to the Cove. A second store was run by the Co-op which started up in 1931. One store closed in 1973, leaving Kyuquot residents with just one general store which carries everything from fresh milk to marine supplies to T-shirts.

Until 1980, children from Walter's Cove attended a small school reached by footpath from the main community. In 1974, they were joined by the Indian children from Houpsitas. A completely modern school was built just above Houpsitas in 1980, and is now attended by children from both Walter's Cove and Houpsitas.

General store and government dock at Walter's Cove, 1988.   Laurie Jones photo.

Old school house, Walter's Cove, 1988.   Laurie Jones photo.

Red Cross Hospital

Situated on one of the small islands near Walter's Cove and Houpsitas is a small outpost hospital built by the Red Cross, in 1937. Now staffed by a single nurse, the small five-bed hospital with accommodation for six opened December 1, 1937 with two nurses. A serious accident had prompted residents to call for a permanent medical facility. The facility was built on a tiny island named Salo's Island after its donor, Mr. Salo.

Red Cross first aid station on Salo Island, 1988.   Laurie Jones photo.

The hospital was closed, in 1940, at residents' request in order to concentrate on the war effort. It re-opened in 1946.

Bunsby Islands

On the rocky shores of the Bunsby Islands, the history of the westcoast has come full circle. Here in an isolated, windswept part of the coast, attempts are being made to revive the sea otter populations. The small mammal whose thick glossy pelt attracted so much attention to the coast in the 18th century, was ruthlessly hunted nearly to extinction by the 1820s. Today, marine biologists have relocated several herds of sea otters from Alaska to the Bunsby Islands, and the rocky islands themselves have been designated a marine ecological reserve.

Aerial view of the Bunsby Islands.   Jim Fiddick photo.

Notes

1. Named Port Brooks after one of the owners of the trading ship, *Princess Royal,* in 1787.

2. Named by George Dixon in 1786.

3. Captain James Cook, *The voyage of the Resolution and Discovery, 1776-1780,* ed. J.C. Beaglehole, (Cambridge: 1967), p. 295.

4. James Strange, *James Strange's Journal and Narrative of the Commercial Expedition from Bombay to the Northwest Coast of America* (Madras: 1928), p. 18.

5. Ibid., p. 53.

6. Ibid., p. 55.

7. Ibid., p. 59.

8. Ibid., p. 53.

9. Esteban José Martínez, *Diary of Voyage...in 1789* (PABC, Victoria), pp. 212-213.

10. John R. Jewitt, *The Adventures and Sufferings of John R. Jewitt: Captive of Maquinna*, ed. Hilary Stewart, (Vancouver: 1987), p. 56.

11. Strange, p. 54.

12. Brooks Peninsula was named by Charles Duncan, captain of the *Princess Royal* who traded along the west coast of British Columbia in the summer and fall of 1787 and again in 1788. Duncan supposedly named the peninsula after one of the ship's owners (Conversation, Richard Inglis, Royal B.C. Museum, July, 1990).

13. Martínez, p. 5.

14. Ibid., p. 7.

15. Orders given to Captain John Kendrick of the ship *Columbia,* in Frederic W. Howay ed., *Voyages of the 'Columbia' to the Northwest Coast, 1787-1790 and 1790-1793* (Amsterdam/New York: 1969), p. 111.

16. Ibid., p. 85.

17. Ibid., p. 190.

18. Ibid., p. 194.

19. Haswell was most likely referring to the Indian village of Acous, located on Ou'ou'kinsh Inlet.

20. Ibid., pp. 190-191.

21. Ibid., p. 191.

22. Ibid., p. 191.

23. Ibid., p. 331 and pp. 400-401.

24. Frederic W. Howay ed., "Journal of the Brigantine 'Hope'," *Washington Historical Quarterly*, Vol. XI., No. 1 (Seattle: January 1920).

25. Susan Kenyon, *The Kyuquot Way*, National Museum of Man, (Ottawa: 1980), p. 42.

26 Ibid., p. 44.

27 Philip Drucker, *The Northern and Central Nootkan Tribes* (Washington D.C.: 1951), p. 111.

28 Conversation, Richard Inglis, head of ethnology, Royal B.C. Museum (Victoria: 1990).

29 Kenyon, p. 44.

30 Kenyon, p. 45, and Wilson Duff, *The Impact of the White Man*, Memoir No. 5, Province of B.C. (Victoria: 1964), p. 23.

31 Kenyon, p. 45.

32 Margaret Sharcott, *A Place of Many Winds* (Toronto: 1960), p. 27.

33 Ibid., p. 29.

34 Ibid., p. 86.

35 Kenyon, p. 45.

36 Drucker, p. 222.

37 Kenyon, p. 223.

38 Ibid., p. 18.

39 Ibid., p. 19.

40 Stewart, p. 98.

41 Kenyon, p. 62.

42 Ibid., p. 25.

43 Ibid., p. 101.

44 Ibid., p. 147.

45 Father Charles Brabant, *Mission to Nootka, 1874-1900* (Sidney: 1977), p. 20.

46 Ibid., pp. 80-81.

47 Reverend Charles Moser, *Reminiscences of the West Coast of Vancouver Island* (Kakawis: 1925), p. 151.

48 Kenyon, p. 55.

49 Ibid., p. 58.

50 Correspondence to the Colonial Office, August 1855.

51 Lewis and Dryden, *Lewis and Dryden's Marine History of the Pacific Northwest*, E.W. Wright ed., (New York: 1961), p. 427.

52 Moser, p. 141.

53 Robert L. Webb, *On the Northwest: Commercial Whaling in the Pacific Northwest, 1790-1967* (Vancouver: 1988), p. 165.

54 J.E. Gilmore, Correspondence, Provincial Archives of B.C. (Victoria: 1950).

55 J.E. Gilmore, Correspondence, Provincial Archives of B.C. (Victoria: 1949).

56 Webb, pp. 233-234

57 Webb, p. 239.

58 Richard Inglis and James C. Haggarty, "Humpback off Port Bow," *Wildlife Review*, Vol. XI., No. 3 (Sidney: 1985), p. 27.

[59] Cecily Lyons, *Salmon: Our Heritage* (Vancouver: 1969), p. 379.

[60] Sharcott, p. 45.

[61] Ibid., p. 115.

[62] Lyons, p. 405.

APPENDIX A

List of Recorded Interviews

The following people were interviewed during the course of the research for this project. They gave generously of their time and their knowledge. Interviews are on audiotape cassette and/or VHS videotape. Tapes and transcripts have been turned over to the Comox-Strathcona Regional District Office in Courtenay, B.C. Interviews followed by (T) are in the Tahsis Community Archives in Tahsis, B.C.

Anderson, Andy and Lorna, 1987.

Anderson, Laura, 1987.

Cawood, Dave and Moya, 1988.

Christensen, J.V., 1987.

Coburn, Wes, 1988.

Crabbe, Jessie, 1989.

Crosson, Jack, 1989.

Crowhurst, John, 1987.

Davies, Kathleen, 1987.

Davies, Bruce, 1988.

Donovan, Bert and Joan, 1988.

Ericson, Eric and Elvera, 1987 and 1988.

Fiddick, Jim and Anne, 1988.

Frumento, Marjorie, 1988.

Fulton, Sandy, 1989.

Funk, Henry, 1987.

Gibson, Gordon, 1986 (T).

Gibson, Jack, 1986 (T).

Grobb, Frank, 1987.

Hanson, Margaret, 1988.

Hansen, Ralph, 1988.

Harlow, George, 1985 (T).

Heevis, Ernie, 1985 (T).

Hill, Charles and Anne, 1987 and 1988.

Hill, Gerry, 1987.

Holst, Cliff, 1988.

Howard, Nick, 1988.

Jack, Ben, 1988.

Johnson, Sam, 1988

Kilmartin, Bob, 1988.

McCrae, Tom, 1988.

McLean, Marion and Shirley Sutherland, 1987.

McLeod, Neil, 1985 (T).

Munro, Jack and Jean, 1985 (T), 1986 (T) and 1988.

Ostergaard, Aksel and Edith, 1985 (T).

Perry, John, 1988.

Shillito, Gail, 1988.

Sinclair, Bunty and Carole, 1987.

Squire, John, 1989.

Stewart, Des and Mae, 1987 and 1988.

Sturdy, Ken and Freda, 1985 (T).

Swanson, Aina, 1986 (T).

Tasker, Ken and Charlotte, 1985 (T).

Tyerman, Wally, 1988.

Wilson, Doug and Betty, 1987.

Young, Budge and Alice, 1989.

BIBLIOGRAPHY

Arima, E.Y. *The West Coast People: The Nootka of Vancouver Island and Cape Flattery*. Province of British Columbia. B.C. Provincial Museum. Victoria, 1983.

Bancroft, Merle F. *Zeballos Mining District and Vicinity*. Geological Survey, Paper 40-12. Ottawa, 1940.

Bergren, Myrtle Woodward. *Tough Timber: The Loggers of B.C. Their Story*. Elgrin Publishers. Vancouver, 1979.

Boas, Franz. *Kwakiutl Tales: New Series: Part I - Translations*. AMS Press. New York, 1969. First published by Columbia University Press, 1935.

Boas, Franz. *Geographical Names of the Kwakiutl Indians*. Columbia University Press. New York, 1934.

Brabant, Father Augustin Joseph. *Mission to Nootka 1874-1900: Reminiscences of the West Coast of Vancouver Island*, ed. Charles Lillard. Gray's Publishing Ltd., Sidney, B.C. 1977.

Brabant, Father Augustin Joseph. *Reminiscences of the West Coast of Vancouver Island*, ed. Charles Moser. Kakawis, B.C. 1926.

British Columbia. *Bulletin*. Bulletin No. 14. Bureau of Provincial Information 1902-1921. Victoria, 1921.

British Columbia. *Archaeological Site Inventory*. Heritage Conservation Branch. Province of B.C. 1982.

British Columbia. *Report of the Royal Commission on Indian Affairs for the Province of British Columbia*. 4 vols. Acme Press. Victoria, 1916.

Canadian Fishing Co. Ltd. *Espinosa Reduction Plant, Records, 1928-1937*. Special Collections, University of B.C. Vancouver.

Canadian Fishing Co. Ltd. *Records: Port Albion*. Special Collections, University of B.C. Vancouver.

Canadian Fishing Co. Ltd. *Records: 1920-1960*. Special Collections, University of B.C. Vancouver.

Canadian Red Cross Society, B.C. Division. "History of Outpost Hospitals and Nursing Stations," March 1967. Unpubl. ms. in Millicent Lindo papers. Provincial Archives of British Columbia. Victoria.

Cook, Captain James. *The Voyage of the Resolution and Discovery, 1776-1780*, ed. J.C. Beaglehole. Hakluyt Society. Cambridge, 1967.

Cook, Warren L. *Flood Tide of Empire: Spain and the Pacific Northwest, 1543-1819*. Yale University Press. New Haven, Connecticut, 1973.

Drucker, Philip. *The Northern and Central Nootkan Tribes*. Smithsonian Institution, Bureau of American Ethnology, Bulletin 144. Washington D.C., 1951.

Duff, Wilson. *The Impact of the White Man: The Indian History of British Columbia, Volume I*. Anthropology in B.C. Memoir No. 5. Province of British Columbia. Victoria, 1964.

Efrat, Barbara I. and W.J. Langlois, ed. *nu-tka: The History and Survival of Nootkan Culture*. Sound Heritage Vol. VII, No. 2. Province of British Columbia. Victoria, 1978.

Flynn, Bethine. *The Flying Flynns: The Remarkable Adventures of an Animal Doctor in the Wilderness.* Seaview Books. New York, 1979.

Flynn, Bethine. *Flynn's Cove.* Porthole Press Ltd. Sidney, B.C. 1986.

Folan, William J. *The Community, Settlement, and Subsistence Pattern of the Nootka Sound Area: A Diachronic Model.* Unpubl. Ph.D. thesis. Southern Illinois University. Carbondale, Illinois, 1972.

Folan, William J. and John Dewhirst, project eds. *The Yuquot Project: The Indigenous Archaeology of Yuquot, a Nootkan Outside Village.* 3 vols. Historic Parks and Sites Branch. Parks Canada. Environment Canada. Ottawa, 1980.

Forester, Joseph E. and Anne D. Forester. *Fishing: British Columbia's Commercial Fishing History.* Hancock House Publishers Ltd. Saanichton, 1975.

Gibson, Gordon with Carol Renison. *Bull of the Woods: The Gordon Gibson Story.* Douglas and McIntyre. Vancouver, 1980.

Gould, Ed. *Logging: B.C.'s Logging History.* Hancock House. Saanichton, 1975.

Greene, Ruth. *Personality Ships of British Columbia.* Marine Tapestry Publications Ltd. West Vancouver, B.C. 1969.

Griffen, George Butler, ed. *Documents from the Sutro Collection.* Publications of the Historical Society of Southern California. Franklin Printing Co. Los Angeles, 1891.

Hacking, Norman R. and W. Kaye Lamb. *The Princess Story: A Century and a Half of West Coast Shipping.* Mitchell Press Ltd. Vancouver, 1974.

Ham, Leonard C. and Geordie Howe. *Report of the 1982 Archaeological Survey of the Nimpkish River Valley and Adjacent Offshore Islands: Permit No. 1982-22.* U'mista Cultural Society. Alert Bay, 1983.

Hanna, Joseph. *Papers, 1914-1915.* Provincial Archives of B.C. Victoria, B.C.

Hines, Ben. *Pick, Pan, and Pack: A History of Mining in the Alberni Mining Division.* Port Alberni Historical Society, Alberni Valley Museum. Port Alberni, 1976.

Howay, F.W. "The Spanish Settlement at Nootka," *Washington Historical Quarterly,* Vol. VIII., No. 3 (July 1917), pp 161-171.

Howay, F.W., ed. "The Voyage of the Hope: 1790-1792," *Washington Historical Quarterly.* Vol. XI., No. 1 (January 1920). University of Washington Press. Seattle.

Howay, F.W., ed. *Voyages of the 'Columbia' to the Northwest Coast, 1787-1790 and 1790-1793.* Da Capo Press. New York, 1969. First printed by the Massachusetts Historical Society. Boston, 1941.

Inglis, Richard. "Rough Outline of the Dogfish Oil Industry on the West Coast of Vancouver Island", unpubl. ms. in the Provincial Archives of British Columbia. Victoria, 1984.

Inglis, Richard. "The Ethnographic History of the Brooks Peninsula Region," unpubl. ms. in the Royal B.C. Museum. Victoria, 1990.

Inglis, Richard L. and James C. Haggarty. "Humpback off Port Bow," *Wildlife Review.* Vol. XI, No. 3 (Spring 1985), pp 25-27. Sidney, B.C.

Inglis, Richard L. and James C. Haggarty. "Cook to Jewitt: Three Decades of Change in Nootka Sound," *Le Castor Fait Tout: Selected Papers of the Fifth North American Fur Trade Conference*, ed. Bruce G. Trigger, Toby Morantz, and Louise Dechene. To be published 1990-91.

Jewitt, John R. *The Adventures and Sufferings of John R. Jewitt, Captive of Maquinna*. Annotated and illustrated by Hilary Stewart. Douglas and McIntyre. Vancouver, 1987.

Keller, W. Phillip. *Splendour From the Sea: The Saga of the Shantymen*. Moody Bible Institute of Chicago. Chicago, 1963.

Kennedy, Des. "Keepers of the Kelp," *Nature Canada*. Winter 1989. Vol. 18, No. 1. pp 20-24.

Kenyon, Susan M. *The Kyuquot Way: A Study of a West Coast (Nootkan) Community*. National Museum of Man, Mercury Series, Canadian Ethnology Service, Paper No. 61. National Museums of Canada. Ottawa, 1980.

Kirk, Ruth. *Wisdom of the Elders: Native Traditions on the Northwest Coast: the Nuu-chah-nulth, Southern Kwakiutl, and Nuxalk*. Douglas and McIntyre with the British Columbia Provincial Museum. Vancouver and Toronto, 1986.

Lillard, Charles. *Seven Shillings a Year: the History of Vancouver Island*. Horsdal and Schubert. Ganges, B.C. 1986.

Lyons, Cicely. *Salmon: Our Heritage, The Story of a Province and an Industry*. B.C. Packers Ltd. Mitchell Press, Ltd. Vancouver, 1969.

Martínez, Esteban José. *Diary of the Voyage of Don Esteban Josef Martínez to the Port of San Lorenzo de Nuca in 1789*. Tr. William Schurz. Unpubl. ms. in the Provincial Archives of British Columbia. Victoria.

Meares, John. *Voyages made in the years 1788 and 1789 from China to the North West Coast of America*. New Israel. Amsterdam, 1967.

Menzies, Archibald. *Menzies Journal of Vancouver's Voyage: I, 1790-1792*. Transcript of the original in the British Museum. Unpubl. ms. in the Provincial Archives of British Columbia. Victoria, 1923.

Mills, John. *Nootka Sound: A Study in Ethnohistory*. Unpubl. Ph.D. thesis. Department of Anthropology, University of Washington. Seattle, 1955.

Moziño, Jose Mariano. *Noticias de Nutka: An account of Nootka Sound in 1792*. McClelland and Stewart Ltd. and Washington University Press. Toronto and Seattle, 1970.

McMillan, Allan D. *Alberni Prehistory: Archaeological and Ethnographic Investigations on Western Vancouver Island*. Province of B.C. Victoria, 1982.

Newcombe, Charles Frederic, ed. *The First Circumnavigation of Vancouver Island*. W.H. Cullin. Victoria, 1914.

Newell, Diane and Logan W. Hovis. *Industrial Archaeological Survey of British Columbia Salmon Canneries Project: A Preliminary Annotated Guide to Bibliographical and Archival Sources*. Unpubl. ms. Department of History, University of B. C. Vancouver, 1985.

Nicholson, George. *Vancouver Island's West Coast: 1762-1962*. Published by the author. Victoria, 1962.

Nootka District General Hospital Association. *Minute Book*. Millicent Lindo papers, 1938-1967. Provincial Archives of British Columbia. Victoria.

Nootka Packing Company (1937) Limited, Nootka B.C. *Records.* Special Collections, University of B.C. Vancouver.

Obee, Bruce. "Sea Otters Return," *Beautiful B.C. Magazine.* Summer 1986. Vol. 28, No 1. pp 16-19.

Orchard, Chauncey Donald. *Papers, 1893-1972.* Provincial Archives of B.C. Victoria.

Ormsby, Margaret. *British Columbia: A History.* MacMillan of Canada. Toronto, 1971.

Pemberton, J. Despard. *Facts and Figures Relating to Vancouver Island and British Columbia.* Longman, Green, Longman and Roberts. London, 1860.

Pethick, Derek. *First Approaches to the Northwest Coast.* J.J. Douglas Ltd. North Vancouver, B.C. 1976.

Pethick, Derek. *The Nootka Connection: Europe and the Northwest Coast 1790-1795.* Douglas and McIntyre. Vancouver, 1980.

Regional District of Comox-Strathcona. *A Report on Land Use and Resources Within the Region 1975.* Comox Free Press. Courtenay, 1975.

Sendey, John. *The Nootkan Indian: A Pictorial.* Alberni Valley Museum. Port Alberni, B.C. 1977.

Sharcott, Margaret. *A Place of Many Winds.* British Book Service (Canada) Ltd. Toronto, 1960.

Sproat, Gilbert Malcolm. *The Nootka: Scenes and Studies of Savage Life*, ed. Charles Lillard. Sono Nis Press. Victoria, 1987. First published by Smith, Elder of London, 1868.

Stevenson, John. *Geology and mineral deposits of Zeballos mining camp, B.C.* Department of Mines. Bulletin 27. Province of British Columbia. Victoria, 1950.

Strange, James. *James Strange's Journal and Narrative of the Commerical expedition from Bombay to the Northwest Coast of America.* Government Press. Madras, 1928.

Studholme, Maude M. "The Latest Gold Rush," *The Canadian Geographical Journal.* Volume 19, No. 2 (August 1939). pp. 134-143.

Suria, Tomas de. *Journal of Tomas de Suria of his Voyage with Malaspina to the Northwest Coast of America in 1791.* A.H. Clarke Company. Glendale, California, 1936.

Turner, Robert D. *The Pacific Princesses: An Illustrated History of Canadian Pacific Railway's Princess Fleet on the Northwest Coast.* Sono Nis Press. Victoria, 1977.

Vancouver, George. *A Voyage of Discovery to the North Pacific Ocean, and Round the World, 1791-1795*, ed. W. Kaye Lamb. 4 vols. Hakluyt Society. London, 1984.

Wagner, Henry R., ed. "Fray Benito de la Sierra's Account...in 1775," *California Historical Quarterly.* September 1930.

Wagner, Henry R., ed. "Journal of Tomas de Suria of His Voyage with Malaspina to the Northwest Coast of America in 1791," *Pacific Historical Review.* September 1936.

Wagner, Henry R., ed. *The Cartography of the Northwest Coast of America to the year 1800*. New Israel. Amsterdam, 1968.

Walbran, John T. *British Columbia Coast Names*. J.J. Douglas. Vancouver, 1971.

Webb, Robert Lloyd. *On the Northwest: Commercial Whaling in the Pacific Northwest, 1790-1967*. University of B.C. Press. Vancouver, 1988.

White, Brian Peter. *The Settlement of Nootka Sound: Its Distributional Morphology 1900-1970*. Unpubl. M.A. thesis. Simon Fraser University. Burnaby, 1972.

Wright, E.W. ed., *Lewis and Dryden's Marine History of the Pacific Northwest*. Antiquarian Press Ltd. New York, 1961. First published by Lewis and Dryden Printing Co., 1895.

Index